DAVID OWEN

COPIES IN SECONDS

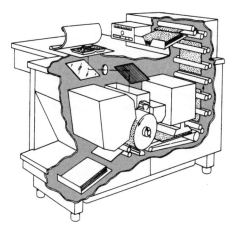

How a Lone Inventor and an Unknown Company Created
the Biggest Communication Breakthrough Since Gutenberg—
Chester Carlson and the Birth of the Xerox Machine

SIMON & SCHUSTER
New York   London   Toronto   Sydney

SIMON & SCHUSTER
Rockefeller Center
1230 Avenue of the Americas
New York, NY 10020

For information regarding special discounts for bulk purchases,
please contact Simon & Schuster Special Sales at 1-800-456-6798
or business@simonandschuster.com

Designed by Jan Pisciotta

Manufactured in the United States of America

10 9 8 7 6 5 4 3 2 1

Library of Congress Cataloging-in-Publication Data
Owen, David, 1955–
Copies in seconds : how a lone inventor and an unknown company created
the biggest communications breakthrough since Gutenberg : Chester Carlson
and the birth of the Xerox machine / David Owen.
p. cm.
Includes bibliographical references and index.
[1. Carlson, Chester Floyd, 1906–1968. 2. Inventors.
3. Xerography—History.] I. Title.
TR1045.O94 2004   686.4'42'092—dc22   [B]   2004049187

ISBN 0-7432-5117-2

For Ann

Contents

PROLOGUE 1

1 COPIES IN SECONDS 3

2 BEYOND THE REACH OF ACCIDENT 15

3 HOW DO YOU KNOW WHAT COLOR IT IS ON THE OTHER SIDE? 49

4 10-22-38 ASTORIA 77

5 FATHERS AND SONS 113

6 THE OX BOX 135

7 THE HOUSE ON HOLLENBECK STREET 161

8 AMERICAN XEROGRAPHY CORP. 183

9 THE 914 199

10 NICKELS 227

11 WHICH IS THE ORIGINAL? 245

12 TO DIE A POOR MAN 259

Sources 285

Index 293

The invention all admired, and each how he
To be the inventor missed; so easy it seemed,
Once found, which yet unfound most would have thought
Impossible.

—*Paradise Lost*

COPIES IN SECONDS

PROLOGUE

WE OURSELVES ARE COPIES. "And God said, Let us make man in our image, after our likeness." A living organism, from its DNA up, is a copying machine. The essence of life—the difference between us and sand—is replication.

Copying is the engine of civilization: culture is behavior duplicated. The oldest copier invented by people is language, the device by which an idea of yours becomes an idea of mine. We are distinct from chimpanzees because speech, through its irrepressible power of reproduction, multiplied our thoughts into thinking.

The second great copying machine was writing. When the Sumerians transposed spoken words into stylus marks on clay tablets, they exponentially extended the human network that language had created. Writing freed copying from the chain of living contact. It made thinking permanent, portable, and endlessly reproducible.

Civilization has evolved at the speed of duplication. One mark in clay became two; two became four; four became eight. Like all doubling, copying accumulates slowly at first but compounds. Less than a millennium ago—forty centuries after the Sumerians—a single literate polyglot theoretically could have read every book in the world; today, copied language constitutes so much of the intangible infrastructure of existence that we consciously register only glimpses of the shadow of its shadow. A newsstand in Manhattan contains more duplicated text than did the legendary Library of Alexandria.

The earliest written documents were simple tallies: so many animals, so much grain. For centuries, that was all the writing in the world. Last week, a small plastic latch broke off my clothes dryer. I copied the number molded into its side and searched for it on Google. Less than a second later, my computer screen filled with a list of suppliers all over the country, with links to their inventories and their prices, along with half a dozen portals into a galaxy of intricately cross-referenced self-promotion. Behind the copied words on the screen lay invisible sentences of ones and zeros, and behind the ones and zeros lay a babel of electrical impulses and magnetic fields: the ultimate modern repository of replicable meaning. I chose a likely supplier, found the part I needed, and with a couple of clicks transmitted a copy of a stored description of myself that was more detailed than any a Sumerian could have produced of anyone he knew: my name, my exact location in the world, a partial history of my material desires, access to my treasure. Two days later, I installed the new part on my clothes dryer.

The world we live in—as distinct from the world we live on—is made of duplicated language. We build our lives from copies of copies of copies.

1

Copies in Seconds

Back in 1985, a friend of mine called to ask if I would send him a copy of a certain newspaper clipping. I said I would. I rooted around in the stuff on my desk and found the clipping near the bottom of a stack of papers. I moved it to the top and made a mental note to take it to the coin-operated copying machine in the drugstore across the street from my wife's and my apartment. Because my office was in a corner of our living room instead of in an office building, I couldn't run down the hall and make a few thousand free copies of the clipping, a recipe, my hand, a newsy Christmas poem describing my family's heartwarming experiences during the previous year, or anything else.

Several days passed. Every time I went out, I either forgot about the clipping or remembered it and decided to do nothing about it. If there's anything I hate, it's carrying a loose, large, irregularly shaped piece of paper while I do various errands. If someone had grabbed me by the cheeks and told me to march right over there and make that copy, I would have replied, like Bartleby, "I would prefer not to." I considered retyping the entire newspaper article—a pleasant way to spend an afternoon. Gradually, the distance between my apartment and the drugstore grew in my mind until it might as well have been the distance between St. Louis and the moon.

Then, early one morning as I lay sleepless in bed, I came to the sudden, powerful realization that I would never make that copy unless I made it on a copier that I myself owned. The necessity for spending large sums often comes to me in such a flash. I now believed, in other words, that walking across the street to pay twenty cents for a single copy was less convenient and more irrational than traveling across town to pay several hundred dollars for an entire machine, which I would then have to find a permanent place for in our apartment.

I knew the machine I wanted. A couple of years earlier, Canon Inc., the Japanese camera and electronics manufacturer, had begun selling the world's first copiers intended for personal use, and I had been trying to think of a plausible-seeming justification for buying one. Canon was promoting the new copiers with an advertising campaign featuring the actor Jack Klugman, whose most recent television role had been the eponymous crime-fighting medical examiner on *Quincy, M.E.* In the Canon commercials, Klugman said that Canon personal copiers were easy to operate and that they used replaceable cartridges containing "the entire copying process."

After breakfast, I took a bus to a discount electronics store on the other side of Manhattan and bought a Canon PC-10 personal copier for $475. (This was quite a bargain at the time; the manufacturer's suggested retail price was just under $800.) I also bought two of the cartridges, for about $50 each, and five 500-sheet packages of ordinary paper for a total of $15.

My Canon personal copier was small—about the size of two toaster ovens. But the box it came in was large—about the size of six or seven toaster ovens. Maneuvering that box and those car-tridges and all that paper into a taxi and then into the elevator and up to our apartment turned out to be quite a problem. I finally made it, though, and I set up the machine without much trouble. I put the clipping on the platen, inserted a sheet of paper, and watched a crisp, clean copy emerge from the other side.

A feeling of well-being and inner satisfaction coursed through my circulatory system. My life had achieved a previously unimaginable level of futuristic-seeming efficiency. I could now enjoy in my own home a pleasure that was then almost unknown among people who, like me, didn't have real jobs. "So long, sucker," I imagined myself saying to the genial Pakistani who ran the drugstore across the street.

I made another copy of the same clipping and threw away the first one. Then I made a third and threw away the second. Then—after a panicky moment in which I wondered whether I had not just satisfied my copying needs in their entirety—I opened the owner's manual and began, page by page, to copy that.

As INEVITABLY HAPPENS with luxuries, my Canon PC-10 became a necessity as soon as it was mine. Much of journalism consists of photocopying things that other people have written and finding slightly different ways to write them again, so having a copier of my own was professionally advantageous. I also found many uses for the machine in my ordinary life: copying documents of interest to my accountant or the IRS; creating a handy record of all my credit card numbers, by copying the cards themselves; making backup copies of medical forms and contest applications; duplicating humorous invitations for two big, boozy parties that my wife and I gave back in the days when we were still young enough to have fun. Using my PC-10 was a nuisance by modern copying standards—the machine didn't have a paper tray, and to make copies I had to feed blank sheets one at a time into a slot at one end—but it seemed revolutionary in comparison with having no copier at all. I stopped thinking not only about the drugstore across the street but also about the upscale copying boutique a few blocks away, on Lexington Avenue, where I had formerly gone to make high-priced backups of especially important documents, such as my will. My PC-10 survived being dropped to the floor, riding to Martha's Vineyard in the back of a station wagon, moving to Connecticut, having coffee spilled on it, and sitting unnoticed for more than an hour directly beneath a cascading leak from our roof, which was being replaced.

When my PC-10 finally wore out, in 1998, after thirteen years of hard use, I replaced it with a Xerox XC1045, which I bought at Staples and brought home in the trunk of my car. My XC1045, which I love even more than I loved my PC-10, has many features formerly found only in top-of-the-line office copiers—an automatic document feeder, a 250-page paper tray, an alternate paper tray, a mode for copying the pages of bound books, automatic and manual exposure controls, an oversize platen, a mode for making copies more economically, and the ability to make a broad range of reductions and enlargements—yet it cost me less than twice as much as my old PC-10 had more than a dozen years before.

My kids, who were born in the eighties and have never known a time when copying someone else's notes for a test was more bothersome than walking across the room and pressing a button, view our XC1045 with about as much awestruck wonder as they view our washing machine. Only with a heroic exertion of sympathetic brainpower can they imagine what life must have been like back in the days when copying an interesting article consisted of calling your grandmother and asking her if she had already thrown away her newspaper. When I needed a copy of my sixth-grade science fair report, back in the mid-1960s, my mother sent the original to work with my father, whose employer had a Xerox machine. My father's access to that machine (or, rather, his access to the secretary who was the machine's sole authorized operator) was another of the semi-supernatural powers he possessed as a result of wearing a suit and working downtown. Yet to my children this all seems like something out of *Little House on the Prairie*.

As for more ancient document reproduction methods—well, forget it. One day not long ago, I happened to mention carbon paper while chatting with my son, who was born in 1988, and he asked me what it was. I told him—thin paper or plastic film coated on one side with gelatinous ink, formerly used in making simultaneous facsimiles of handwriting or typing—and he said, "Cool."

"But you've seen carbon paper before, of course."

"No."

"But you remember when credit card slips had little sheets of carbon paper in them, don't you?"

(Glancing toward the door.) "No."

My son's unfamiliarity with carbon paper seems all the more surprising when you consider that the stuff was fairly common in our house until he was nearly in first grade. I bought one of the very first personal computers, the original IBM PC, in 1981. It came with 64 kilobytes of random-access memory—about what a wristwatch contains today—and cost more than $4,000. I also bought a printer the size of a Weber grill. It had a thimble-shaped character element, which printed by impact, the way a typewriter does. It also had an elaborately geared, toothed, and belted attachment that locked onto the top and hoisted a continuous stream of computer paper from a big box—the kind of paper with tear-off perforated strips along the sides. The printer was so slow and cacophonous that when I needed two copies of something I had written, I didn't simply print it twice, the way I do now with my laser printer, but instead switched from regular computer paper to three-part carbon computer paper, which in a single pass produced an original plus two duplicates. If I was printing something long, like a book chapter, I would sometimes go for a walk while the printer was banging away, because the noise at close range was unendurable.

While thinking about that old printer of mine, I realized that my son doesn't just lack an appreciation of how hard it used to be to make copies; he also doesn't really know what an *original* is, or was, in the sense that older people understand it. When he writes an essay for school, he composes and continuously revises the text on his computer and then either prints it on the day it's due or e-mails it to his teacher. If he has to make further revisions later, he doesn't look for his jar of correction fluid; he just edits the computer file and then prints or e-mails it again. He never really produces a first draft, a revised draft, a final draft, or a copy in the antique sense. His paper, between the moment he begins writing it and the moment his teacher gives him a grade, simply exists in a fluid succession of related states. His understanding of "copies" and "originals" is as different from mine as Werner Heisenberg's understanding of the electron was different from Niels Bohr's.

You don't have to be as young as my son to have a hard time appreciating what it was like to live in a world where making more than one of something was a novelty, if not an ordeal. Most of us old-timers have forgotten what the pre-Xerox era was like, too, and can no longer relate to the astonishment we felt when the technology was new. That astonishment was, well, astonishing. Shortly after the first Xerox office copier was introduced, in 1960, a journal for librarians pointed out, in the tone that Christopher Columbus must have used to describe the coast of San Salvador to Queen Isabella, that the curious new machine might be used to make copies of old books. In an article about the Xerox Corpora-

tion which *The New Yorker* published in 1967—seven years later—
the writer John Brooks described a still more remarkable application:

> One rather odd use of xerography insures that brides get the
> wedding presents they want. The prospective bride submits her
> list of preferred presents to a department store; the store sends
> the list to its bridal-registry counter, which is equipped with a
> Xerox copier; each friend of the bride, having been tactfully
> briefed in advance, comes to this counter and is issued a copy of
> the list, whereupon he does his shopping and then returns the
> copy with the purchased items checked off, so that the master
> list may be revised and thus ready for the next donor. ("Hymen,
> iö Hymen, Hymen!")

In the early days of the automobile, people no doubt bothered to
point out that the new invention might be employed to "facilitate
travel" and so on. Brooks's amazement was unbounded. He mar-
veled that police officers "in New Orleans and various other
places" sometimes used Xerox machines to make pictorial records
of objects confiscated from prisoners; that some hospitals copied
"electrocardiograms and laboratory reports"; and that stock bro-
kerages had begun using Xerox machines in the distribution of
"hot tips."

THE FIRST OFFICE COPIERS WERE, as is well known, monks.
When Johannes Gutenberg invented movable type, in the early
1400s, monkdom trembled. Carbon paper, the typewriter, and
blueprints, among other things, were invented in the nineteenth
century. The decades flew by. Relatively convenient copying began to be possible only in the early 1950s, half a millennium after

Gutenberg, when the world's first true office copiers were introduced. The new machines had names like Thermo-Fax, Dupliton, Dial-A-Matic, Autostat, Verifax, and Copease, and all of them were reasonably compact and inexpensive to buy. Their chief drawbacks were that they cost a fortune to operate (since they used expensive chemically treated papers) and that the copies they made were hard to read, smelled bad, didn't last very long, and had a tendency to curl up into tubes.

Office copying as we know it didn't arrive until 1960, when a small photographic supply company in Rochester, New York, shipped the first Haloid XeroX 914 Office Copier. (The second capitalized *X* is a flourish that the company later dropped.) The 914's manufacturer, which had started life as the Haloid Company, is known today as the Xerox Corporation. The 914 employed a copying process that was revolutionarily different from anything used in machines made by other companies; that process was called xerography, and unlike all competing techniques, it made sharp, permanent copies on ordinary paper. The 914, furthermore, was simple enough for a child to operate. Essentially overnight, people began making copies at a rate that was orders of magnitude faster than anyone had believed possible. Even when the machines didn't work properly—and they often didn't—users became convinced that Xerox copiers were indispensable. Before long, Thermo-Fax, Dupliton, Dial-A-Matic, Autostat, Verifax, Copease, and all the other machines based on different copying technologies had disappeared.

Xerography, unlike most mid-twentieth-century technological innovations, has never been superseded. My Canon PC-10 was a xerographic copier, and my Xerox XC1045 is a xerographic copier, and the copier in your office is a xerographic copier. All these machines, no matter which company's nameplate is affixed to the front, are direct descendants of the 914. Indeed, the vast majority of the documents that a typical American office worker handles in an ordinary day are produced xerographically, either on copiers manufactured by the Xerox Corporation and its competitors or on laser printers, which also operate xerographically and were invented, in 1969, by a Xerox researcher. (Most of the relatively few nonxerographic plain-paper copiers in the world—found mainly in private homes—are ink-jet machines, which typically operate much more slowly than xerographic devices do and are more expensive to run.)

People often assume that xerography must be related to conventional photography, but it's not. It is unlike any technology that preceded it, and it was not a refinement of a previously existing process. Its central component is a surface known as a photoreceptor. In the 914, the photoreceptor was a thin layer of selenium applied to the outside of an aluminum cylinder. Selenium is an unusual element in that it acts as an electrical insulator in the dark and as an electrical conductor in the light. If you place a selenium photoreceptor in a dark room and spray a uniform electrostatic charge onto its surface, the charge will remain until you turn the lights back on, at which point the selenium will become conductive and carry the charge away into the (grounded) aluminum cylinder underneath.

If you shine a light on a document in such a way that an image of the document is projected onto a charged selenium photoreceptor, the selenium coating will retain its charge in those areas where no light falls—that is, in those areas that correspond to the dark ink on the document—and lose it everywhere else. If you then sprinkle an oppositely charged powdered resin onto the selenium coating, the resin will stick to the areas where the charge remains, in the same way that house dust sticks to a staticky balloon. Doing so will produce on the surface of the selenium a visible mirror image of the original document. You can then transfer the resin to a sheet of paper and melt it, making a permanent copy. (In a laser printer, the light that shines on the photoreceptor comes from a digitally controlled laser, but the other components and steps are the same. In some xerographic devices, the light source is a fiber-optic array.)

Xerography is unusual among modern inventions in having been conceived by a single person. There was no one in France or Russia who was working on the same thing. The Chinese did not invent it in the eleventh century BC. The inventor was a shy, humble patent attorney named Chester Carlson. He grew up in almost unspeakable poverty, and he made his discovery in solitude. For nearly a decade after he thought of xerography, the process—which he initially called electron photography and then called electrophotography—was his private obsession. He offered his idea to two dozen major corporations, all of which expressed what he called "an enthusiastic lack of interest" and thus missed an opportunity to manufacture what *Fortune* magazine would later describe as "the most successful product ever marketed in America." So persistent was this failure of capitalistic vision that by the time the 914 Office Copier went into production in 1960, the original patent covering its internal processes had expired. In fact, Carlson's idea was so unusual and nonintuitive that it could conceivably have been overlooked entirely. Scientists who visited the drafty warehouses in Rochester where the first machines were built sometimes expressed doubt that the process was even theoretically feasible.

It is often interesting to speculate what life would be like if some conspicuous element of it were removed. Suppose, for example, that the universe contained no solid material that was also transparent—no glass or plastic or anything similar. Without such a substance we would have no windshields, no light bulbs, no contact lenses, no television sets, no optical telescopes, no see-through shower curtains, and so on. What would we do? The loss of xerography would be less dramatic but would still be profound. We would have fewer lawyers, larger forests, smaller landfills, no Pentagon Papers, no laser printers, more (fewer?) bureaucrats, shorter (longer?) meetings, better memories, more secrets, fewer cartoons on our refrigerators, less to read at work every day (along with more time in which to read it), and a lot less information in general.

The invention of the Xerox machine was an epochal event in the history of communication and, therefore, in the history of civilization. It gave ordinary people an extraordinary means of preserving and sharing information, and it placed the rapid exchange of complicated ideas within the reach of almost anyone—a potent and, indeed, subversive capability, whose reach and ease of use have been exceeded only relatively recently, by the World Wide Web and e-mail. In the former Soviet Union, whose totalitarian rulers maintained their power in part by monopolizing access to information, copiers were guarded more closely than computers, and individual copies were numbered, so that they could be traced.

Yet today we take xerography almost entirely for granted. The only way to regain an appropriate sense of its importance is to go back to the beginning.

in various liquids, stretched and dried on a wooden frame, scraped smooth on one side with a circular knife, and scoured with a pumice stone. Parchment is the reason college diplomas are called sheepskins, although many years have passed since any graduate received anything but paper. Closely similar to parchment was vellum, which was calfskin prepared in the same manner (though scraped on both sides).

Parchment and vellum were later supplanted by paper, which was invented by the Chinese four thousand years ago and then—one and two and three millennia later—imported, imitated, and reinvented by the rest of the world. Like papyrus, paper receives its strength and flexibility from compressed masses of plant fibers arranged in opposition to one another; in paper, the arrangement is more chaotic. In medieval Europe, the most common fiber source for papermaking was linen and cotton rags, which were wetted and left to molder, pounded until their threads had become unwoven and unspun, and soaked and stirred in giant vats. The resulting pulp was strained through sieve-like molds, then squeezed in screw presses until almost all the water had been removed. Even the best paper was inferior to parchment and vellum as a surface for writing, but it was cheaper. Its proliferation in Europe in the Middle Ages was made possible by a sudden huge increase in the availability of inexpensive recyclable rags: the heaps of unwearable clothing left by victims of various plagues. Today, most paper is made of fibers that originated in trees, a source that was suggested to early papermakers by the nests of wasps.

For the human copying machines of the medieval world, the crucial office supply was always light. An order's scriptorium—its copy center—was often situated within a colonnaded cloister walk, giving scribes maximum uninterrupted exposure to the sun. The walk's open side also admitted winter weather, and the scribes, who worked at their writing tables for six hours or more a day, suffered from stiff backs, cold fingers, and frozen ink. The earliest inks took their color from candle soot and other readily available forms of carbon, and were ephemeral. Later inks were better. Among their most important ingredients were iron and one of several tannin compounds extracted from oak galls, which are tumorlike growths that oak trees generate in response to infestations by parasitic wasps. (Wasps were second only to humans among contributors to early copying technology.)

When multiple copies of a single book were required, one monk dictated to others; when a scribe copied directly from a book, he dictated quietly to himself, sounding out the words as he worked. Silent reading was a late innovation in Europe; it didn't begin to catch on widely until the tenth century, although there were isolated instances before then. The future St. Augustine was astonished the first time he saw someone reading without moving his lips, in Milan in the fourth century. ("When [Bishop Ambrose] read his eyes would travel across the pages and his mind would explore the sense, but his voice and tongue were silent," Augustine wrote in his *Confessions*, which has been called the first Western book almost certainly intended by its author to be read in privacy by individuals rather than declaimed.) Except for the dictating and the sounding out, though, talking was forbidden in scriptoria. To circumvent the ban, monks devised systems of hand signals, and jotted notes in the margins of the pages on which they were working—two of the earliest known attempts to combat the monotony of copying.

Over time, scribes became specialized, like the tools on an assembly line. One of them might do only body text, another only dropped capitals, another illustrations. Some proofread. (Meticulous checking was crucial, because uncaught errors cascaded through subsequent iterations.) The steady accretion of duplicates stimulated further demand; the ability to make copies caused more copies to be made. Copying also moved beyond the monasteries. Secular scribes were common near commercial centers and universities—exactly the sorts of places where you'd be most likely to find a Kinko's today.

THE THIRD GREAT MILESTONE in the history of copying was the invention of mechanical printing—the duplication of text or images by transferring them from one surface to another rather than re-creating them by hand. Rudimentary printing, of pictures, probably originated in Buddhist monasteries in India around the middle of the first millennium, and from there it spread to China and the rest of Asia, where the technology was soon adapted to duplicating text. (If you broaden your definition, you can extend printing's origin back much further. Around 1700 BC, someone in Crete used stamps to impress hieroglyphs on both sides of a clay disk; a signet ring is a printing press.) By the year 1000, books assembled from page-size wood-block prints were relatively common in China.

In the West, the invention of mechanical printing is almost always attributed to Johannes Gutenberg, a fifteenth-century German.* Most of the little we know about him—that he may also have invented a new kind of mirror to sell to religious pilgrims, that he may have surrendered some cases of metal type to settle a lawsuit—comes from court records. In a world in which copies

---

*The Dutch, but almost no one else, often credit a Dutch contemporary of Gutenberg's named Laurens Closter; some other scholars think the first modern book was actually printed by Johann Fust, a onetime business partner of Gutenberg's. But the true innovator, and the source of Fust's knowledge of the new technology, was almost certainly Gutenberg himself. (Crude versions of movable type had been used earlier in China and Korea, but written Asian languages, with their thousands of unique ideographs, were poorly suited to the idea. Typesetting as we know it was a European innovation.)

had to be made by hand and were therefore rare, one of the best ways to keep a name alive was to involve it in litigation, since courts were among the few places where documents were created and preserved. Court records constitute almost all we know about William Shakespeare, too (except for his plays, which were printed).

Gutenberg is usually referred to as the inventor of the printing press—and he was—but his history-transforming innovation was movable metal type. Four hundred years later, Thomas Carlyle would write: "He who first shortened the labor of copyists by device of movable types was disbanding hired armies, and cashiering most kings and senates, and creating a whole new democratic world." Movable type survived for more than five centuries in a form Gutenberg would have recognized. His system involved casting individual characters in metal molds; arranging the castings, later called "sorts," in lines within page-size forms; and using a screw press (like the ones that were used to remove water in papermaking) to transfer ink from the type to sheets of paper. The process was fantastically labor intensive by modern printing standards. In the early years, a skillful worker might cast four thousand sorts in a day, which sounds like a lot but would have been enough to typeset only two or three pages of the book you are reading. Sorts could be rearranged and reused—that was Gutenberg's breakthrough—but not until a printer had made all the copies he needed of the page into which they had been locked.

We tend to think of technological revolutions as absolute—one day, monks; the next day, printing presses—but most innovations are adopted gradually, and few fully supplant the processes they theoretically make obsolete. For editions of fifty or even a hundred copies, a well-run fifteenth-century scriptorium could be more efficient at producing books than a well-run fifteenth-century printing shop, and competition between scribes and printing presses continued for decades. More than fifty years after the publication of the book we call the Gutenberg Bible, the issue was still alive even in Gutenberg's own country, where printers were more numerous than they were anywhere else in the world. In 1494, a quarter century after Gutenberg's death, the Abbot of Sponheim—a German cleric, whose interests included not only copying but also shorthand, cryptography, and the possibility that angels might be employed to carry secret messages over long distances—wrote a treatise called *De Laude Scriptorum* ("In Praise of Scribes"), in which he argued that monks should not allow the invention of printing to stop them from copying books by hand. He contended that handwritten books would last longer than printed ones, and that hand copying itself was a virtuous activity because a copyist could pause in the course of his work to pray. To ensure that his treatise received the readership it deserved, the Abbot had it printed.

WHEN GUTENBERG MADE BOOKS, he reproduced illustrations the way the Chinese did: with carved woodblocks, which he incorporated into his page forms. Printing from woodblocks and printing from metal type are both subsets of a single general printing technique, called relief printing: the ink is applied to surfaces that stand out in relief, or protrude, from a nonprinting background, and when paper is pressed onto those surfaces and then pulled away, much of the ink comes with it.

Around the time of Gutenberg's birth, an Italian invented a method of reproducing images which solved the same problem from the opposite direction. The method is called intaglio. An intaglio engraver creates a printable surface not by removing the nonprinting background areas, the way a woodcarver or a type founder does, but by carving away the lines of the image itself, usually on a plate made of polished copper or some other soft metal.

After the desired text or image has been engraved (in reverse), the plate is inked and then wiped clean, so that the ink remains only inside the carved indentations, below the surface of the plate. A piece of paper is then pressed firmly against the plate, causing the ink in the indentations to transfer to the sheet. The finely detailed engravings in old books are often examples of intaglio printing; so are engraved wedding invitations and all U.S. currency. (On an engraved wedding invitation or a reasonably recent dollar bill, the areas directly behind any printed characters or images appear slightly depressed, you'll notice if you look closely, because those areas were squeezed into the indentations in the plate.)

The next great step forward in duplication was the invention of lithography, or "stone writing." Because lithography was invented after printing and copying had become comparatively common, we know much more about its creator and the circumstances of his discovery than we do about Gutenberg. In 1795, a twenty-four-year-old German playwright and former law student named Alois Senefelder—who looked like a slightly scruffy version of Beethoven—was experimenting with printing methods. His father, a noted actor, had died a few years before, leaving Senefelder largely responsible for the support of his mother and eight siblings. His inaugural effort as a professional writer—a play called *The Connoisseur of Girls,* which was first performed in 1789, shortly before his father's death—had been a financial success, but since that time he had had difficulties with publishers, and he set out to devise an economical means of printing his works himself.

Senefelder was an engagingly open-minded researcher; at one point, he explored the possibility of fashioning printing plates from what was almost baked pastry. He also reasoned that stone might make an inexpensive and easy-to-use engraving medium for intaglio printing, and he tried his idea several times, with mixed success. Then, one day, his mother asked him to quickly make a list of the items in a load of clothing she was about to send out for laundering. "I happened not to have even the smallest slip of paper at hand," he wrote, "as my little stock of paper had been entirely exhausted by taking impressions from the stones; nor was there even a drop of ink in the inkstand." His mother was in a hurry, though, so he dipped a pen in a waxy, experimental ink (which he had recently created for use in his intaglio experiments) and wrote the list on the polished surface of a large piece of Kelheim limestone, intending to copy it later with a pen and paper.

As soon as the laundry was out the door, though, Senefelder looked at the waxy marks on the stone and was inspired: perhaps the stone could be used to make relief prints instead of intaglio ones. He bathed the limestone surface in a solution of nitric acid, figuring the acid would etch away stone everywhere except in the places where the waxy ink protected it. After five minutes, he removed the acid and rinsed the surface—but was disappointed to find that the stone appeared to have been affected very little, rather than being deeply etched, as he had hoped. He applied printer's ink to the written image anyway, and the ink, which was oil based, stuck readily to the wax. After the stone had dried, Senefelder pressed a piece of paper onto its surface, then peeled away a print—a lithograph. Although the difference in relief between the etched and unetched parts of the stone was less than a hundredth of an inch, Senefelder estimated, the stone plate printed as effectively as a carved block of wood.

Senefelder's subsequent printing results were not uniformly encouraging—"I was soon deterred from farther improving on the press, as, on one occasion, I had a very narrow escape from being killed by the great stone of 300 pounds, which always fell from a height of ten feet"—but he kept tinkering. Eventually he realized that the crucial contribution of the acid rinse lay not in lowering the profile of the nonprinting areas, as he had believed at first, but in enhancing the stone's ability to become saturated by water, making it repellent to oil-based inks, which therefore adhered only to the waxy image to be reproduced. This is the central principle of lithography. Senefelder received the first of several patents in 1799; adapted the process to plates made of metal and plates made of a vellumlike "artificial stone paper"; founded a successful printing company, called Senefelder, Gleissner & Co., in 1806; and published a comprehensive, chatty reference work on his invention in 1817 (and later translated it into English).

Lithography revolutionized printing. It also represented the first reasonably economical method of duplicating ordinary documents—a capability that Senefelder himself believed to be "the principal and most important part of my discovery." To quickly make a hundred copies of an advertising circular, say—or of an essay denouncing your nation's government—you could write your text on an ordinary sheet of paper using Senefelder's waxy "chemical ink"; press the still-wet written surface onto a polished stone plate, thereby transferring the image, reversed, to the stone; and proceed by the lithographic printing method that Senefelder had devised. "In order to multiply copies of your ideas by printing," he wrote, "it is no longer necessary to learn to write in an inverted sense; but every person who with common ink may write on paper, may do the same with chemical ink, and by the transfer of his writing to the stone, it can be multiplied *ad infinitum.*" This capability of lithography anticipated a phenomenon familiar to anyone who has ever been buried beneath piles of unnecessary copies while working on a committee: "All resolutions, edicts, orders, *&c.*, agreed to in the cabinet meetings, are written down on paper by the secretary with chemical ink; in the space of an hour fifty impressions may be had and distributed at pleasure."

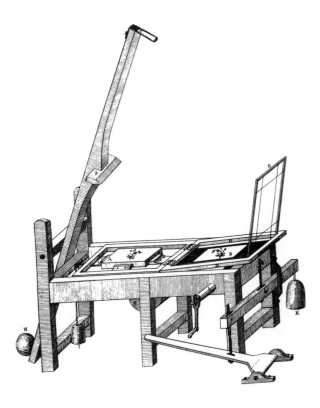

Senefelder's lithographic printing press.

Today, only artists—and not many of them—still use stone plates in making lithographs, but direct descendants of Senefelder's invention are employed in printing virtually every newspaper, magazine, and book that you read, including this one. Lithography also played an essential role in the development of xerography and in the survival of the first commercial Xerox machine—as a later chapter will explain.

•   •   •

IN 1612, A GERMAN JESUIT PRIEST named Christoph Scheiner published a series of letters arguing that sunspots—which had recently been observed by Scheiner himself and by his fellow astronomer Galileo, among others—were not features of the sun's surface, as Galileo correctly believed, but rather were planets or other satellites, which became visible from Earth as their movements through the heavens caused them to eclipse the solar disk. The issue was theologically important because Christian doctrine in those days was generally considered to work better if the sun was a perfect, unblemished orb. Scheiner was wrong about sunspots, but he was nevertheless a gifted scientist. He wrote an important work about sundials, made several improvements in the telescope, and correctly determined the retina's role in vision.

Scheiner also built a copying machine. (Germans are more abundant than even wasps in the history of copying technology.) In 1603, at the age of thirty, he built a "pantograph," a brilliantly simple device that employed principles of Euclidean geometry to make duplicates, enlargements, and reductions of existing images.

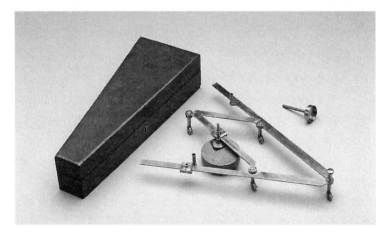

Pantograph owned by Thomas Jefferson.
THOMAS JEFFERSON MEMORIAL FOUNDATION, INC.

A pantograph consists of four rods arranged in a parallelogram and joined, at the points where the rods intersect, with pivoting hinges. Tracing a drawing with a stylus inserted at one position in the device causes a pen at a second position to reproduce the drawing in perfect proportion. A pantograph can also be used to reproduce writing, by simultaneously creating an original and an exact facsimile.

Many writers have credited Scheiner with inventing the pantograph, but Leonardo da Vinci, Michelangelo, and various ancient Greeks, among many others, used pantographs, too, or devices similar to them. And even Scheiner's pantograph was directly inspired by someone else, an artist acquaintance of his named Georgius, who had "boasted to me of possessing an admirable invention, namely, a compendious method of delineating any object most easy, sure, and speedy to practise; so that whoever would take a drawing from any original, did it by regarding the original alone, without needing to look at the copy." Based on Georgius's description, Scheiner deduced the principle and built one of his own.

During the next two centuries, the pantograph was improved, forgotten, and reinvented several times. (Repeated reinvention of useful objects was a common phenomenon in the centuries before easy document reproduction improved civilization's ability to remember previous innovations.) Christopher Wren—most famously the architect of St. Paul's Cathedral in London, but also a noted astronomer, mathematician, and inventor—patented a pantograph in 1631, claiming that it was useful in "diminishing the tedious labour of transcriptions of the greater sort of deeds, indentures, conveyances, charters, and all other duplicates." In 1648, William Petty, who was then a professor of anatomy at Oxford University, invented a version that he described as "an instrument of small bignes," which could be used to "write two copies of the same thing at once." (Petty illustrated his anatomical lectures with a pickled human cadaver, which he had "brought by water from Reading," according to a reminiscence by a near contemporary.) Similar devices were made and used by others. One was invented in the late 1770s by Erasmus Darwin, who was a grandfather of Charles Darwin. Erasmus described his creation, which he called a bigrapher, as "a pen with two beaks," and he constructed several versions, which he used to make duplicates of his own letters. In 1763, a Frenchman named Cotteneude invented a

Early sixteenth-century scribe, apparently using a pantograph.

three-pen pantographic copier and referred to it both as a *copiste habile* and a *polygraphe;* the latter name stuck and was adopted by others, both in French and in English, although Cotteneude's device didn't work very well. Among the main difficulties faced by all early designers and users of pantographic copying devices were the limitations imposed by the inconsistent size and quality of quill pens, which were cut by hand from goose feathers. ("Pen" comes from the Latin *penna,* meaning "feather," and penknives are called penknives because their original purpose was to cut pens from quills. The German word for "pen," and for "feather," is *feder.)*

In 1803, a significantly better version of the polygraph was created by John Isaac Hawkins, a clever and ambitious young English expatriate living in the United States. Hawkins manufactured and marketed his device in partnership with Charles Willson Peale, an American friend of his, who had been experimenting for some time with copying machines of his own. Like all polygraphs, Hawkins's looked like a big, complicated mousetrap—or like an old-fashioned swing set intended for children the size of Barbies. In one version, two pens were suspended side by side in an elaborately articulated wooden frame and were separated laterally by slightly more than the width of a sheet of paper. (There were also models with three, four, and five pens.) Moving either pen in any direction caused the other to move in tandem: east and west, north and south, and, most crucially, forward and up and down into a pair of inkwells, which were set into the center of the frame. In his application for a British patent, Hawkins wrote that the device could be used to make multiple facsimiles of letters, drawings, and paintings; to rule sheets of paper with straight, parallel lines; to draw single or multiple portraits, landscapes, and images in perspective; to make enlargements and reductions; and to create "secret correspondence"—distorted script that could be rendered legible only by using a second machine to "retract" it.

One of Thomas Jefferson's polygraphs.
Thomas Jefferson Memorial Foundation, Inc.

Among Hawkins and Peale's earliest and most enthusiastic customers was Thomas Jefferson, who had an insatiable passion for cool gizmos and had become acquainted with Hawkins while purchasing an earlier creation of his: a five-and-a-half-octave piano, which Jefferson wanted for one of his daughters. (Hawkins's numerous other inventions include a method of waterproofing fabric, an improved method of distilling liquor, and a technique for making paper from corn husks.) Jefferson loved his polygraph. "I think this is the finest invention of the present age," he wrote in his diary in 1804. "As a secretary to copy for us what we write without the power of revealing it, I find it a most precious possession to a man in public business." He eventually owned so many polygraphs—some of which are now displayed at Monticello—that he is often credited with having invented the device. He did not, but he did suggest numerous improvements, quite a few of which were incorporated into subsequent versions, and he maintained a supply of spare parts so that he could make repairs and adjustments.

Jefferson, even before he owned a copying machine of his own, was one of the first people anywhere to understand the sweeping historical, cultural, and political significance of office copying. In the early 1760s, as a teenage undergraduate at William & Mary College, he had undertaken an ambitious project to preserve a large number of early-Colonial-era legal documents, which had been carelessly stored at the Public Record Office in Williamsburg. (He wrote out fresh copies of crumbling old manuscripts, and sewed vulnerable pages in protective oilcloth wrappers.) A few years later, in 1770, a catastrophic fire at his family's home, Shadwell, destroyed most of his own written records, along with those of his parents—a loss that sharpened his already acute sense of the potentially disastrous impermanence of unique paper documents. In later years, he devoted much effort and ingenuity to copying and preserving his correspondence and other writing, and he borrowed back letters he had written years before, in order to make facsimiles for his files.

The source of this busywork was Jefferson's conviction that democracy and copying are intertwined: copying turns information into public information. Silvio A. Bedini, in a 1984 book called *Thomas Jefferson and His Copying Machines*, quotes an eloquent letter on the subject which Jefferson wrote in 1791 to a historian named Ebenezer Hazard, who shared at least some of Jefferson's concern: "Time and accident are committing daily havoc on the originals deposited in our public offices. The late war has done the work of centuries in this business. The lost cannot be recovered; but let us save what remains: not by vaults and locks which fence them from the public eye and use, in consigning them to the waste of time, but by such multiplication of copies, as shall place them beyond the reach of accident."

IN THE HANDS OF A careful user, a well-calibrated polygraph could produce permanent copies that were indistinguishable from originals. Bedini writes that many of the polygraphic copies Jefferson made "have remained fresh and totally legible" after two centuries, even in those instances where the tip of the copying pen became snagged in the fibers of the paper on which the facsimile was being produced—a common occurrence: "Remarkably, the polygraph resumed operation after such accidents, writing on after blank or blot." Many of Jefferson's copies, Bedini says, are known to be copies only because Jefferson himself so labeled them.

Users who were less mechanically adept than Jefferson generally felt less enthusiastic about polygraphs, and the devices consequently never found a mass market. (Unlike almost all successful office machines, the polygraph was meant to be operated not by clerical underlings but by their impatient, time-pressed bosses—a bad marketing strategy.) Vastly more popular, and ultimately more significant, was a copying machine that Jefferson himself had used for two decades before rejecting it in favor of the polygraph: the copying press. Although few people today know that this device ever existed, for more than a century it was the most important mechanical office copier in the world.

The copying press principle was both very simple and very old. As soon as people began to write with ink, they noticed that a reversed image of fresh handwriting could be made if a second sheet of paper (or a shirtsleeve or a hand) was pressed against it while the ink was still wet. In the late 1770s, James Watt—the inventor of the modern steam engine, the originator of the concept of "horsepower," and the man after whom the metric system's base unit of the rate of energy consumption was named—elevated that principle into a piece of office equipment.

Watt's interest in copying technology was personal. His steam engine company required, every day, a large and steadily increasing number of copies—of bills, of inventories, of ordinary correspondence—and Watt yearned to find a mechanical replacement for the burgeoning corps of human copyists he was forced to employ. Watt was a friend of Erasmus Darwin's, and both men were members of the Lunar Society, an association of fourteen learned friends who met once a month for several hours of vigorous discussion (about science, manufacturing, philosophy, and other subjects) and drinking. When Darwin, having just thought of the principle behind his bigrapher, announced at a Lunar Society meeting in 1779 that he had conceived of a device for duplicating script, Watt responded, "I hope to find a better solution of the problem. I will work out my ideas tonight and will communicate them to you tomorrow." The result was the copying press, which Watt patented and began to manufacture in early 1780.

You've probably seen a copying press without realizing what it was, very possibly in an antiques store or at a flea market, where it was almost certainly called a "book press." The most popular models were cast-iron screw presses, which were equipped with a heavy iron pressure plate that could be lowered, and raised again, by turning a horizontally mounted iron handle or wheel—the sort of wheel you might use to shut off a steam valve or batten down a hatch on a submarine. Other models exerted force not by lowering an iron plate but by rotating a heavy cylinder, which operated like a rolling pin or like the mangle on an old washing machine. A user took a freshly written document, placed a moistened sheet of translucent paper against the inked surface, and squeezed the two sheets together in the press, causing some of the ink from the original to penetrate the second sheet, which could then be read in the proper orientation by turning it over and looking through its back.*

---

*Watt, who died in 1819, spent the last years of his life working on a pantograph-like device for making three-dimensional copies of sculpture. You can see his prototype at London's Science Museum, where his workshop has been replicated.

Copying press with rolling-type moistening attachment, 1886.

To make good reproductions in this manner, a user needed not just a copying press but also the right kind of ink, the right kind of paper, and a number of other items, all of which Watt's company and several competitors supplied. Several pieces of standard nineteenth-century office equipment which now mystify people are in fact copying press accessories that were once widely used: flat drawers and divided shelves for filing individual press copies or storing bound copy books; heavy iron stands for supporting screw-type presses (and resisting their considerable torque); brushes and iron water bowls used in wetting pages; "blotter baths"; "dampening chambers"; and "drying books."

The earliest customers for Watt's invention included Benjamin Franklin, who ordered three of the devices in 1780. Franklin—whose first job was as a printer's apprentice and who, throughout his life, gave his occupation as "printer"—had long been interested in the copying problem, and, a few years later, invented a somewhat quirky method of his own. That method involved writing on a metal or stone plate with a viscous ink similar to Watt's; sprinkling fine sand, emery, or iron filings onto the ink while it was still wet; using a press to squeeze the dusted plate against a woodblock so that the granular material was transferred to and partially embedded in the wood; and using the treated woodblock as a relief printing plate, by inking the surface of the embedded material, which stood slightly higher than the background. The prints thus made were crude and often hard to read, and the method couldn't be used to make copies of correspondence, since there was no original; but the project was typical of Franklin, who was always fiddling with something.

Adam Smith ordered a copying press, along with a ream of copying paper, in 1780. George Washington was given one in 1782 and later bought another. Jefferson acquired his first in France in 1785, having learned of the invention from Franklin. Four years later, when Jefferson was about to take office as the first secretary of state, he bought one for the State Department as well. This was the first office copier owned by the United States government and one of the first copying presses owned by any government anywhere in the world. Jefferson also designed a portable version (similar to ones manufactured by others, including, eventually, Watt himself), and he carried it with him on the road in much the same way that a business traveler nowadays carries a notebook computer. In fact, Jefferson's model, which included a built-in miniature roller press, wasn't all that much bigger than a jumbo laptop. And its cabinet, which was made of wood and had brass fittings, contained storage compartments for Jefferson's razors, strop, shaving brush, toothbrush, comb, and nightcap. By the late nineteenth century, portable copiers that could be tucked into a coat pocket had become popular among salesmen and others who traveled frequently. One such device consisted of a wooden dowel along the length of which one edge of a flexible tablet of copying paper had been attached. A freshly written sheet was placed between two leaves in the tablet, and the tablet was then tightly rolled up, by hand, around the dowel.

Portable copying press, 1899.

PEOPLE IN THE DOCUMENT BUSINESS distinguish between copiers and duplicators. Describing the difference is harder to do with definitions than with an inexact analogy: If you gave birth to identical triplets, the three babies would be duplicates; if you then cloned one of the triplets, the fourth baby would be a copy. In this sense, a printing press is a duplicator, while a standard Xerox machine is a copier. A duplicator produces identical documents, of which none is truly the "original"; a copier makes facsimiles of documents that already exist. With a duplicator, there is always an intermediate phase—a woodblock, a page form filled with metal type, a lithographic plate—between the source document and the duplicates. Once you've written a letter on a sheet of paper, you can't reproduce it simply by feeding it into a printing press; you have to transfer your text to a printing plate of some kind first, then use that plate to make prints—each of which is then a duplicate of every other rather than a copy of anything.

This distinction is impossible to honor strictly, but it is historically significant nevertheless. After the era of monastic scribes—

who acted as copiers when they reproduced existing books and as duplicators when a roomful of them transcribed another monk's dictation—duplication was a vastly easier problem to solve than was true copying. In fact, until 1780, when Watt invented his copying press, all the world's copying machines were actually duplicators: engraved copper plates, Gutenberg's printing press, all pantograph-based devices (which produced equivalent duplicates rather than facsimiles of preexisting originals). Watt enabled people, for the first time in history, to mechanically make a facsimile of a document already in hand. This new capability was sharply limited, because a copying press could copy only originals that had been written very recently and with a modified ink, and each such original could be reproduced only a limited number of times. Still, it was something brand new in the world.

Like the printing press before it, the copying press failed to put scribes entirely out of work, and the two technologies, one mechanical and one human, coexisted for most of the nineteenth century. Even in the late 1800s, labor was so inexpensive that significant numbers of businesses continued to rely at least in part on human copying machines. The work was drudgery, of course; when a mid-nineteenth-century fiction writer needed a wretched character, an easy choice was a copyist: Gogol's Akaky, Dickens's Cratchit, Melville's Bartleby. (The job still exists on a limited scale today, in any small business that tracks its accounts manually in double-entry ledger books rather than electronically on computers.)

Nor were copying presses immediately displaced by some brand-new successor technology. The presses were so widely used, and for so long, that James Watt's entry in the 1899 edition of the British *Dictionary of Biography* could describe his invention, 119 years after he had filed his patent, as "universally employed." Few people today know what copying presses were, yet the date of their extinction is quite recent. The last president whose White House correspondence was copied on a copying press was not Abraham Lincoln or Andrew Johnson but Calvin Coolidge, who left office in 1929. And copying presses continued to be used elsewhere, though mostly in very limited applications, for another thirty years after that. Indeed, until the mid-twentieth century there were instances in which a copying press (which, after all, transferred the exact image of its original) was the only available means, other than taking a photograph, of creating a legally indisputable perfect copy—a function that in 1960 would be taken over, once and for all, by the Xerox machine.

IT TOOK TWO NEW INVENTIONS working together to begin to displace the copying press as the world's foremost device for reproducing routine office correspondence. The first was carbon paper, which was invented in 1806 by an Englishman named Ralph Wedgwood; the second was the typewriter, which was introduced in the 1870s. Neither carbon paper nor the typewriter alone would have been sufficient, but the two inventions together eventually put copying press manufacturers out of business.

Ralph Wedgwood was a black sheep member of the famous pottery family and therefore also a relative of Charles Darwin's. (Darwin's maternal grandfather was Josiah Wedgwood.) He called his invention Wedgwood's Patent Stylographic Manifold Writer, and originally intended it as a writing aid for the blind. The system's central element was a sheet of ink-soaked paper, which Wedgwood called "carbonic" or "carbonated" paper. Thomas Jefferson, America's original copying evangelist, tried it and didn't like it very much, although he acknowledged that a traveler might find it useful. "The fetid smell of the copying paper would render a room pestiferous if filled with presses of such paper," he wrote in a letter to Charles Willson Peale, who had been worried about the competition.

Wedgwood's system, in addition to smelling bad, was harder to use than later carbon papers would be. The main difference was that Wedgwood's paper, having been fully saturated with a pigmented oil, was inky on both sides. A user placed a sheet of it between a sheet of translucent paper and a sheet of regular paper, and wrote on the translucent sheet with a stylus made of metal, glass, or agate. Pressure from the stylus, which wasn't inked, produced a reversed image on the back of the translucent sheet and a properly oriented image on the front of the regular sheet. The regular sheet was treated as the "original"—it was the page that went into the mail—while the translucent sheet, which had to be flipped over in order to be read in the correct orientation, was filed. This awkward-seeming system was made necessary by quill pens, which couldn't be pressed hard enough to cause Wedgwood's carbon paper to leave a legible image.

By midcentury, pens and carbon paper had both been improved to the point where carbon copies could be made in the manner familiar to twentieth-century users. The 1881 edition of a popular reference book, *The Household Cyclopedia of General Information*, contained a recipe for making your own: "A mixture of equal parts of Frankfort black, and fresh butter is now to be smeared over sheets of paper, and rubbed off after a certain time. The paper, thus smeared, is to be pressed for some hours, taking care to have sheets of blotting paper between each of the sheets of black paper." Frankfort black was a popular nineteenth-century pigment, originally imported from Germany. According to a 1913 dictionary, it was prepared by "burning vine twigs, the lees of wine, etc."

Wedgwood made some money from his invention, but carbon paper didn't really flourish until it was paired with the typewriter, which struck paper with enough force to create an attractive original and several acceptable facsimiles. The first truly practical typewriter was the Sholes & Gliddon, introduced in 1874 by E. Remington & Sons, a manufacturer of sewing machines and guns. (The earliest model looked like a sewing machine—it had a treadle-powered carriage return—and sounded like a gun.) Among the first customers was Mark Twain, who was almost as much of a gadget-loving early adopter as Thomas Jefferson. Twain paid $125 for his machine, which typed only in capital letters. Late in his life, he claimed (in an unpublished autobiography) to have been "the first person in the world to apply the type-machine to literature"—since in 1874 he had hired a typist to make a copy of part of the manuscript for one of his books, most likely *The Adventures of Tom Sawyer.* (Twain is also often said to have been the first person in the world to have had a telephone installed in his home.)

Twain actually despised his typewriter, which he found complicated and frustrating, and soon got rid of it. When Remington, in 1875, asked him for an endorsement, he wrote, "GENTLEMEN: Please do not use my name in any way. Please do not even divulge the fact that I own a machine. I have entirely stopped using the Type-Writer, for the reason that I never could write a letter with it to anybody without receiving a request by return mail that I would not only describe the machine, but state what progress I had made in the use of it, etc., etc. I don't like to write letters, and so I don't want people to know I own this curiosity-breeding little joker. Yours truly, SAML. L. CLEMENS." Remington happily, and quite understandably, reproduced this note (under the heading WHAT "MARK TWAIN" SAYS ABOUT IT) in all its advertising.

The function performed by the carbon-paper-and-typewriter combination fell somewhere between copying and duplicating. Carbon paper isn't really a copying device, since you couldn't use it to (for example) make a copy of the crossword puzzle in today's newspaper. But it produced as many as ten duplicates without an intermediate step, and it economically performed almost all the same functions that a copying press did. As a result, the copying press gradually disappeared, not only from offices but also from the collective memory of the world.

ONE OF THE MOST IMPORTANT nineteenth-century advances in copying technology didn't involve the creation of a new device— although it did enhance all existing copying devices (and several still-to-be-developed ones). This was the invention of aniline dyes, the world's first synthetic coloring agents. In 1856, an eighteen-year-old English college student named William Henry Perkin was experimenting with coal-tar derivatives in an effort to create a substitute for quinine, which was made from the bark of a Peruvian tree and was then the only treatment for that great scourge of the far-flung British Empire, malaria. At the conclusion of one unsuccessful experiment, Perkin noticed a dark residue in the bottom of a test tube. Later, by accident, he discovered that the residue stained cloth bright purple. This substance came to be called mauveine, or aniline purple, and it was soon followed by numerous similar substances in various shades.

Aniline dyes—which were far more vivid and uniform than natural colorants, such as Frankfort black—transformed fashion (Queen Victoria wore mauve to her daughter's wedding, in 1858), interior decoration (the colors that defined Victorian homes were the colors of aniline dyes), chemistry (Perkin had shown that a test tube could make a man rich), and industry (the mass production of fabrics and other colorful consumer products became increasingly practical and profitable).*

---

*An interesting book on this very topic not only could be written but has been: *Mauve: How One Man Invented a Color That Changed the World*, by Simon Garfield.

Copying also changed. "Aniline dyes were swiftly adopted for copying inks"—the kind used with copying presses—"because they possess great tinctorial power, a property required in order to create multiple copies," Barbara Rhodes and William Wells Streeter write in a wonderfully comprehensive book called *Before Photocopying: The Art & History of Mechanical Copying, 1780–1938.* ("Tinctorial power" could also be called "stainability.") The new dyes "were also thought to increase the 'delicacy' of the copied image, retaining more of the original character of the handwriting than was possible with the diffuse lines of iron-gall copying inks." Copying presses, carbon paper, and typewriters all produced sharper images when vivid aniline dyes were used in place of old-fashioned natural pigments. The existence of the dyes also made possible the invention of the copying pencil—a very hard pencil whose graphite-and-clay-based lead was suffused with synthetic colorant. A letter written with a copying pencil could be copied on a copying press, just as one written with copying ink could be. A copying pencil could also be pressed hard enough to make a legible impression with carbon paper.

Early synthetic dyes, like many newly discovered and widely embraced nineteenth-century chemical innovations, also posed serious unanticipated health risks, of which most users remained unaware for decades. Aniline dyes were deadly poisons and could cause serious injury if, say, a user of a copying pencil accidentally stuck himself with its point. An 1899 issue of *Scientific American*, as quoted by Rhodes and Streeter, described a particularly gruesome poisoning case, involving a typewriter and a woman in Cincinnati: "Her fingers were stained by the blue ink used on the typewriter ribbon, and in trying to break a small blister on her lip she placed the stained finger on it, and very soon she felt a slight pain in her face. This was followed in a short time by a slight swelling. The pain then became almost unendurable and her lip began to swell badly and turn black.

Everything that medical skill could do was done, but she got rapidly worse and died in great agony. The poisoned lip had swollen to gigantic proportions and nothing could reduce it."

A MAJOR BENEFICIARY of the invention of synthetic dyes was a document reproduction technique known as stencil duplicating. Its earliest form was invented in 1874 by Eugenio de Zuccato, a young Italian studying law in London, who called his device the Papyrograph. Zuccato's system involved writing on a sheet of varnished paper with a caustic ink, which ate through the varnish and the paper fibers, leaving holes where the writing had been. This sheet—which had now become a stencil—was placed on a blank sheet of paper, and ink was rolled over it so that the ink oozed through the holes, creating a duplicate on the second sheet. One year later, the man who invented everything, Thomas Edison, introduced a stencil duplicating device of his own: Edison's Automatic Press and Electric Pen. This was a stylus with a sharp tip that moved rapidly up and down, like the needle on a sewing machine. The tip was powered by an electric motor the size of a fishing reel which was mounted at the other end of the pen. By carefully maneuvering the pen around an impervious sheet, a user could create a perforated stencil through which ink could be pressed. (In his patents, Edison cited the "cartoons" used by artists beginning in the sixteenth century to transfer large designs to canvas: full-size paper sketches, which the artists pricked with pins and dusted with powdered charcoal or graphite, creating a dotted outline).* Duplicates made with Edison's Electric Pen had a dis-

---

*The English word *cartoon* comes from an Italian word meaning simply "card" or "chart" and therefore refers to the medium rather than the message. The Italians took their word from the Greek *khartës:* "papyrus leaf."

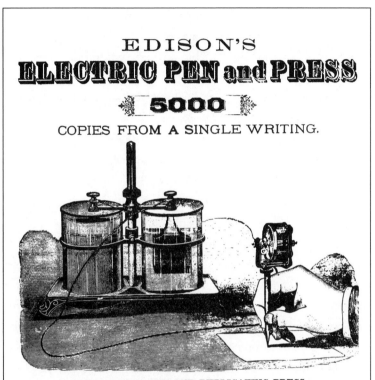

Advertisement for Edison's Electric Pen, c. 1880.

tracting pointillist quality but were otherwise legible. The battery, which was connected to the motor by wires, was a machine in itself: two humidor-size jars containing water and sulfuric acid, mounted on an iron stand. This ungainly contraption was "the first electric motor and associated battery ever to be manufactured and sold as a working unit," according to W. B. Proudfoot, the author of *The Origin of Stencil Duplicating*.

In the 1880s, Albert Blake Dick—the famous A. B. Dick, whose name brought joy to any schoolboy who suddenly discovered it (as I did) on the side of a machine in the office of his school's secretary—thought of placing a sheet of impervious paper (usually waxed) on top of a filelike metal plate and then "writing" on the paper with a metal stylus in such a way that the sharp points on the plate perforated the sheet, which could then be used as a duplicating stencil. Dick was a lumberman. Like James Watt a century before him, he originally intended merely to address his own company's copying needs. When he applied for a patent, he discovered that Edison had invented but never developed a similar idea. The two men met to discuss a licensing agreement, and Edison said, "Dick, I would give everything I own to be a young man like you again because there is so much I want to accomplish before I die." (Dick was thirty-three at the time, and Edison was forty-two.) Dick called the new device a Mimeograph and had the marketing wisdom to give all the credit to his famous partner. Edison Mimeographs in a variety of shapes and sizes sold well for decades—by 1940, roughly half a million were in use in the United States—and A. B. Dick and his descendants eventually forgot all about two-by-fours.

Among Dick's competitors during the late nineteenth century and early twentieth century was the Gestetner Co., which was based in England. In 1881, David Gestetner patented a device he called the Cyclostyle: a stylus with a small toothed wheel at the

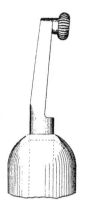

Gestetner's Cyclostyle, 1881.

tip. "The waxed paper or stencil was placed not on a file plate; but on a smooth surface such as a sheet of tinned metal or zinc (a soft metal)," Proudfoot writes, "and the Cyclostyle was held in the hand like a pen. Indeed it was a pen—a wheel pen—and the teeth of the wheel, cut in the rim, effectively punctured both wax and paper, forming good perforations through which the ink could freely pass."

Another competitor was the gelatin duplicator—more commonly known as the hectograph. It was invented in 1878 and was used for so long in so many versions that you don't have to be a grandparent to remember taking a school exam that had been printed on one, or using one to publish a neighborhood newspaper, or making signs and posters on a REMCO Hectographic Copier (a children's toy sold in the late 1960s).* The hectograph's name was derived from the Greek word *hekaton*, meaning "hun-

---

*The company's slogan in that era was "Every boy wants a REMCO toy—and so do girls." The company is part of another company now, but it still exists.

dred"—the number of legible copies that could supposedly be made from a single original. In Germany, hectographs were known for a time as Schapirographs.

The idea behind the hectograph was so simple that a determined kid with sympathetic parents might hope to make one for himself. The key component was a shallow, page-size tin or tray containing a mixture of gelatin and glycerin and (sometimes) a few other ingredients; it looked like a mean, unappetizing plate of grayish Jell-O. A user created a duplicating master by writing or drawing on a sheet of paper using hectographic ink, which was similar to the copying ink used with copying presses and contained an aniline dye. Once the ink had dried, the gelatin pad was moistened with water, and the paper was pressed, ink side down, against it. Some of the ink transferred to the gelatin, which kept it damp. Copies were made by pressing blank sheets of paper against

Hectograph.

the pad, a process that could be repeated until the last of the ink was gone. The hectograph soon evolved into more convenient versions, in which the gelatin pad was replaced by a waxed-paper master sheet, and the liquid ink was replaced by a form of carbon paper, which made distinctively purple impressions on the master. Rotary spirit duplicators, the best known of which were produced by the Ditto Co., employed versions of both innovations and were therefore direct descendants of the hectograph. The "spirit" in that name refers to methyl alcohol, a small amount of which was applied to each sheet of copy paper as it entered the machine, dampening it just enough to dissolve a bit of the waxy purple ink from the master, which was attached to a rotating drum. The alcohol gave the copies a characteristically terrible smell, adored by schoolchildren of my generation.

In all of the nineteenth century, only two true copying technologies (as opposed to duplicating technologies) were devised, and both of them had severe limitations insofar as documentary reproduction was concerned. One was photography, about which I'll have more to say in another chapter. The other was blueprint-

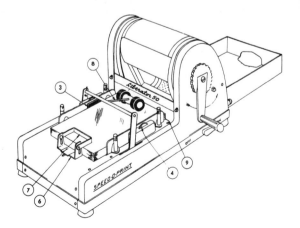

Speed-0-Print stencil duplicator, 1950.

ing, which was invented in 1842 by an Englishman named Sir John Frederick William Herschel and was used mainly to reproduce engineering and architectural drawings. (A related process, called diazo, actually was used for ordinary office copying, but not until well into the twentieth century.) Blueprinting was fairly common in Europe after 1842 but was not introduced in the United States until 1876, when a Swiss exhibitor demonstrated it at the Philadelphia Centennial Exposition. To create a blueprint, a draftsman made a drawing on translucent paper; the paper was pressed, in a frame, against a sheet that had been treated with potassium ferrocyanide and ferric citrate or similar photosensitive chemicals; the paired sheets were exposed to sunlight or (after the introduction of electrical service) to a bright arc light. This exposure eventually caused the treated paper to turn dark blue except where the dark lines of the original blocked the light. Blueprinting had inherent limitations that made it all but useless for ordinary office copying: it took forever; the original was often ruined, since it was usually oiled to make it more translucent; and the chemicals smelled so horrendous that many architects and engineers preferred to use gigantic copying presses instead.

And that, more or less, is where copying technology stood in 1906, the year Chester Floyd Carlson, the inventor of xerography, was born.

3

How Do You Know What Color It Is on the Other Side?

ALL FOUR OF CHESTER CARLSON'S GRANDPARENTS emigrated from Sweden to the United States in the mid-nineteenth century. For the most part, they came seeking religious freedom. (Carlson's grandfather on his father's side, for example, had been disinherited by his own father after becoming interested in baptism by immersion and other practices proscribed by the Swedish National Church.) They settled, at different times, on what turned out to be neighboring homesteads in Grove City, Minnesota, a tiny Swedish farming community about seventy-five miles west of Minneapolis.

Chester's father, Olof Adolph Carlson, was born in Grove City in 1870. He hated farming and hated working for his father, and he fled as soon as he was twenty-one. He learned to cut hair in a barbershop in Elgin, Illinois—where he also briefly attended a "business college"—then drifted west, traveling partly by bicycle, giving haircuts along the way. He ran a barbershop in Ogden, Utah, which in the 1890s was a booming frontier railway junction. Then he took to the road again, probably spurred by reports of gold discoveries in Alaska. He covered his expenses by cutting the matted hair and beards of miners in camps in southeastern Washington, and eventually found steady work in a barbershop in Seattle. Sometime afterward, his old Grove City neighbor Ellen Josephine Hawkins—who was three months younger and had been a friend throughout his childhood—traveled to Seattle to attend a convention of Swedish Baptists. They renewed their acquaintance and married shortly afterward.

A relative later described Olof as "brilliant"—a reader and a deep thinker, although his formal education was sketchy. Ellen was bright, cheerful, and reasonably attractive, and she had an indomitably optimistic outlook. She was the third eldest in a family of ten children (four boys and six girls) "and was looked up to by her sisters as one of the wisest and as a sort of leader," Chester Carlson wrote later. She also had a "great capacity for personal sacrifice of her own self-interest for others, and for endurance of hardship."

Ellen had many opportunities to demonstrate these noble qualities, because the Carlsons' life together was unlucky from the start. Chester's birth—in Seattle, on February 8, 1906—was preceded by that of a stillborn boy and followed by that of a stillborn girl. When Chester was an infant, Olof came home from work one day with what at first seemed to be a cold and then seemed to be pneumonia but turned out to be tuberculosis. Olof also suffered increasingly from arthritis in his spine, and the two illnesses combined to incapacitate him—especially in later years, when they were accompanied by what was almost certainly a severe, unremitting depression. Chester knew his father only as an invalid, never as a provider, and remembered him later as "a bent walking skeleton, who had to spend the greater part of his time lying flat on his back." Olof was strikingly handsome when he was young but looked eighty by the time he was forty-five. In a family photograph taken when Chester was nine, Olof lurks in the background, a wraith suspended from a pair of crutches, his sunken cheeks gnawed by shadows. His forehead is lowered and his chin is drawn back: he is straining for breath. He looks old enough to be his son's grandfather.

Olof's ill health dominated Chester's childhood. When Chester was three and a half, in 1909, Olof moved the family to Kingsburg, California, where one of his brothers owned a vineyard and where he hoped the mild climate would help him. It did not. Four months later, thinking dry air might bring relief, he moved the family again, to what must have been a religious camp or a sanitarium, called Camp Freedom, in the desert near Yuma, Arizona. The Carlsons lived there in a two-story wood-framed tent erected among sand dunes, and Olof spent much of every day lying on a cot in the tent's ovenlike interior, hoping to bake the disease from his lungs. He had a deep, excruciating cough, and each cough wrenched his spine. One day, in agony, he suddenly cried out that he wished he could die, and Chester, who was now four years old, heard him and was deeply frightened.

In 1910, after eight months in Arizona, Olof moved the family again. "My father had been roped in on a crazy American land colonization scheme in Mexico," Chester wrote later. "I suspect he sunk the bulk of his remaining savings into it, sight unseen. We traveled to the site, which was several hundred miles down the west coast of Mexico, with all our personal belongings. On arrival we found that the 'farm' my father had presumably bought was nothing but dry adobe clay and cactus, totally unproductive."

The property was near the town of Abuya, in the state of Sinaloa. Olof, who was no longer physically able to cut hair, had been attracted to the scheme in part by promises of plentiful, inexpensive Mexican labor. The promises turned out to be false but irrelevant, since the land was too poor to have occupied even a single worker. The Carlsons bought a cow and some chickens but had no hope of planting crops, and they were barely able to feed themselves. Then the rainy season arrived, and the parched ground was transformed into thick, gluelike mud. Water stood a foot deep on the floor of the two-room adobe hut in which they lived, and they were forced to take refuge in bed—the only dry surface in their home. Periodically, the cow and chickens became stuck in the mire, and Ellen had to wade outdoors to free them. And that wasn't the worst of it. "My father's health deteriorated further," Chester wrote later, "my mother contracted malaria, and we were beset by scorpions, tarantulas and snakes, chicken thieves, and eventually the threat of danger from the Mexican revolution."

The Carlsons lived in Mexico for seven months, a period that Chester described later as "probably the most grueling and depressing time in my young life, although much more so for my parents, who protected me from the worst." Ellen, in particular, strove to shield her son from their destitution. She remained cheerful during her own serious illness, and Chester said later that throughout his childhood she had always somehow managed to make the family's poverty seem like a game—a challenging puzzle that could be solved with good spirits and ingenuity. In Mexico, furthermore, Chester, for just the second time in his life, had other children to play with. (The first time had been during the family's four months in Kingsburg, where he had enjoyed what he would later describe, in the heartbreakingly flat tone that characterizes nearly all his written childhood reminiscences, as "the first experience I had had with playfellows.") The Carlsons' Mexican farm was situated near the farms of four or five other American families, all of whom had been duped by the same land fraud, and one of the other fathers started a small school, in which Chester constituted half the kindergarten. It was at this school that he made his first real friend, a little girl named Pauline Nickerson, who was so fond of him that five years later she was still sending him letters.

The turmoil that became the Mexican Revolution commenced in November 1910, and American officials advised all U.S. citizens to leave the country. Olof, who was now nearly penniless, abandoned his adobe hut and booked passage on the only form of transportation he could afford, a rusting freighter bound for Los Angeles. Baggage wasn't a problem, because the Carlsons' remaining possessions fit easily into a single trunk. At sea on Christmas morning, the freighter's captain, feeling sorry for his youngest passenger, gave Chester the only present he would receive that day: a chocolate bar.

It may be impossible for an American born after 1935 to imagine a society with no public safety net. When the Carlsons debarked in Los Angeles during the final week of 1910, they were alone, impoverished, and homeless to a degree that is scarcely conceivable in America today. They later qualified for minimal relief from the county, and Olof for a time received a small disability stipend from a barbers union, which he had joined as a young man, but there was no government agency or program from which they could seek assistance with food, housing, or medical care. They moved in briefly with a sister of Ellen's, but her house was small and she had financial difficulties of her own. With the sister's help, though, Ellen—who was still suffering the effects of her malaria and of a dispiriting variety of other ailments, including headaches and gastrointestinal troubles—found work as a doctor's housekeeper, and the doctor, taking pity, allowed the family to move into a single room in the back of his house. The Carlsons lived in that room for more than a year.

Chester was now five years old and increasingly conscious of the scale of his family's misfortunes. "I was beginning to become aware that I was somehow 'different' from other children, whose fathers worked for a living, and that I was somehow an 'Outsider,' " he wrote later. At around the same time, he suffered two painful and potentially serious accidents—a fall against a bronze fixture in a bank lobby and a blow to his head from a playground swing—both of which, he later speculated, might have been caused "by unconscious self-destructive wishes prompted by growing awareness of our family situation." He was a shy, soft-spoken, well-behaved little boy, who, deep within himself, couldn't help sharing his parents' deepening despair about the precariousness of their existence.

In the spring of 1912, shortly after Chester had turned six, Olof moved the family to San Bernardino, which was then a small town sixty miles east of Los Angeles. He rented, for $12 a month, a decrepit house on what Chester later described as the wrong side of the tracks, and Ellen did her best to support the family, by taking in sewing and doing other odd jobs. Chester attended the local school and enjoyed what felt to him like the ordinary pleasures of childhood. Three years later, though, Olof—now believing that cold, rather than heat, might improve the condition of his lungs and spine—moved the family to the village of Crestline, in the mountains outside of town. There they lived in a decaying shed, which had been built as a warehouse for cement during the construction of a dam nearby and, the summer before, had housed a grocery store used by dam workers and by tourists staying at a nearby campground. The Carlsons did what they could to insulate a single small room in the back, mainly by stuffing newspapers into the many gaps between the boards, and heated the space with a balky stove. The snows that winter were three and four feet deep. Each morning, Ellen used a hand mirror to flash a signal to a worried storekeeper in the valley below, to let him know that they had survived another night.

In Crestline, Chester attended a one-room school with a handful of other children, and, once again, he was delighted to have playmates—until the day after Christmas vacation, when he returned to the schoolhouse to find that he had suddenly become the entire student body. The fathers of all the other children had been employed by the reservoir company that was building the dam, and a court order issued the previous year had brought construction to a halt. Now their jobs had definitely ended, and they had all moved away.

The teacher, whose contract ran for the rest of the school year, stayed on to teach her single pupil. At recess each day, Chester would wander alone in the empty schoolyard or sit on the front step. He had no one to talk to and nothing to do. "Sometimes I'd look inside, and there was the teacher at her desk, her chin in her hand, staring at the wall," he recalled later. He described these final months of fourth grade as "one of the loneliest periods in my life" and said that his isolation from other young people at that time "marked the beginning of a considerable setback in my social development among children of my age." When the school year ended, Olof—who had now abandoned all hope of improving his health—moved the family back into the valley, where for the next eight years they lived in a grim succession of run-down houses.

Even as young Chester was worrying that the circumstances of his life had made ordinary companionship with other children impossible, his family's poverty was forcing him prematurely to join the world of adults. He began working odd jobs for money when he was eight. By the time he was twelve or thirteen, he was rising each morning at four o'clock so that he could work for two or three hours before school; when classes ended in the afternoon, he went to work again, traveling from job to job on a battered bicycle. (His bike was stolen a few years later, making it impossible for him to get to work on time, and one of his employ-

ers replaced it with an old one that someone else had discarded—
out of pity for his family's situation, Chester came to believe.) He
sold soda water, pulled weeds, picked fruit, harvested potatoes,
swept sidewalks, washed store windows, sold fish, and raised
guinea pigs for a research laboratory. He was a bill collector, a bill
passer, and a mail boy, and he worked as a janitor for a number of
local businesses, among them a bakery, a bank, a building and loan
association, a newspaper, and the local prizefight arena. (He was
entrusted with the keys to the bank and the building and loan,
since he went to work each morning long before any other employee was around to let him in.) On a few widely separated occa-
sions, Olof felt well enough to attempt to earn some money. He
tried giving haircuts at home for a brief time, and he once bought
a horse and wagon in the hope of earning a living by collecting and
selling junk. But these efforts never lasted more than a few weeks,
and they were never profitable. Chester—who was earning $50 or
$60 a month by the time he entered high school—had become his
family's principal provider.

Despite this growing burden, Chester managed to make good
grades, especially in his science classes, and he began to think seriously about how he might use his talents to construct a better life.
Briefly he thought he might be a novelist, and for an English class
assignment he wrote a brooding short story in which he used the
word *dank* several times. ("Too dank," was his teacher's comment.)
He considered gold prospecting, publishing, and several other oc-
cupations but eventually decided that his best chance would be to
invent something valuable. "It looked very doubtful if I could ever
go to college," he said later, "and still my interests were in things
that almost required a college education to make anything out of
them. Invention was one chance to start with nothing and end up
with a fortune." He pursued this theme again several years later: "I
had read of Edison and other successful inventors, and the idea of

making an invention appealed to me as one of the few available means to accomplish a change in one's economic status, while at the same time bringing to focus my interest in technical things and making it possible to make a contribution to society as well." When he was twelve, he told his cousin Roy that he was going to invent something big someday, and Roy took his ambition seriously.

Roy was an important figure in Chester's life. He was five years older, but he found Chester to be a more stimulating companion than any of his contemporaries, and on Sundays when he was in college he used to ride his bike eleven miles from Redlands to visit him. The two often talked about science, and Roy said later that he learned something new from every conversation. One day, he recalled, he pointed out a blackbird to Chester, who responded, "How do you know it's a blackbird?"

"Because I see it is black," Roy said.

"On this side it's black," Chester said, "but how do you know what color it is on the other side?"

Chester would say later that his loneliness as a child had led him to develop independent habits of thinking, and that those habits had informed his scientific imagination as an adult. At fifteen, he began jotting down ideas for inventions and making other notes in a pocket diary, a practice he maintained for the rest of his life. He sketched concepts for a rotating billboard, a machine for cleaning shoes, a trick safety pin (which could be made to look as though it had pierced a finger), a fastener for bags and clothing, a new type of lipstick, and a disposable handkerchief made of soft paper.* He also made drawings of interesting devices invented by

---

*Carlson may have been inspired by Kleenex facial tissues, which were introduced in 1924 as a "sanitary cold cream remover"; sales of Kleenex remained modest until six years later, when the tissues were repositioned as disposable handkerchiefs. (Times change. In 2003, an eleven-year-old niece of mine saw her grandfather using a handkerchief and asked, with astonishment, "Is that a *cloth* Kleenex?")

others, including a stencil duplicator with a revolving print drum, a device very much like machines then marketed by A. B. Dick.

Chester had been fascinated by printing and the graphic arts since early childhood. When he was ten, he created a newspaper called *This and That*. He wrote out the first issue by hand ("Rule— Do not read this in school") and solicited contributions from his friends: "This is a new paper being started by Chester Carlson. If you wish to have a story, a drawing or any other thing put in this paper, write it so I can understand it on a paper, give it to ME and I will have it in the next paper I publish." He solved his duplication problem in the same way that virtually every office worker of that era did: by including a routing list on the original and asking each reader to pass it along after finishing it. (The order of circulation: Damon, Gladys, Fredrick, Marion, Thirza, Charlesa, "ME.")

Chester's favorite plaything was a rubber stamp printing set, and the possession he coveted most was a typewriter. An aunt gave him one for Christmas in 1916, when he was ten—but it was a toy rather than the genuine office model he yearned for, and he was secretly disappointed. Still, he made heavy use of it. It was a Simplex, a so-called index typewriter, which had a manually operated print wheel instead of keys, produced capital letters only, and was small enough to carry in a large pocket. (The mechanism was very similar to that of the much later Dymo label maker, which embosses raised white letters on colored plastic tape; with a Simplex, too, you typed by squeezing.) The Simplex Typewriter was actually a clever piece of engineering and an excellent value. It did a passable job of typing—although keeping letters in straight lines was a problem—yet cost as little as a dollar, while real machines sold for a hundred or more. Simplex Typewriters were manufactured in dozens of models beginning in 1891, and they were popular not only with children ("They teach—They entertain") but also with traveling salesmen, who used them to type orders and in-

Simplex Typewriter, c. 1916.
Jim Paisley

voices while on the road. The fourth issue of *This and That* was typed on Chester's Simplex, with help from his friend Norman Borden, who also wrote articles for the paper and, occasionally, figured in the news:

SAYS ARM IS BROKEN.

IN PLAYING AT RECESS M. JONES BENT N. BORDEN'S ARM
IN SOME WAY. NORMAN SAID IT BROKE HIS ARM BUT
TEACHER SAYS IT WAS ONLY SPRAINED. SOME SAY SMALL
BONE IS BROKEN.

When Chester was in high school, his numerous employers included a local printer. Sweeping the floors around the typesetting machines and printing presses gave Chester many opportunities to observe the technology of printing, and his fascination deepened. One week, his employer allowed him to take home an old, barely functioning printing press in lieu of a paycheck. Chester refurbished the machine and used it to publish a crude magazine called *The Amateur Chemists' Press*, which he intended to sell to other science-minded students at a subscription price of sixty-five cents for six

FOR SALE
GOOD RANCH AND HOUSE ALSO
BARN AND PEACH TREES WITH
HORSE AND WAGON.
CALL SUNSET 868-R.

FOR SALE
GOOD HORSE AND SUHY.
CALL SUNSET 858-R.

PUZZLES
TO DO THIS PUZZLE COPY IT DOWN ON A PAPER THE
WAY IT IS HERE AND SEE IF YOU CAN PUT THE RI-
GHT LETTERS WHERE THEY BELONG. IF YOU CAN SEND
OR GIVE THEM TO CHESTER CARLSON.
TH-- P-P-- -- -R-E.
ANSWER NEXT WEDNESDAY.
ANSWER--FROM LAST WED.--BANKER-A MAN THAT OWNS
A BANK.

FOR SALE - OL
5 DAY OLD KID, NANNY $1
CALL EDITORS.

FOR SALE--CHEAP
BANTAM HEN AND COCK
HEN LAYING.
CALL T. STEVENS

A BAD BOY.
THERE IS A BAD BOY ALWAYS HURTING THE LITTLE ON-
ER AT SOHOOL THE BOYS WILL KNOCK THEM DOWN
AND SIT ON THEM AND MAKE THEM CRY. AND THEN
LAUGH AT THEM AND KNOCK THEM DOWN AGAIN. ONE
DAY WHEN SOME BOYS WERE FIGHTING A BOY GOT HIS
ARM AND HE COULD GO TO SCHOOL FOR A DAY.
D. M. EVERETT

OLD MOTHER WITCH
FELL IN A DITCH
PICKED UP A PENNY
AND THOUGHT SHE WAS RICH

"This and That," typed on Chester's Simplex.

months. Almost immediately, though, he scaled back his ambitions: setting the type for a single issue had required a week of close, tedious work, and the press, which was powered by a foot pedal, was hard to operate. After two or three issues, thoroughly exasperated, he dropped the project. "I was impressed with the tremendous amount of labor involved with getting something into print," he said in 1965 in an interview with Joseph J. Ermenc, a professor at Dartmouth College. "That set me to thinking about easier ways to do that, and I got to thinking about duplicating methods."

Thinking about duplicating methods would become the work of his life, of course, but his thoughts on that subject couldn't take him very far at the time, because his schoolwork and his jobs kept him occupied. He seldom enjoyed more than brief periods of true leisure, and he had no social life. He was a little over six feet tall, had blue eyes and wavy blond hair, and was frequently described as handsome, but he was athletically inept, and in groups of other teenagers he was quiet and retiring to the point of invisibility. "I felt inferior not only economically, but physically as well," he wrote in 1963. "I was in good health but physically the least muscular in my class, and was awkward and given to social blunders. I felt I was the lowest in the pecking order and something of a 'laughing stock' among other students." He did join the Boy Scouts and the YMCA. "But I was never invited to parties, nor did I have time or money for most of the other pleasures of my schoolmates." His best friends were a casual girlfriend named Kitty and a former neighbor, an older boy who had dropped out of high school, found a job as a railroad machinist, and developed a local reputation as a juvenile delinquent. The two boys had almost nothing in common except comparably lonely lives at the perimeter of adolescent society. They hung around together on weekends and occasionally went for aimless drives in a car belonging to the friend's mother.

Then, catastrophically, Chester's already diminished world collapsed. During his junior year in high school, when he was seventeen years old, his mother—who since his infancy had been his
one source of happiness, encouragement, stability, and love—died
of tuberculosis, at the age of fifty-three. Her death devastated
him; twenty-five years later, he was almost physically unable to
speak of it, and haltingly told his wife, "That is the worst thing
that ever happened to me. I so wanted to be able to give her a few
things in life." His mother's death also meant that the task of supporting and nursing his father, with whom his relationship had
grown increasingly strained and whom he couldn't help blaming
for his mother's death, now fell entirely to him. Almost immediately, he developed a severe abscess on the side of his foot "which
crippled me for several months," but he had to continue working.
He took on more jobs, including one that a sympathetic teacher
arranged for him as a laboratory assistant at a cement mill, where
he sometimes worked three 8-hour shifts in a row. He managed to
cover his expenses and save a bit more than $100.

This relatively secure period didn't last long. Olof—extending
what by then had become the one clear pattern of his life—squandered the bulk of Chester's savings, plus an unexpected small in-
heritance of his own, by investing without Chester's knowledge in
an ill-considered health food business, for which his own physical
condition proved to be an almost perfectly effective negative advertisement. (In a two-page "personal history" that Chester wrote
in a pocket notebook five years later, he described this period simply as "Pa gone crazy 1924–5.") To cover their meager living costs,
Chester now had to go work at the county farm—the "poor farm."
By the time he graduated from high school, he and Olof had been
reduced to living in a former chicken coop, whose single room had
a bare concrete floor. Chester—hoping to muffle the sound of his
father's coughing and to lessen his own chance of contracting the

disease that had killed his mother—slept outside, on a narrow strip of packed earth between the chicken coop and a board fence that ran along the alley, in a sleeping bag that he himself had made. ("It wasn't as bad as it sounds," he recalled.) Later, he built himself a hut from scrap lumber and moved into that.

CHESTER HAD PROMISED HIS MOTHER before she died that he would finish high school, and he kept his promise. For some time, he had dreamed of attending the California Institute of Technology—an ambition that had arisen during a visit to his school by a group of Caltech students—but he felt now that he had no hope of meeting the cost of further education, and he resigned himself to the idea that his high school diploma would be his last. At an opportune moment, though, he and Olof were visited by his Uncle Oscar, one of his mother's four brothers, who was the principal of a public high school in Minnesota. Oscar urged Chester to make any sacrifice to continue his education and told him that if he delayed matriculation in the hope of accumulating money for tuition he would almost certainly never go. Inspired by this advice, Chester took a postgraduate year at his old high school, to fill in required courses he had missed, and applied to a cooperative work/study program at Riverside Junior College, fifteen miles from San Bernardino. Students in that program worked and went to class in alternating six-week periods, and earned a two-year associate's degree in four years. Chester, after being admitted, moved himself and his father into a cheap one-room apartment in Riverside. With help from the school, he found a job in the lab at another cement plant. He also got a job at a cannery, and another in the kitchen of a nearby inn.

At Riverside, Chester began as a chemistry major but soon switched to physics, largely out of admiration for his physics professor, a charismatic young man named Howard Bliss, who also ran the work/study program. Bliss was Chester's first real mentor—maybe his first real father figure—and Chester said later that he was the best teacher he had ever had. Bliss, in addition to recognizing and cultivating the academic talents of this shy, hardworking student, gave Chester glimpses of an existence far less suffocating than the one he had known. Bliss was an avid, eccentric outdoorsman—he sometimes slept in the back of his truck rather than inside his house with his wife—and he frequently led groups of students on hikes and camping trips. Chester went along on many of these, including a week-long expedition through Death Valley. The trips provided his only genuine relief from his oppressive responsibilities. Bliss also introduced Chester to photography—a field that would later influence his thinking about copying, though mostly in a negative way, because his one effort at developing and printing his own pictures came out so poorly that he gave it up.

Bliss's most important contribution to Chester's future lay in urging him not to abandon his aspiration to attend Caltech. With Bliss's encouragement and guidance, Chester completed Riverside's academic program in three years instead of four, receiving his degree in the spring of 1928. He also accumulated several hundred dollars in savings. He took two additional calculus courses during the summer after graduation and was admitted to Caltech in the fall as a junior.

Before Chester left Riverside, Bliss enumerated what he believed to be his student's weaknesses as a scholar and as a person, and made suggestions for eliminating them. Chester noted all this in his pocket diary, along with comments of his own. For example, Bliss told him that he lacked self-confidence and proposed the following "pill" as a solution (as recounted by Chester): "Put on a bold front, change tone of voice, call other fellows crazy once in a while. (Note: I feel self-confident, but perhaps I don't show it to others.)" In addition, Bliss—in a series of instructions that Chester labeled, in his notebook, "Suggestions on Proposed Method of Procedure at Caltech"—advised him to cultivate the acquaintance of faculty members, take part in campus activities, keep a financial record, and not try to hold down a job during the first term. Thus prepared, Chester moved himself and his father to Pasadena, where he found a cheap apartment for the two of them; his father, still unable to work, contributed by doing the cooking.

Despite personal difficulties and a crushing work schedule, Chester had greatly enjoyed his three years at Riverside, where, he recalled later, he "made several good friends and had many good times." At Caltech, in contrast, he often felt lonely and over-whelmed. He was ashamed of his now threadbare and unfashion-able clothing, and he told no one that he was living with an ailing parent. Even worse, he found his classmates—math and science whizzes, most of whom were no more socially adept than he was—to be numbingly uninteresting outside of class. "Right now I am sorry I went to Caltech," he wrote in his notebook toward the end of his third semester. "I should have gone to Berkeley. True, the technical education here is probably better, but I am literally starved socially; I am becoming a social dunce." Old photographs show that he had a girlfriend—and that he himself had become dashingly good-looking—but he never mentioned the girlfriend in his journals or in any of his later autobiographical writing.

His most pressing personal concerns at Caltech were financial. Tuition alone, at $260 a year, exceeded his total earnings, and his school workload, which was much heavier than at Riverside, left him little time to earn money. He mowed lawns and did similar odd jobs on weekends, and he worked at a cement mill in Los

Angeles when school ended for the summer, but his income covered less than a third of his and his father's expenses, and he soon
had to borrow money from the school and from every remotely
solvent relative he dared to approach—obligations that he
recorded meticulously in his notebook. By the time he graduated,
with good but not exceptional grades, he was $1,500 in debt.

At the end of his first term at Caltech, Carlson had written in
his notebook, "God, what a weakling I am. I can't buckle down to
study, to work hard, or anything. I can't concentrate, waste 10
minutes out of every 15 of an hour of study. . . . When I make a little failure at anything I lose heart and quit if I can. Otherwise I go
on halfheartedly. I am the opposite of the best ideal of a fine man.
Why, my voice, even, is squeaky." By the end of the next semester,
his mood had improved, and he had begun to sound, at least occasionally, like a reasonably confident and ambitious young man. "I
think it would be a good idea to have a definite objective for my
lifework," he wrote. "Therefore I plan to break other business
connections and go fully into a project of organizing a business for
inventing, research on inventions, and the buying and development of patent interests at or before the age of thirty. Among
other things careful investigations would be made of present industrial processes and machinery with an effort to invent new improved ones. Close contact would always be kept with both the
latest developments of science and the latest needs of industry."
More than a year before, in the same pages, he had stoically identified what he believed to be a key to success and personal fulfillment: "It has ceased to be mere interesting speculation with me
and has become more and more an accepted 'fact,' that the most
pleasure we get from life is 'sweating.' " Decades later, he would
often say that his two years at Caltech, though difficult and lonely,
had been crucial to his success in life. The courses he took—in
physics, chemistry, mechanics, electricity, magnetism—all con-

tributed to his discoveries and gave him a grounding in science which he believed he could not easily have obtained elsewhere.

CARLSON GRADUATED FROM CALTECH IN 1930, one of the least auspicious moments in American history to be looking for a first job. Unemployment was at a record high and rising. Banks were failing at the rate of dozens per month, and then at the rate of hundreds per month. Industrial investment throughout the country had essentially ceased. Early in his final semester, Carlson sent letters to more than eighty potential employers. "I wrote to any company that I thought might be interested in physical chemistry, and a few to companies interested only in straight chemistry," he told Joseph Ermenc in 1965. "I got only two or three replies and one interview. At the interview the man was friendly and sympathetic but I never got the job." In the spring, with no other prospects, he signed up to meet on campus with a representative from Bell Telephone Laboratories, which was one of the few big companies still recruiting college students. He felt afterward that he hadn't made much of an impression, but the company offered him a job, as a "research engineer" in New York.

The salary was $35 a week. He moved his father back to a rented house in San Bernardino and found a neighbor to shop for him and look in regularly. "By this time his health had stabilized to the extent that he got no better nor much worse as the years went by," Carlson recalled later. "He was crippled by arthritis and the TB was still with him, but he could take care of himself as far as housework was concerned." Carlson packed his few possessions into a single suitcase and hitched a ride east with a young couple he knew, who were on their honeymoon. The young couple's future appeared no more certain than his did at that moment, and they were happy to have a passenger to help buy gas for their Hudson sedan. They camped along the way, to save money, and visited Yellowstone Park. The trip took a month.

During the next two and a half years, Carlson lived at the Brooklyn Central YMCA (and held his living expenses under $20 a week); in a rooming house at 270 Henry Street, in Brooklyn (where his rent was less than $1 a day); and in the home of his Aunt Ruth, in Passaic, New Jersey. Ruth was one of his mother's five sisters. She was the aunt who had given him the toy typewriter when he was ten, and she had also been his main benefactor during his two years at Caltech, when she had lent him more than $200. On New Year's Eve in 1932, he moved from Passaic into the city itself, renting a bedroom in the Greenwich Village apartment of a science-fiction writer and playwright named Slater LaMaster, who was sixteen years older and had just been divorced. (Three years before, LaMaster had published a book called *The Phantom in the Rainbow*, which a modern rare-book dealer's listing describes as a "weird mystery novel involving a hashish eater.") One month later, Carlson moved again, into the apartment of Lawrence Dumond, a reporter for the *Daily News*, who had advertised for a roommate. The apartment was small, just a single room with no kitchen, but the two men were a good match because Carlson worked during the day and Dumond worked at night. They saw each other mostly on weekends, when they would sometimes play mental chess as they walked to breakfast at a diner in Sheridan Square.

Carlson's research job at Bell Labs, meanwhile, turned out to be a deep disappointment. "To my mind, it was practically the back door of the laboratories," he told Dumond seventeen years later. "It was one of the least desirable jobs, both as to job and location of work. We were down in the basement of the old annex building, four or five men all by ourselves. The place looked more like a little factory or workshop." The tasks they were asked to perform—rudimentary quality tests on samples of granular carbon, a coal-based material used in telephone microphones—seemed demeaning to Carlson while nevertheless confirming an earlier suspicion of his that he was too clumsy and uncoordinated to be much use in a laboratory. (In an inventory of his personal flaws that he made in a notebook at Caltech, he had written, "Ability in doing things with hands or things requiring muscular coordination or strength very low. 'I can't even saw a board straight.' Therefore work in a laboratory would be out of the question.") Deciding, after a year, that the job would not lead to a career, he applied for a transfer to the company's patent department—representatives from which had made a pitch to the workers in his lab not long before—and went to work there as an assistant to one of the company's patent attorneys. "This sounded more interesting to me," he explained later. "I thought it would be a chance to get a bird's-eye view of everything that was going on in the labs." Such knowledge, he felt, would be useful to him when he himself became an inventor, as he still hoped to do.

Inventing was very much on his mind during those first years in New York. In his notebooks he recorded more than four hundred ideas for potentially lucrative products, among them a raincoat with gutters to channel water away from trouser legs; a toothbrush with replaceable bristles; a see-through toothpaste tube, made of cellophane; a perforated-plastic filter tip for cigarettes (which he tested, to his own satisfaction, over a period of several days); hollow glass blocks for constructing transparent structural walls; a metal-engraving machine that could be operated like a typewriter; an improved cap for ginger ale bottles; a matchbook with a cellophane cover, which would reveal at a glance how many matches remained; a replacement shirt button attached to an adhesive cloth disk; and a "pivoted pen," whose nib was mounted on tiny ball bearings. He discovered that some of his ideas—such as the raincoat with gutters—had already been patented; he never found the time or had the money to pursue any of the others. But he kept writing down new ideas and noting areas that he thought might merit further consideration: "Means for utilizing beet sugar refineries during idle season."

As he was considering these inventions, though, he continually returned to an earlier notion of his—one that dated back to his youthful interest in printing. The patent department at Bell Labs, like patent offices all over the country, required large numbers of copies of the patent documents it handled. "They were sent to associates in foreign countries, to companies, to inventors, and others," he said in an interview many years later. "We would need a dozen or more copies of every specification. To make twelve copies with carbon paper is pretty difficult. Often it involved two typing operations. A specification would be typed and then some-one would just have to sit down with a typewriter and retype the whole detailed specification of many pages. Then typographical errors would creep in and two girls would have to read them back to each other. It was a very tedious thing."

Thinking about the copying problem began to occupy more and more of his spare time. In an interview with Dumond in 1947, he explained, "The need for a quick, satisfactory copying machine that could be used right in the office seemed very apparent to me—there seemed such a crying need for it—such a desirable thing if it could be obtained. So I set out to think of how one could be made." During the years when he was living with Dumond, he made some tentative experiments with what he hoped might be an improved stencil sheet for mimeograph machines, but he had no success. With growing conviction, he began to think that what he and the rest of the world needed was not an improved duplicating system but rather a true copying machine: a device that could take an image from one piece of paper and print it on another without a long series of messy and expensive intermediate steps.

• • •

In the fall of 1932, Carlson received word from California that his father was extremely ill. He negotiated an emergency two-week leave from Bell Labs and booked the cheapest transportation he could find. "I rode the bus night and day," he recalled later, "and the day I arrived they told me my father had died the day before." The bus ride to San Bernardino had taken nearly a week. Carlson quickly made funeral arrangements, dispatched his father's few tattered possessions to the dump, and got back on the bus. The round trip gave him many opportunities to contemplate his increasingly unhappy situation.

As the Depression deepened, Bell Labs began laying off large numbers of workers and reducing the hours of those who remained. Carlson was cut to five days a week from five and a half, then cut to four, and he worried that he could be let go at any time. He ended up being fired, in the summer of 1933, for participating in an extracurricular "business scheme" with several other Bell Labs employees, who, like him, were interested in finding a "hedge against the depression," he wrote. (The "scheme" had involved starting a company that would market physics-related inventions, but it came to nothing.) Being out of work was a severe personal crisis, because he was still more than $600 in debt. "That was the period when many a Phi Beta Kappa was to be found in Bowery pawn shops," he said many years later, "and engineers were peddling apples on street corners." He told his cousin Roy that this period of financial uncertainty was more difficult and worrisome to him than his destitute boyhood had been. He looked up patent attorneys in the phone book and called on them in person. After about six weeks of knocking on doors, he was offered a job at a firm called Austin & Dix, and at a salary that was slightly higher than what he had been earning at Bell Labs. A year later—having been warned by Mr. Austin that business was deteriorating—he moved to the patent office of P. R. Mallory & Company, a manufacturer of electrical and electronic components (and the predecessor of the modern Duracell battery division of Gillette).

Although Carlson's professional life during the early thirties was filled with uncertainty, his social life had become increasingly agreeable to him. Dumond was nearly as shy as he was, but the two men together managed to bolster each other's courage, and on weekends they went to dances and other social activities in attempts to meet young women. "Chet had much greater success than I did," Dumond said forty years later. "His shyness and good looks—he was good-looking—and his bashfulness, I guess, just drove the girls crazy." The two men developed a widening circle of friends, and in the fall of 1933 they moved, along with a new friend of Carlson's named Phil Helsley, into a four-bedroom apartment at 139th Street and Broadway, where Helsley's girlfriend and two other young women lived in an identical apartment on another floor. Dumond's mother (who had followed her son to Manhattan from Michigan and had been living until now in a separate apartment) moved into the fourth bedroom in the men's apartment and did most of the cooking for all six young people—who treated both apartments as home, played cards until late at night, gave parties, screened a friend's extensive collection of marginally dirty movies, and, in a mild way, anticipated by more than half a century the concept of the television show *Friends.*

"This happy group"—as Dumond referred to it later—remained intact for most of a year, until, one by one, the members moved on, mostly to marriages. In the fall of 1934, Carlson himself left, to marry a young woman named Elsa von Mallon, who had given him her telephone number after dancing with him to

Duke Ellington records at a party at the YWCA. Elsa was "vivacious, very pretty," according to Dumond, but the marriage was not happy. Carlson later told his cousin Roy that he had been attracted to Elsa in part because she didn't insist on being taken out—something he couldn't afford to do—and that the main force propelling them toward marriage had been inertia. Chester and Elsa were both only children; beyond that, they had little in common. Elsa herself once told Roy, "I don't know what to do or say—he's so much smarter." Carlson had virtually no capacity for small talk, and he never discussed his emotions or feelings. He and Elsa spent most of their time together in silence. He later described their marriage as "an unhappy period interspersed with sporadic escapes."

The newlyweds moved into a small apartment that Elsa's parents owned in Jackson Heights, in Queens—another source of tension and distress. "I had just finished paying off the last of my college debts," Carlson wrote twenty years later in a letter to Dumond, "and for the first time in my life thought I should be able to lift my nose an inch off the grindstone. But I had just got married and was expected to provide the wherewithal for a very stuffy kind of life which seemed an awful letdown and blind alley. In addition I was being constantly and viciously heckled by my mother-in-law and felt little companionship in the home." Elsa's mother, who had been born in Germany, felt that her daughter had made a poor choice of husband, and she didn't conceal her opinion. "She made my life very unhappy for the next few years," Carlson wrote.

Partly in the hope of advancing to a higher salary level in his patent work and partly to give himself an excuse to spend his evenings away from home, Carlson in 1936 enrolled in night classes at New York Law School. He did most of his studying on weekends at the New York Public Library on Fifth Avenue between 40th and 42nd Streets, where he copied by hand long passages from law books that he couldn't afford to buy. His copying gave him writer's cramp, and sitting for hours at a desk in the library's reading room hurt his back—a deeply worrisome sign, since he had begun to notice in himself symptoms of the spinal arthritis that had crippled his father. The pain and tedium of copying legal texts by hand made him think again about the desirability of inventing a device that, unlike carbon paper or a stencil duplicator, could be used to reproduce text that already existed.

When his hand hurt too much to write, Carlson sometimes turned his full attention to the copying problem. Inventing an office copier would solve all his difficulties, he believed, since doing so would eliminate the necessity of copying text by hand and would also generate the income that his young wife and her mother seemed to require. In addition, it would remove entirely the necessity of pursuing a law degree—a degree that he felt was likely to doom him to spending the rest of his career in patent work.

His approach to the problem was characteristically disciplined. He made frequent visits to the library's science and technology department and "got out everything I could find on printing and duplicating," he told Ermenc. He would take an armload of books and scientific journals back to his desk, where he would steadily work his way through the volumes, occasionally writing notes in one of his pocket notebooks. When he found what he thought might be a promising idea, he would sometimes attempt an experiment at home. Mostly, though, he read and thought, turning the problem over in his mind, thinking back through the courses he had taken at Caltech, looking for a clue that might somehow lead him to a solution.

This process continued intermittently for a little over a year and included many abandoned lines of inquiry. Then, one day in 1937 as he was thumbing through an obscure German scientific journal, he found a brief article by a Hungarian physicist who had been experimenting with the transmission and development of photographic images—and suddenly he thought of a way in which the thing might be done.

4

10-22-38 ASTORIA

AROUND 1800, THOMAS WEDGWOOD—a son of the famous potter and therefore a relative of the inventor of carbon paper, of the inventor of the bigrapher, and of the author of *The Origin of Species*—came within a few miles of inventing photography when he placed small objects on a sheet of paper he had treated with a solution containing a silver compound and exposed the arrangement to sunlight. The light caused the paper to darken except where the objects covered it, as in those famous shadow prints made in the 1920s by the avant-garde photographer Man Ray.

The silver compound Wedgwood used was one of several so-called silver halides, whose crystals darken if they are exposed to light and then immersed in certain chemicals. That's what happens when photographic film or prints are developed.* Wedgwood

---

*It's also roughly what happened to Stan Jones, a Montana candidate for the U.S. Senate in 2002, whose skin turned blue gray after he repeatedly consumed a homemade silver solution that he had hoped would strengthen his immune system. Jones's condition, which is irreversible, is called argyria.

and his friend Sir Humphry Davy—a pioneering chemist and electrical experimenter, who, among a great many other things, discovered nitrous oxide (and was the first person ever to become intoxicated by it)—presented a paper on the phenomenon in 1802 but knew of no way to permanently fix the images they had created. Those images gradually disappeared into featureless blackness as the entire paper darkened under subsequent exposure to light. (Wedgwood kept his unspoiled prints in his cellar and showed them to others only briefly and by candlelight.) Wedgwood died in 1805, at the age of thirty-four, before he could find an answer, and Davy went on to other projects, leaving the concept temporarily orphaned.

About a decade after Wedgwood's death, a Frenchman named Joseph Nicéphore Niépce, who was looking for a method of creating lithographic printing plates which didn't require artistic skill, succeeded in using a box with a lens attached to it to make a persistent image of a birdhouse, on a sheet of paper he had treated with silver chloride. Disappointed that the image was a negative one (with light and dark areas reversed from the original, as always happens with silver compounds), Niépce turned his attention to other light-sensitive substances and succeeded in devising a different etching technique, which involved masking a metal plate with a bitumen compound, projecting an illuminated image onto it, and bathing the plate in acid—a technique very similar to ones in use today.

If Thomas Wedgwood had come within miles of inventing photography, Niépce came within feet. And although he never fully pursued his first experiments, he did help to make the eventual breakthrough. During a visit to Paris in 1827, he met Louis Daguerre, an artist and set designer, who had been absorbed by a similar quest. The two men had lengthy conversations in Paris, corresponded after Niépce went home, and signed a ten-year partnership agreement in the hope of making a fortune from their discoveries. Niépce died four years later, but Daguerre continued to work on their ideas, and in 1837 he made the world's first true photographic print, on a copper plate coated with a silver compound—a daguerreotype. It was a truly revolutionary invention, one that permanently changed the way people everywhere see everything. (One small but compelling example: Photography has transformed people's sense of their own childhood, since their earliest memories often consist mainly of events and images made familiar by snapshots.)

The emphasis of early photographers was almost always on pictorial images—and their pictures were so arresting and so intricately detailed that mid-nineteenth-century painters feared for their careers—but some people soon understood that cameras also had the potential to become documentary copying machines. Turning that potential into products took longer than a modern reader may suppose, though, for several reasons: early emulsions required inconveniently long exposure times; no one had yet invented a source of sufficiently intense artificial light; there were limitations on focal length and maximum print size; and making pictures of any kind was still relatively difficult and expensive. As a result, the photography-based copying of documents didn't begin to become truly practical until the early twentieth century, nearly seven decades after Daguerre made his landmark print.

The first photographic copying machine was built in 1906— the same year Chester Carlson was born—by an Oklahoma City inventor named George Beidler, who called his machine the Rectigraph. Beidler was an eccentric genius: he mixed his company's photographic chemicals himself to keep others from learning their formulas, effortlessly switched his pen from his right

hand to his left when his right hand was tired, and had such a difficult and disagreeable personality that the golf professional at a
country club he belonged to tried to isolate him from other members by having his foursome tee off ahead of everyone else.

Early Rectigraph.
Xerox Corp.

Beidler's machine was not remotely an "office copier" in the
modern sense. A Rectigraph cost several hundred dollars—the
equivalent of thousands of dollars today—was so large that it almost needed a room of its own, and depended on two commodi-
ties not universally available in American offices in 1906: electric
power and running water. Rectigraph machines therefore typi-

cally resided in specialty shops. You sent something out to have it Rectigraphed, rather than going down the hall (or reaching across your desk). The key component was a camera the size of a kitchen stove, with a big black bellows for adjusting the focus. The process was a direct-to-paper photographic method, with no intermediate negative, so the color scheme of the copy was always the reverse of that of the original: black type came out white, white backgrounds became black. (I still have a copy of my birth certificate which looks like this.) To create a copy that looked like the original, you had to make a copy of the first copy—a negative of a negative. Beidler quickly attracted a major competitor, the Photostat Corporation, which had a licensing and manufacturing relationship with Eastman Kodak.* Making copies with either company's machines took time and cost money, so businesses usually sent out drawings and written documents to be reproduced only when they felt they couldn't make do with a faster, cheap alternative, such as carbon paper, a copying press, or a typist with a high threshold of boredom.

---

*Photostat eventually became a generic term, along with "photocopy," for any copy made by a photographic process—thus extending a tradition, which was already a century old at that point, of muddling the distinctions between copying terms. Lithographs were sometimes called "polygraphs" in the early years of both processes; much later, polygraph was appropriated for lie detectors. Mimeograph, which was originally an A. B. Dick trademark, gradually became a generic term not only for stencil duplicators and the copies they made, but also for spirit duplicators and the copies they made—as did another trademark, Ditto. "Photocopy" was once used only for copies made by photography-based machines like Rectigraphs and Photostats; later it became the preferred generic term, rather than the trademark-weakening Xeroxes, for copies produced by xerographic machines. Xerox itself proposed the term *xerocopy*, but it never caught on, even at Xerox. In 1978 and 1979, I worked briefly at *New York* magazine, where xerographic copies were sometimes referred to as "photostats," in the same way that older people sometimes call their television set "the radio." People at *New York* also used the term *photostat* for any print made on the magazine's actual Photostat machine, which belonged to the art department and was used to reproduce page layouts back in those dark days before digital scanning.

• • •

W HEN C HESTER C ARLSON, working in the patent office at P. R. Mallory, needed a copy of a drawing in a patent application, his only option was to have a photographic copy made by an outside company that owned a Photostat or Rectigraph machine. "Their representative would come in, pick up the drawing, take it to their plant, make a copy, bring it back," he recalled later. "It might be a wait of half a day or even twenty-four hours to get it back." This was a costly nuisance, and it meant that what we now think of as a mindless clerical task was then an ongoing corporate operation involving outside vendors, billing, record keeping, and executive supervision. "So I recognized a very great need for a machine that could be right in an office," he continued, "where you could bring a document to it, push it in a slot, push a button, and get a copy out."

As Carlson began to consider how such a machine might work, he naturally thought first of photography. But he realized quickly that photography had distressingly many inherent limitations. Reducing the size of a bulky Photostat machine might be possible, but a smaller machine would still require coated papers and messy chemicals—the two main reasons making Photostats was expensive and inconvenient. Photography, furthermore, was already so well understood that it was unlikely to yield an important discovery to a lone inventor like Carlson. People had been using cameras for more than a century, and the laboratories at Eastman Kodak were filled with well-financed researchers, yet no one, so far, had come up with a method of making photographic prints on ordinary paper. Carlson reasoned that silver halide photography almost certainly did not hold the solution to the copying problem—and that if it did somehow hold the solution, he himself would be highly unlikely to find it.

Having eliminated conventional photography as a field of investigation, Carlson next considered the possibility of making copies chemically—perhaps by using a mild solvent to partially dissolve the text or image of an existing document, so that an impression of it could be made by pressing a blank piece of paper against it, as with a copying press. But there are hopelessly many different writing and printing media—water-based inks, oil-based inks, graphite, charcoal, crayon, and others—and Carlson knew that no single solvent would work with all of them. Besides, even if a single practicable solvent could be found, using it would unavoidably harm the original document, and the reproduced image would be reversed, like a reflection in a mirror. Chemistry alone, he decided, could not provide the answer.

If ordinary photography was messy, and chemical processes ruined originals, what was left? "The only thing common with the different inks, pencils, and papers is that they reflect light in different ways from the image areas and from the background areas," he said later. We easily distinguish text from the paper it's printed on, because the ink absorbs most of the light that strikes it (and therefore appears black), while the paper reflects the light (and therefore appears white). A nondestructive copying process, Carlson reasoned, would almost certainly have to take advantage of this contrast—just as conventional photography does. But how? Were silver halides the only materials that changed when exposed to light? Carlson went back to the library and soon found a book called *Photoelectric Phenomena*, which had been published a few years before.

Photoelectricity is so hard to understand that Albert Einstein won the Nobel Prize in 1921 for having explained it in 1905. (Incidentally, Einstein, like Carlson, was a physicist who worked in a patent office.) To simplify a great deal, a photoelectric material is one that sheds electrons when light shines on it. The phenomenon was first noticed in 1887 by the German physicist Heinrich Hertz (whose name is preserved in the standard scientific term for "one cycle per second"). Hertz observed that the sparks thrown off by an induction coil in his laboratory got smaller when he darkened the room (as he had done in the hope of seeing the sparks better). Einstein's explanation, which became part of the basis of quantum mechanics, was that when light, behaving like a stream of particles, collides with electrons on the surface of a photoelectric material, it knocks significant numbers of the electrons loose and thereby stimulates increased electrical activity: bigger sparks. A related phenomenon is photoconductivity, which Carlson read about in the same book. A photoconductive material is one whose ability to transmit electricity increases when it is illuminated. This happens because light, behaving like a stream of particles, jostles the electrons on the material's surface and thereby increases the material's ability to conduct a charge.

"I thought that if a layer of photoconductive material could be placed in contact with a sheet of paper that had been wetted with a chemical, the paper would change color if electricity flowed through the sheet," Carlson said later. Working in the kitchen of his apartment, he saturated a sheet of ordinary paper with a solution of potassium iodide and starch, placed the treated paper on a copper plate coated with cuprous oxide (a photoconductor), placed a printed document on top of the treated paper, and shone a bright light through the back of the document. As he explained on another occasion, he was hoping that the sheet of paper "would be darkened by the photoelectric currents that I thought would be produced during exposure," and that an image of the printed document would form on the treated paper. But nothing happened.

"That led me to take a somewhat deeper look into the needs of the process," he recalled in 1964; "e.g., I recognized that photoelectric currents are bound to be rather small, but, on the other hand, electrochemical effects which I was trying to use require rather large currents to cause any substantial darkening of a layer."

Furthermore, a current large enough to darken paper would also most likely be large enough to set it on fire, among other undesirable results. He concluded that his idea was "even less satisfactory than the known photographic methods that were then used," and turned his attention from amperage to voltage. "With high voltage, the current could be small but still the energy could be high," he realized. "This led me to the idea of electrostatics."

Electrical phenomena are conventionally divided into two broad and confusingly overlapping categories: current electricity and static electricity. Current electricity is what makes electric appliances work; it consists of continuously flowing electrical charges. Static electricity is what causes your hair to stand up when you run a plastic comb through it; it consists of opposite electrical charges that are separated or imbalanced (and that produce transitory electric currents—sparks, lightning—when the voltage is sufficient to ionize the air separating them). Scientists have been known to come to blows over these definitions. For the purposes of understanding xerography, it's enough to say that the most important difference has to do with amperage, which can be thought of as analogous to volume in the flow of water, and voltage, which can be thought of as analogous to water pressure. Generally speaking, an electric current involves relatively high amperage at relatively low voltage, while electrostatic phenomena involve high voltage at low amperage. (The electric current you experience when you stick a butter knife into a wall receptacle is just 110 volts, but it's more than enough amps to kill you; the harmless electrostatic shock you receive when you shuffle across the carpet and touch a metal doorknob is many thousands of volts but virtually zero amps.) Carlson realized that if he could devise a copying process based on voltage rather than amperage, he might be able to build a machine that would neither set paper on fire nor electrocute its operator.

Carlson returned to the library. And there, while working his way through a pile of foreign technical journals, he came across a brief article by a Hungarian physicist named Paul Selenyi. Selenyi had been trying to devise a way of transmitting and printing facsimiles of graphic images, such as news photographs. His method, which he had tried with some success, involved using a directed beam of ions to lay down a patterned electrostatic charge on the outside of a rotating drum that was covered with an insulating material—something like the way a cathode ray tube creates a picture on a television screen, by scanning a beam of electrons repeatedly across it one line at a time, or like the way an ink-jet printer sprays ink in an intelligible pattern onto a sheet of paper.

"He had developed, essentially, a triode in air," Carlson said later. "It embodied a heated cathode enclosed in a metal cup which had a small hole in it. Then there was a drum coated with hard rubber or some kind of insulating varnish that rotated very close to that hole. The heated cathode created ions within the metal cup and the metal let varying proportions of ions through a little opening. They were deposited on the rotating, insulating drum by a bias field that was applied. Then, after the image had been scanned, he simply dusted the drum with a fine powder and the image became visible." The powder stuck to the ions on the insulating surface of the drum in the way that beach sand sticks to wet spots on a bathing suit. A transmitted photographic image that Selenyi had generated in this manner was reproduced in the journal; it was grainy, and the scanning lines were quite noticeable, but the image was reasonably distinct.

Using finely divided powders to make visible images of electrostatic charges was an old idea in physics; it had first been done in 1777, when George Christoph Lichtenberg, a German professor, noticed that house dust adhered to an electrostatically charged piece of amber in a distinctive arrangement, which later became known as a "Lichtenberg figure." Carlson knew about Lichtenberg figures, and Selenyi's work reminded him of them. Suddenly, he saw that he might be able to make copies by employing a similar phenomenon in combination with photoconductivity. Instead of trying to use light to generate an electric current in a sheet of paper placed on top of a photoconductor, as he had done in his kitchen experiments, he would use light to remove electrostatic charges from the nonimage areas of a uniformly ionized photoconductor. Then he would make the pattern visible by dusting it with powder, and transfer the powder to a sheet of untreated paper.

Photoconductivity was the key. Carlson knew he needed to find a material that would act as an electrical conductor in the light and as an electrical insulator in the dark. If a grounded metal plate coated with

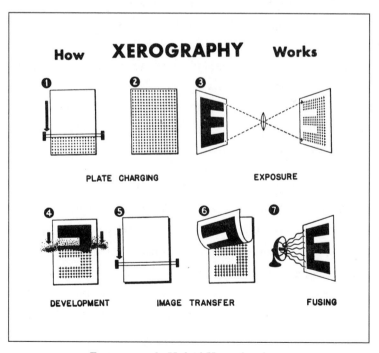

From an early Haloid Xerox brochure.
XEROX CORP.

a thin film of such a material could, in the dark, be given a uniform electrostatic charge—perhaps by using an electrostatic generator to spray ions onto its surface—then exposing the plate to light should cause the charge to drain away. And if that light could be shone on the charged plate not uniformly but in the image of a printed page, then the charge should drain away only from the illuminated parts of the plate (the parts corresponding to the reflective white background of the page) and persist in the parts that remained dark (the ones corresponding to the black ink). Dusting the entire plate with an oppositely charged powder should then make the latent image visible, because the powder would adhere only to the places where charges remained. That powder would form a mirror image of the original page and could then be transferred to a sheet of paper: a copy.

Carlson's knowledge of electrostatics had arisen partly from personal experience. Back in his physics class at Riverside Junior College, a student had asked the teacher one day whether static electricity had any commercial use, and the teacher had said that it did not. "But at that time I was working for a cement plant," Carlson recalled later, "and I could think of one commercial use for it—in separating dust from the flue gases and separating smoke from the air." The plant where Carlson worked had been sued by neighboring orange growers, whose trees became coated with the fine white dust that billowed from the plant's smokestacks. The plant had been able to eliminate the problem and satisfy the growers by installing two sets of electrodes in the flues—one to give escaping dust particles an electrostatic charge and the other, of the opposite polarity, to pull the charged particles out of the air. The copying process that Carlson had now conceived would operate in a similar manner—except that the electrostatic charges he had in mind would be used not simply to attract dust randomly but to form it into a comprehensible pattern.

• • •

FEW BIG INVENTIONS truly have a single inventor; most technological revolutions are essentially collective efforts, arising in several minds and in several places at more or less the same time, generated as much by cultural pressures as by spontaneous individual insight. If Gutenberg hadn't thought of movable type in the early 1400s, someone else would have, because other advances in printing technology, along with an accelerating increase in the demand for books, had made a breakthrough of some kind inevitable. Carlson, in contrast, was genuinely alone. He always credited Selenyi with having inspired him, but Selenyi never saw the connections that Carlson did. As a matter of fact, in the years following Carlson's discovery, the few people who came up with truly similar ideas were able to do so only after studying Carlson's patent specifications, and their innovations were merely variations on themes he had long since defined. Carlson alone thought of a way to make copies easily and quickly on plain paper; no one yet has come up with a better way of doing it.

"Xerography had practically no foundation in previous scientific work," Dr. Harold E. Clark, a Xerox physicist, told John Brooks in 1967. "Chet put together a rather odd lot of phenomena, each of which was obscure in itself and none of which had previously been related in anyone's thinking." Carlson himself believed that his lonely upbringing had contributed to his success: spending so much time in his own company had given him an acquired immunity to conventional thinking. "The result was the biggest thing in imaging since the coming of photography itself," Clark continued. "Furthermore, he did it entirely without the help of a favorable scientific climate. As you know, there are dozens of instances of simultaneous discovery down through scientific history, but no one came anywhere near being simultaneous with Chet. I'm as amazed by his discovery now as I was when I first heard of it."

Carlson at first called his idea "electron photography," and then he decided upon "electrophotography." As soon as the elements had come together in his mind, the process seemed so intuitively obvious to him that he worried some other researcher would follow the same line of reasoning and beat him to market with a functioning product. He called his old roommate Dumond—who had been fired from his job at the *Daily News* and was now managing a small investment fund for some midwestern businessmen—and asked him to meet him at a local Automat. (Carlson had recently served as the best man at Dumond's wedding and, as a prank, had hidden a wound alarm clock in the newlyweds' honeymoon luggage.) Over coffee, Carlson described the idea behind electron photography and then asked Dumond to sign and date a document stating that Carlson had explained the process to him and that he understood it.* Carlson wanted this affidavit as proof of his priority, in the event that someone else should think of a similar idea while he was working on a patent application. Dumond happily complied. Carlson also asked his employer to grant him permission to apply in his own name for a patent for an "improvement in photography"—

---

*In 1947, during another conversation with Dumond, Carlson explained his basic idea with an odd but oddly memorable analogy—perhaps the same one he used that day at the Automat: "Imagine there was a field with a ditch running across it full of water, but it had a few stepping-stones from place to place. There is a crowd of people lined up on one bank waiting to get across, but it is dark. They could not see the stones, and had to wait. Suppose there is a flash of lightning for a moment. It enables a few of them to see the stones and jump across. Soon as the light disappeared, the ones behind would be blocked. Where they never got any light, the people would wait indefinitely. But in sections of the ditch where there is able to be a light all the time, the whole crowd of people would soon get across and there wouldn't be any left on the other side. That's a funny kind of illustration, but it's a pretty close analogy. Each person could be comparable to one unit of electrical charge, or one electron. Where all the electrons escaped it would leave an uncharged plate."

which, he explained, was unrelated to his work at the company—and Mr. Mallory himself approved his request (in a letter headed "Dear Carlson").

With these documents in hand, Carlson went to work on his patent application, a task for which his job, his legal studies, and his methodical temperament suited him perfectly. He filed his first application in the fall of 1937 and followed it a little over a year later with an improved and expanded version. That expanded patent, which was issued in the fall of 1942, has been regarded ever since as a model in the genre: Carlson knew how to protect an invention. In just a dozen pages and a few simple drawings, he lucidly anticipated and described virtually every aspect of what would ultimately become known as xerography.

Confident that he had now done everything he could to protect himself from competing inventors and manufacturers, Carlson set out to establish that his idea would actually work. In this, he was far less successful. He was positive, he said many years later, that he had truly solved the copying problem, and he was equally confident that his invention would one day be a commercial success. But his efforts to prove the practicality of his idea—to actually make a copy of something—were painfully unproductive. He could see the process in his mind, and he could understand how its elements fit together. But he couldn't make it work.

One of his difficulties was the manual ineptitude that he had noted in his college diary (and which had contributed to his decision to transfer out of his experimental job at Bell Labs). Another was the circumstances under which he was trying to work. Since January 1938, he and Elsa had been living with Elsa's parents in a small house in Jackson Heights. He conducted his experiments in the house's old coal cellar when he could, but there were times when he needed running water and an open flame, and that meant he had to share the kitchen with his wife, who resented the intru-

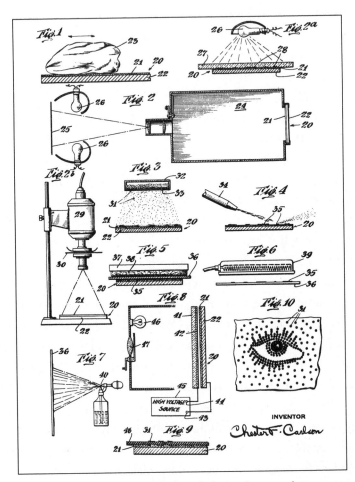

*Illustration from Carlson's second electrophotography patent,
filed April 4, 1939.*

sion. He stocked a single shelf with a modest selection of experimental supplies: a jar of chemically pure crystalline sulfur (a photoconductor), which he had bought at a chemical supply house called Eimer & Amend; a few business-card-size zinc engraver's plates; and a miscellaneous collection of parts from which he hoped to fashion an electrostatic generator. He concentrated at first on

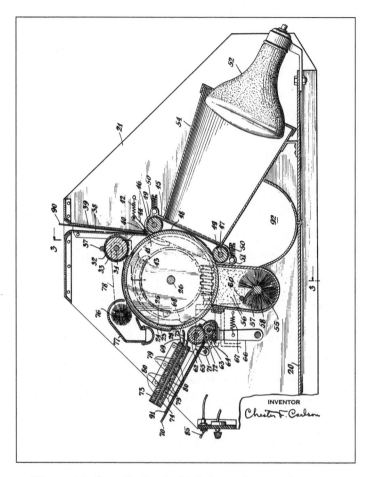

Illustration from Carlson's third electrophotography patent,
filed November 16, 1940.

coating one of the plates with sulfur, by sprinkling crystals on the
zinc and using a pair of pliers to hold the plate over one of the
burners on the kitchen stove. He found that if he held the plate at
the right distance from the flame and kept it moving, the crystals
would eventually liquefy and spread across the plate—although
the usual result of these efforts was not a uniformly coated plate

but a sulfur fire, which filled the kitchen with acrid fumes and made the entire building smell like rotten eggs. These accidents annoyed his wife and drew bitter complaints from his mother-in-law. "My experiments became very unpopular around the house," he told an interviewer later.

His attempts to make a suitable developing powder were unpopular as well. "I decided that the way to do it was to spray-dry a solution of a dyed resin in a highly volatile solvent in a spray booth or chamber and collect the deposit," he recalled later. "Well, in an apartment I didn't have a very convenient spray chamber, so I decided to use the bathtub. I got an air brush, which is a form of spray gun, and I produced a solution of resin and dye and acetone, and I pulled the shower curtains around the tub, and I sprayed the solution into the space above the tub, and it settled down and I swept it up. Unfortunately, the tub was not very clean after that."

Carlson eventually realized that his apartment made a poor laboratory and that he needed help with his experiments. In the fall of 1938, nearly a year after filing his first patent application, he rented a room on the second floor of a house owned by his in-laws, at 32-05 Thirty-seventh Street in Astoria, Queens. The room had once been the kitchen of an apartment, which was now occupied by a beauty parlor, and there was a bar downstairs. But the room contained a sink and a gas connection, the house was a fifteen-minute walk from home, and the rent (payable to his mother-in-law) was just $15 a month.

Next, he set out to find an assistant. He returned to the library and searched through the classified advertisements in the back pages of scientific magazines. The American economy had been paralyzed for most of a decade, and many scientists were unemployed, but few of them, apparently, saw any point in advertising for work. Carlson could find only one ad that seemed promising. It was in a magazine called *Electronics*, and it had been placed by an Austrian physicist named Otto Kornei, who had recently immigrated to the United States and had had no luck in finding work. Kornei had decided, in desperation, to spend the last of his minimal savings in publicly seeking a job. Carlson's response was the only one he received.

CARLSON'S OWN FINANCES IN 1938 were far from robust. His final salary at Bell Labs, in 1933, after a companywide wage cut, had been $100 a month. He was making roughly three times that much at Mallory, and he was earning regular raises, but he could not afford extravagances. His budget in 1935 had added up to a little over $230 a month, including $45 for rent, $20 for entertainment for himself and Elsa, and $50 for groceries. Now he was bearing the additional expense of law school. The salary that Carlson offered to Kornei was small in absolute terms—just $90 a month for a period of six months, plus an expense budget of roughly thirty cents a day—but it represented a major portion of his resources. Elsa was already annoyed by his copying obsession; she can't have been pleased that he had now decided to devote more than a third of his gross income to pursuing it.

Kornei was scarcely more enthusiastic. He was a skilled experimental scientist, and he had spent the previous two years, in Vienna, working as an electrical engineer. In a better economy, he would have had his choice of good jobs at big companies. Instead, he found himself being interviewed for a virtually imaginary position by man who not only wasn't a research scientist but held a mundane job in a corporate back office. The offered salary was low even by the standards of the Depression, and Carlson's so-called laboratory looked more like a janitor's closet—which, in fact, it had once been. Carlson, furthermore, was not a salesman. He was thirty-one years old but looked and acted older, and he dressed like an actuary. He showed Kornei his patent application and gave him a lucid explanation of his idea, but he was too reticent to be able to convey more than a fraction of the excitement he felt about electrophotography, much less to inspire someone else to share it. Carlson augmented the offered salary by promising Kornei 20 percent of the first $10,000 in Carlson's net proceeds from the invention, and 10 percent after that. Kornei agreed to the terms but viewed the offered royalty less as a deal-clinching inducement than as additional evidence that his employer was living a fantasy.

Nevertheless, Kornei turned out to be an ideal assistant. He went to work on October 6, 1938, and in just a few days he made more concrete progress with electrophotography than Carlson himself had managed in more than a year of fumbling experimentation. Coating a zinc plate with a thin, uniform layer of sulfur—a task that had virtually defeated Carlson—turned out to be easy for Kornei. He also showed Carlson that there was no need to build or purchase an electrostatic generator, since they could create a sufficient electrical charge by rubbing the coated plate with a pocket handkerchief or a scrap of fur. And almost immediately he had some limited success in partially discharging coated plates by exposing portions of them to sunlight. That experience persuaded him that he needed a stronger and more reliable light source than the sun shining through the window, and he told Carlson on October 19 that they needed to invest in a Mazda No. 2 Photoflood lamp. Carlson agreed.

The following Saturday, Carlson visited the lab, as he did each weekend. Kornei had already coated a zinc plate with sulfur, and he had ground down the surface with emery paper and polished it with precipitated chalk. He had also purchased a small quantity of lycopodium powder—the extraordinarily fine yellow spores of a plant known as club moss or Christmas tree fern, and the same substance Paul Selenyi had used to develop his facsimile images.*

Kornei arranged these materials on a table. "He pulled down the window shade and charged the sulphur surface in the darkened room by rubbing it with a cotton handkerchief," Carlson wrote later. "Then he laid a transparent celluloid ruler having black scale markings on the charged plate and turned on an incandescent lamp (photo flood lamp) for about 10 seconds." The lamp was positioned about a foot above the ruler and the charged plate. "He then turned off the lamp and carefully removed the ruler. Nothing was visible on the plate in the subdued light of the room, but an electrostatic image was there. He sprinkled a little lycopodium powder from a cloth-covered test tube onto the sulphur surface then gently blew away the loose powder. There, adhering to the plate, was a perfect image of the scale of the celluloid ruler, every line and inch number standing out sharply as little ridges of powder."

Carlson raised the shade and held the plate to the light. "The powder image was adhering to the plate by virtue of relatively small, but nevertheless real, electrostatic forces," he wrote. "Kornei then drew his finger over the surface of the plate wiping away the pow-

---

*Lycopodium powder is so fine that it is used as a dusting agent in a variety of scientific experiments, and is so water-repellent that it was once sold as baby powder. (If you sprinkle lycopodium powder on water, it will float on the surface indefinitely; if you then stick your hand into the water through the film of powder, the lycopodium will coat your hand like a glove and keep your skin dry.) It's also explosively flammable and was the key ingredient of early flashbulbs. Practitioners of homeopathic medicine value lycopodium powder as a treatment for hair loss, depression, constipation, hemorrhoids, loss of sexual appetite, prostatitis, psoriasis, "right side symptoms," and a long list of other ailments.

First xerographic copy, 1938.
Xerox Corp.

der image." Kornei took a glass microscope slide and, using India ink, wrote the place and date on it: "10-22-38 ASTORIA." He then closed the shade again, rubbed the sulfur-coated plate with his handkerchief, placed the inscribed slide on the charged surface (as he had previously done with the ruler), turned the flood lamp back on for another ten seconds, and dusted the plate with lycopodium powder. "The letters came out clearly," Carlson wrote, "proving that the plate could be re-used without difficulty."

They repeated the experiment several times, to convince themselves that it worked, then walked to Carlson's apartment and got some waxed paper. Back in the lab, using Kornei's slide once more, they went through the steps again. This time, though, they didn't wipe away the developed image from the surface of the sulfur-coated plate. Instead, Carlson cut out a small rectangle of waxed paper and pressed it against the image, so that most of the lycopodium powder stuck to it. He then placed a warm metal plate against the back of the waxed paper, softening the wax so that the powder became embedded in it. Carlson was now holding the world's first xerographic copy.* He gazed at the paper for a long time, and held it up to the window. Then he took his assistant to lunch.

Carlson felt elated. And, indeed, the sudden appearance of a re-produced image on a photoconductive plate seems almost magi-cal. Charging and exposing a plate makes no change in its appearance, yet if you then sprinkle powder over the surface and blow, an exact facsimile of the original image appears all at once, just as if it had been printed there. In two weeks of experimenta-tion, Kornei had fully justified Carlson's confidence in the process he had conceived. Electrophotography worked, and it worked ex-actly as he had predicted it would. All that remained to do was to refine the basic process and incorporate it into a functioning office machine.

Yet Kornei, in contrast with his employer, felt distinctly let down: the piece of waxed paper didn't look like much to him. True, a graphic image had been reproduced successfully. But the facsimile was pale and less than perfectly sharp, and the back-ground area appeared speckled and blotchy because some of the lycopodium powder had remained stuck to the discharged por-tions of the plate. Lycopodium powder, furthermore, was not an ideal developing material, because it was so light. Kornei had darkened the yellow spores with an aniline dye dissolved in alco-hol, but doing so had created a clumpy grayish material that worked less well as a dusting agent than undyed powder did. And transferring a developed image to waxed paper was relatively easy, since the wax was slightly adhesive—but how could an image be permanently bonded to plain paper, as Carlson wanted to do?

Even more discouraging were the inherent difficulties of work-ing with electrostatics. Moisture in the air can increase the conduc-

---

*You can see it today at the Smithsonian Institution.

tivity of materials that act like insulators in dry weather, causing charges to bleed away from surfaces on which they would otherwise accumulate. Kornei had found that he was sometimes unable to reproduce the results of earlier experiments—"the reason is not clear at all since all efforts are in vain," he wrote in his laboratory notebook—and the explanation for some of those failures may have been at least partly humidity related. He also found, during later experiments, that on some days images would inexplicably develop negatively, with the powder adhering to the background rather than the image.* And all these difficulties would become more troublesome as the experiments became more ambitious.

Kornei worked for Carlson for another five months, completing the employment period he'd agreed to, and during that time he made a number of significant advances. He discovered that anthracene (a derivative of coal tar) was a more sensitive photoconductor than sulfur, and he devised several methods of laying it down in thin, uniform layers. He found a reliable way of executing an idea that Carlson had described in his patent application: using electrophotography to create masters for lithographic printing (in one case by using an acid-resistant developing powder on an anthracene-coated etching plate). He experimented with alternative developing agents, including ordinary talcum powder and the natural resins copal, gum damar, and dragon's blood—none of which worked very well. (These resins are derived from the gummy sap of three tropical trees.) And he conducted some promising experiments connected to another idea of Carlson's—applying electrostatics to the recording and transmission of pictures—which was the subject of Carlson's second patent.

---

*It turned out that the developing powder, which was ordinarily electrically neutral, had picked up a charge. Kornei solved the problem by storing the powder in a metal container with a wire-mesh top, which discharged the powder as he shook it onto an exposed plate.

Yet despite all this, Kornei felt deeply discouraged. Carlson's basic idea clearly worked, but even under the relatively controlled and benign conditions in the Astoria laboratory, there were bafflingly many complications. If day-to-day changes in the weather and the random accumulation of haphazard electrostatic charges could upset the process, how could anyone hope to build a commercially viable machine, which would have to work year-round in every office environment? Electrophotography seemed to Kornei more like a clever novelty than a breakthrough in document reproduction. When his employment agreement expired, in March 1939, he told Carlson that he had accepted a job offer from the Brush Development Company, in Cleveland. Brush was an electrical engineering company and was involved in the development of magnetic audio-recording tape—a research area that seemed likely to make better use of Kornei's considerable skills as an engineer. (Researchers at Brush were also working on microphones, oscillographs, and torpedoes.)

The two men remained on cordial terms, and corresponded for a time. But Kornei had no faith in or enthusiasm for electrophotography. Shortly before he moved to Cleveland, he and Carlson met in New York and decided to dissolve their agreement, which had not only given Kornei 10 percent of Carlson's future proceeds from electrophotography, if any, but had also given Carlson sole ownership of any inventions that Kornei might make while working in Carlson's lab. Kornei was eager not to surrender the rights to one such invention, and in July he wrote a letter releasing Carlson from his side of the agreement, adding, "You, in turn, have agreed to leave me the unrestrained right to my idea concerning the scanning of a photoconductive layer with an electron beam (put down in my notebook for you by the end of last March)." Carlson wrote back that he would "very gladly accept" this request.

Kornei never pursued his scanning idea, as things turned out. And his decision to nullify the royalty agreement was one that he would come to regret.

Shortly after Kornei had moved to Cleveland, Carlson graduated from law school. That accomplishment didn't excite him, though, and he didn't rush to take the bar exam (although he did pass it the following year). Meanwhile, his relationship with his wife was becoming increasingly unpleasant. His work with Kornei, far from discouraging him, had persuaded him that he would need to make further financial sacrifices in pursuit of his idea—a major point of contention. He had shut down his beauty parlor laboratory, saving $15 a month in rent, but had moved all his scientific materials into their apartment, where he built a small workbench inside a closet. He and Elsa tried to revive their relationship by spending two weeks together in Florida, but the underlying resentment and incompatibility remained. In the summer of 1940, Elsa's parents took a meandering car trip to California, and Elsa went with them while Carlson stayed at home—a trial separation, in effect, and a portent of what was to come.

Even when Elsa was physically present, Carlson avoided her company, spending the weekends working in his makeshift laboratory and doing additional research at the library. He also wrote letters to more than twenty companies—including IBM, General Electric, RCA, and A. B. Dick—in the hope that one of them would be interested in commercially developing electrophotography. He later described the response to these letters as "an enthusiastic lack of interest," although a number of companies actually did invite him to make a presentation.

Kornei, before moving to Cleveland, had assembled a demonstration kit consisting of a few coated plates, a container of dusting powder, and other supplies. Carlson now used that kit in making his pitches, but the results were discouraging. Typical of the people he met with was a representative of a major office equipment company, whom Carlson described as an "old Photostat salesman." As Carlson said later, "After my demonstration of the process to him and telling him what I thought it would do he blamed me for wasting his time and was very scornful of the whole thing."

There were two main problems: the results of the presentation were mediocre, and Carlson was too soft-spoken to overcome the natural skepticism of his interviewers. "After talking to a number of people in industry, I found that my little crude demonstration did not impress them," he said later. "A technical person could usually understand it, but few of them saw the potential in it. Businessmen were not very impressed with it. It was hard to find anyone who could visualize what could be done toward the engineering development of the process."

Carlson's luck changed somewhat in November 1940, when his first patent was issued and *The New York Times* ran a brief story on the front page of its second section. That article generated several inquiries, including one from an executive at IBM, who told Carlson that he was excited by the idea. "So a day was arranged, and I went to his office, and set up my meager equipment," Carlson recalled later. "At the appointed time, eight or ten men filed into the room and sat down, and I gave them my demonstration. After that, I explained what I thought were some of the potentials of the process, and then I asked them if there were any questions. Not a word was said. After a few minutes, at the signal from the director of market research, they all got up and walked out of the room, and that was essentially the end of it."

Nevertheless, Carlson followed up with a letter offering IBM "an exclusive license for the U.S. and Canada under all my patents and applications for the field of photographic copying of documentary material and all applications to business machines and a non-exclusive license for all other fields," including pictorial photography, x-radiography, facsimile transmission, and the creation of masters for lithography and other forms of printing and duplication. In exchange, Carlson sought a minimum annual royalty of $10,000 against 5 percent of IBM's proceeds from sales and rentals—a requirement that would expire at the end of one year if the actual sales and rentals fell short of that minimum and IBM chose to make its license nonexclusive. In other words, Carlson was offering IBM the exclusive right to develop what would become the Xerox machine, in a deal from which the company, if it changed its mind, would be able to walk away after a year without forfeiting more than a single $10,000 advance against revenues. (Had IBM agreed to the deal, "Xeroxing" might be known today as "IBM-ing.")

A month later, Carlson wrote again, to ask why he hadn't received a response. A leisurely exchange of letters ensued—assurances from IBM that the matter was being considered, anxious expressions of frustration from Carlson. Then, on March 13, 1941, IBM's director of market research wrote, "With reference to the subject of Electron Photography which you brought to our attention, please feel assured our review of this matter is progressing, but it has occurred to me to suggest that if you could bring your model, if available, to our office for demonstration, it would supply our people with complete information."

This, finally, was the inescapable problem: Carlson didn't have a working model of the machine. He had decided, after making his first few pitches using Kornei's kit, that he was unlikely to find a buyer for his idea until he could produce a device that was actually capable of making a copy. About a year before, he had hired the Precision Instrument Company, in Brooklyn, to build a machine like the one he later depicted in the drawings included in his fourth patent application, which he submitted in November 1940 (and which was approved four years later). That machine was about the same size as a lawn mower engine, which it also resembled. In many of its internal details, however, it was remarkably suggestive of xerographic copying machines that would not be manufactured until decades later: the photoconductive surface was applied to a rotating drum rather than a flat plate; the drum was cleaned, after exposure, by a rotating fur brush; the fusing mechanism—which was intended to permanently bond the developed image to a sheet of paper—was a radiant heater through which a copy was supposed to pass just before exiting the machine; and the whole thing was compact enough to fit easily on a desk. All these features, though, were essentially chimerical. "I think they gave the job to the youngest apprentice in the shop," Carlson said later. "He did his best, but after the machine was completed, it didn't work."

Carlson took his nonfunctioning model to a more experienced machinist, in Manhattan. This time there were long delays—the entire American manufacturing sector was switching to war-related production, and projects like Carlson's were not a priority—but the second machinist eventually did solve several of the mechanical problems that had defeated the first, and Carlson was at last able to conduct a test. "I started it up," he recalled in 1965, "and as the cylinder, wrapped with anthracene-coated aluminum foil, rotated, a nearly perfect image of a [small part of a] full-size page appeared on the plate. However, the machine hadn't been completed to the point where it would transfer the image to a sheet of paper and fix it, so no copies were preserved. Also, the machine got badly gummed up with powder after a few operations and a mercury switch blew out. The model maker was called to war work and I was left with a half-complete model, which I still have.* I was also in the hole several thousand dollars, and no one seemed interested in taking up the idea."

In this recounting, Carlson suggested that his problem was merely one of "completing" the machine. This was true in a sense, but it grossly understated the scale of what remained to be done. No machinist in the world could have produced a working copier from Carlson's drawings—among other reasons, because the processes they described violated any number of physical laws. Carlson made it sound as though image transferring and image fixing were merely features that the model maker hadn't got around to adding, but, in fact, both of those functions presented major mechanical and scientific perplexities, which would ultimately be solved only through the efforts of large teams of physicists and engineers working over a period of years. Later writers have sometimes suggested that Carlson succeeded in making a few (unfused) paper copies with his model, but he never came close. The "nearly perfect image" he mentioned was merely a dusted image on the foil-covered surface of the drum, and it was only about five inches square. He had not yet devised a means of transferring that image to a sheet of paper, or to anything else.

The model, in other words, was a hopeless mess. Carlson's investment in it was substantially less than the "several thousand dollars" he recalled in 1965, but it still amounted to two or three times his annual salary, and he couldn't afford to spend more. He now had virtually nothing to show for his work up to that point, other than an enhanced awareness of the difficulties that lay ahead, and he had no idea what to try next.

---

*This device has been at the Smithsonian since 1968. When the mercury switch exploded, Carlson said, "the mercury flew all over the room."

This was essentially where matters stood in the spring of 1941 when IBM's director of market research cheerfully suggested that perhaps Carlson would like to swing by with his model and crank out a few copies for the boys in engineering. Carlson's heart must have sunk when that letter arrived. The correspondence continued sporadically for two more years, with IBM always expressing interest but asking to see the model, and Carlson always managing to sound impatient yet evasive. Both parties had reasonable points. IBM's interest in the model had been stimulated by Carlson himself, since he had said that he had one and that he would be happy to demonstrate it as soon as he had incorporated a few additional "improvements." Yet Carlson was also correct when he wrote to IBM, in the spring of 1943, "The development work required is largely the mechanical problem of working out the best design of machine to perform the process. This could be done more expeditiously by your laboratories, in consultation with me, than by me alone." The process Carlson had conceived was too complex to be fully developed by any lone inventor; the fact that he needed help did not discredit his idea. Someone at IBM needed to make an imaginative leap—yet no one did.

Three months later, Carlson did go back to IBM, at the company's invitation, to make a more modest presentation. But he had nothing new to show other than a somewhat improved version of his original kit, and the two sides remained at an impasse. And Carlson had similar experiences with other companies as well. The Charles Bruning Company—a manufacturer of duplicating machines and supplies—expressed strong interest in Carlson's ideas, which he had described in a letter to the company's president in November 1943. Bruning followed up several times, always hoping to set up a demonstration. "Inasmuch as we have been unable to find your name in the Manhattan phone book," the company's technical director wrote in December, "may I suggest that you telephone me at BArclay 7-8300, extension #25, to arrange the details." Carlson wrote back a week later to say that he would call soon, but he never did. Bruning's technical director, who also ordered a copy of the patent, tried again in the fall of 1944, having not heard from Carlson in nearly a year. But the requested meeting never took place.

When Carlson said later that his efforts to sell his idea had been met by indifference and scorn, he was only partly correct. Most of the two dozen companies he contacted expressed at least some interest, and a few were persistent in following up. But Carlson had trouble advancing the discussion beyond an initial meeting, since he could show little empirical support for his ideas. Many of the people he talked to were willing to be persuaded but found his presentations underwhelming. This was not an irrational reaction. Erik M. Pell, a retired Xerox physicist, has written, "His cousin Roy later said that he, himself, perceived no 'commercial value to Chet's invention because of its low image quality.' The copy speed was reasonable only for contact exposures, charging was clumsy, ineffective, and impractical, transfer to a damp or waxed sheet was unattractive, and the final image was fuzzy. Whether it would work on a damp day was anyone's guess, and the guess was likely to be that it would not."

It is conceivable that Carlson would have had better luck if he had been more of a showman. The men he had met with had all had a "rather naive approach to the method of deciding on the value of a new invention," he said in 1947, and he added, "I honestly believe that if I had brought them a large chromium-plated machine with red and green lights on it they would have been more enthusiastic about the process, whether it worked or not. In all cases there was, insofar as I can tell, not a single clear analysis of the relative value of the invention. The decision was almost invariably based on extraneous facts that had no bearing on the question involved. Even some highly trained engineers dismissed it as unworthy of serious consideration without actually understanding the situation."

There's also a possibility that Carlson would have had better luck if he had entirely skipped his doomed effort to build a functioning model and concentrated instead on making a foolproof page-size photoreceptor plate, which he could have used in a conference room to (for example) produce a clear facsimile of the letterhead of whichever executive was interviewing him. The useless model made his copying process seem like a con: Carlson was always having to make excuses for the machine and thereby inevitably suggesting that the basic idea was faulty, too. Compounding all these difficulties was the war, which had curtailed nearly every large company's commitment to nonmilitary research and development.

Carlson had personal troubles as well. Elsa's mother died in the spring of 1941, and the following October the couple moved, along with Elsa's father, to another apartment in Jackson Heights. This living arrangement placed additional strains on a relationship that was already in serious trouble. Exactly two years later, the couple separated. "The separation is no fault of Elsa's," Carlson wrote to his cousin Roy, "but was my own wish inasmuch as we had very little in common and little of an intellectual nature to sustain mutual interest in each other." Carlson also wrote, "In the beginning years [Elsa] had many justifiable faults to find with me, which usually came to me through her mother, [but] she eventually settled down to a commendable effort to be what she thought I wanted her to be. However, in my unhappiness and insecurity (socially) I finally decided that life would be too dreary if we had to continue together and on my initiative I suggested we separate. This was a cruel thing to do, particularly with so little discussion, but I was determined and we separated." Elsa later traveled to Las Vegas with another man, intending to divorce Carlson there, but then the other man disappeared and Elsa returned to Jackson Heights—to Carlson's disappointment. ("I thought I was off the hook," he told Roy.) They finally divorced in 1945.

Meanwhile, Carlson had been made the head of Mallory's patent department, and his growing responsibilities at work left little time for electrophotography. His health was poor, too. His arthritis troubled him, and he had begun to slouch when sitting and to appear slightly hunched as he walked—symptoms that would worsen as he aged. His condition was aggravated, he felt, by the long periods he spent standing on cold Manhattan street corners, waiting for a bus to take him back to Queens. While he waited, he inevitably brooded about the future of his invention. He remained convinced that his ideas were correct, but there were times, he said later, when he came close to giving up.

The solution arrived unexpectedly. One day in 1944, a young engineer from the Battelle Memorial Institute—a private, non-profit research and development organization in Columbus, Ohio—visited Carlson's department at Mallory. The U.S. Patent and Trademark Office had recently ruled unfavorably on one of Mallory's patent applications, which had been based on metallurgical research performed by Battelle, and the company was thinking of filing an appeal. Mallory was interested in engaging the Battelle engineer, whose name was Russell W. Dayton, as an expert witness, and Dayton had come to New York to discuss the case.

Carlson and Dayton spent most of the day together. Late in the afternoon, with an hour left before the departure of Dayton's train, Carlson decided that Dayton was "the kind of fellow who looked like he was interested in new ideas" and brought up electrophotography. He began by asking Dayton if Battelle ever developed ideas generated by others. Dayton said that it did not, and explained that the institute mainly performed contract research for large corporations and for the government—the same kind of research it had been doing for Mallory—as well as doing some original industrial research of its own. But Dayton told Carlson he was nevertheless interested in hearing about his invention.

"I described the idea to him simply as a scientific curiosity and gave him a copy of my patent," Carlson wrote later. Dayton took the patent with him on the train back to Columbus. A few weeks later, he and Carlson met again, at a patent hearing in Washington, D.C. When the hearing was over, Dayton asked Carlson to walk with him around a block near their hotel. "Then he explained to me that he had shown the patent to his associates at Battelle," Carlson continued, "and that they were interested in talking to me with a view to making some arrangements for further development of the idea." Carlson had suffered so many disappointments already that he was careful to keep his hopes in check. Still, he couldn't help thinking that perhaps this was the break he had been waiting for.

5

FATHERS AND SONS

GORDON BATTELLE WAS BORN IN 1883. He was the son of a wealthy Ohio industrialist, the grandson of a Methodist preacher and Civil War chaplain, and the great-great-grandson and great-great-great-grandson of militiamen who fought at the Battle of Lexington, during the Revolutionary War. He went to work for his father's steel business after college, and later set out to distinguish himself in his father's eyes by revitalizing some unprofitable zinc mines the company owned in northwest Missouri. He moved to Joplin, hired consultants, and funded the research of a former university professor, who was experimenting with new ways of processing ore. These efforts were partly successful, and Gordon, partly vindicated, became obsessed with establishing an independent industrial research laboratory—an unusual idea at the time. "Gordon would get steamed up and go on talking about it until my wife would say, 'I'm going out to the kitchen to get a glass of water,' and she'd disappear," a neighbor said. "He would talk on and on, but I had to go to work in the morning, even if he didn't."

Gordon's father died in 1918, making Gordon rich and elevating him to the presidency of several companies. Five years later, Gordon himself died, at the age of forty, after undergoing an operation to remove his appendix. He had never married. In his will he left his entire estate, $1.5 million, for "the foundation of a 'Battelle Memorial Institute,' " which would be dedicated to "education in connection with and the encouragement of creative and research work and the making of discoveries and inventions in connection with the metallurgy of coal, iron, steel, zinc and their allied industries," among other things. The institute's original trustees included President Warren G. Harding, a family friend, who died before the board could meet, and Gordon's mother, who died two years later. Gordon's mother left an additional $2.1 million to the project. The institute—with a brand-new building and twenty employees—opened during the summer of 1929, just in time for the Crash. The first director was Horace Gillett, who had previously run the United States Bureau of Standards and had once worked for Thomas Edison. A laudatory historical booklet commissioned by the institute in the early seventies says, "What Arthur Murray was to ballroom dancing, Escoffier was to *haute cuisine*, and Emily Post was to social graces, Gillett was to metallurgy."

By the 1940s, Battelle (which had survived the Great Depression in part because its trustees, shortly before the stock market collapsed, had shifted a significant portion of its endowment into government bonds) employed more than two hundred engineers and other workers, and had established itself as a hands-on industrial consulting agency, which a manufacturer might hire to help it build (for example) a pump with valves capable of withstanding extremely high temperatures. Battelle's scientists also made their own discoveries, including several involving new alloys, and during World War II they performed research for the U.S. military.

(Battelle developed an improved type of armor for American tanks, and it fabricated uranium fuel rods used in the Manhattan Project.) By 1944, when Chester Carlson mentioned his invention to Russell Dayton in his office at P. R. Mallory, Battelle had been expanding into fields that were only tangentially related to metallurgy. One of those fields was the graphic arts.

Carlson traveled to Columbus to pitch his idea in the spring of 1944. The group that met with him included Dayton, several of the institute's other top scientists and engineers, and Clyde Williams, who had succeeded Gillett as Battelle's director. Carlson made his standard presentation and, as he was accustomed to doing at such meetings, used Otto Kornei's demonstration kit to make a small, somewhat blurry copy, essentially repeating the Astoria experiment. During previous demonstrations, this had always been the point in his spiel when the people he was talking to would cough into their fist, rearrange a pile of papers, look down at the table. At Battelle, though, the reaction was different. Dayton took the copy Carlson had made and held it up to the other men. He said, "However crude this may seem, this is the first time any of you have seen a reproduction made without any chemical reaction and a dry process."

It was also the first time Carlson had made his presentation to a group of knowledgeable people who understood what he was talking about and believed there might be something to it. Shortly after the meeting, Roland M. Schaffert, one of the engineers present, wrote an internal memo that was both favorable and prescient. "Mr. Carlson's invention on electrophotography appears to have possibilities, and if it can be made to work in a usable manner, broad commercial application can be expected." Schaffert was the head of Battelle's graphic arts group. He had come to the institute from the Mergenthaler Linotype Company, which manufactured typesetting machines.* In his memo, he identified two of the biggest challenges that had to be met before a working product could be manufactured: attaining "sharper definition of the electrical image" and "development of some workable technique for transforming this image into a printable substance." He suggested first concentrating on finding a better photoconductor than sulfur or anthracene, both of which required lengthy exposure, then tackling the printing problem. "It may be that ionized ink particles could be attracted to the electrical image as well as powder," he wrote.

The challenges Schaffert had identified were serious ones—but his recognition of them as challenges proved to Carlson that Schaffert had looked past the crudeness of the result and understood the idea behind it. The rest of Schaffert's memo was encouraging, too. Schaffert (correctly) foresaw a number of potential applications: copying and duplication (and the replacement of carbon copying, stencil duplicating, spirit duplicating, and the making of Photostats); simplified creation of lithographic and hectographic masters; creation of relief and intaglio printing plates; and the direct printing of original text. All of these were applications that Carlson had described in his patents, and Schaffert, by enumerating them, was endorsing them, Carlson believed. "This process looks like a

---

*The linotype machine, which was invented in 1886 by a (German-born) American printer named Ottmar Mergenthaler, partially automated the typesetting process invented by Johannes Gutenberg. It allowed an operator to set a complete "line of type" at one time, by pressing leverlike keys on a machine the size of a church organ. The machine would arrange a sequence of brass letter molds and spacers in a justified line and then flow molten lead over the molds. The lead quickly hardened into a rectangular slug, with printing characters standing out in relief from the uppermost edge. These slugs were arranged into columns—and the columns were arranged into pages—and the brass molds were routed back into the machine to be reused. When I was a college newspaper editor, in the early seventies, linotype machines were still widely used in the printing business but were beginning to be supplanted by so-called cold, photography-based typesetting systems. *The New York Times* was typeset on linotype machines until 1978.

good research gamble," Schaffert concluded. "It would seem that the success or failure of the process might be determined during the early stages of the research work."

BY THE FALL OF 1945, Carlson and Battelle had settled on a business arrangement. "The first agreement was essentially an agency agreement," Carlson said later. "I appointed them as the exclusive agent for my patents and inventions in this field and they promised to put into the package any inventions they made. They promised to use diligence to obtain licenses. They agreed to do some research, although there was no dollar value put on the amount of effort they were to put into research. We were to share any return on royalties that would come out of the commercial development on a sixty-forty basis, sixty percent for Battelle and forty percent for me."

The deal required both parties to seek additional investors, and Carlson believed that Battelle's formal commitment to the idea would give potential licensees confidence that their money wouldn't be wasted. That turned out not to be the case, however. Carlson and various Battelle employees went back to all the companies Carlson had talked to in the past and made the pitch again—and they approached a number of other companies as well, including every significant American manufacturer of printing, duplicating, and photographic equipment—but they had no success. Schaffert said later, "In our constant attempts to obtain sponsors and licensees, we demonstrated the process to the representatives of the Eastman Kodak Company, the Harris-Seybold Company, and others. I personally showed what we had to a member of the research staff of Kodak when he came to Columbus to give a talk to the Central Ohio Camera Club. I explained some of the potentialities that I thought existed in the process. He made a statement that his company was interested only in photographic film and cameras. So that was that. Looking back, I feel it was perhaps fortunate that these people did not become interested at the time. It is conceivable that in our eagerness to get financial help we might have sold the process too cheaply."

Battelle itself initially seemed to exhibit no great enthusiasm for the idea, either; its total investment in electrophotography research in 1944 added up to just $702, which was very little more than Carlson had paid Otto Kornei back in 1938 and 1939. The next year, as Battelle's wartime assignments ended, expenditures on electrophotography rose to roughly $7,000. This still seems like an almost comically small sum, even by the standards of the time, but it was nevertheless enough to finance several major technological advances in the development of Carlson's idea.

The first of these advances involved the method of applying an electrical charge to the photoreceptor—a task that Kornei had accomplished by rubbing it with his handkerchief and that Carlson's model had accomplished by rubbing it with a revolving fur brush. Carlson, in his patents, had suggested that a better possibility would be so-called corona charging, which would involve showering ions onto the surface of the photoreceptor by running a high-voltage electrical current through a bare conductor stretched above it. (St. Elmo's fire—the eerie glow sometimes seen dancing around the mast of a ship or the wing of an airplane in a lightning storm—is a corona effect.) The first corona charger that Battelle devised consisted of a wire threaded through dozens of sharp sewing needles. The results were mediocre until Battelle's engineers, following a suggestion of Carlson's, moved the needle array farther from the plate—a counterintuitive idea that ought not to have worked (the engineers felt) but did.

Battelle's second great discovery was one that Carlson had not anticipated. In all of Carlson's early demonstrations, the dusted image had been transferred from the photoreceptor to a piece of paper by a physical process: Carlson either used an inherently sticky paper (such as the waxed paper that he and Kornei had bought for their first experiments) or used regular paper and made it sticky by moistening it with water (the technique depicted in Carlson's patent drawings and used in his nonfunctioning model). Both of these techniques had serious drawbacks: waxed paper wasn't much of an improvement over photographic paper—what secretary would want a file cabinet filled with waxed-paper sheets?—and wet paper would have fouled the photoreceptor, played havoc with electrostatic charges inside the machine, and wrinkled as it dried.

Schaffert soon thought of a better method: transferring the image from the plate to the paper by using the same electrostatic force that had put the image on the plate to begin with. After making the image visible by sprinkling a powdered resin on the exposed photoreceptor plate, Schaffert placed a sheet of ordinary paper on top of the plate, then ran the corona charger over the back of the paper. The charge thus applied to the back of the paper, being opposite to the charge on the resin, drew the resin particles from the plate to the front of the paper and held them there, almost as though the charger were a magnet and the resin particles were iron filings. "That causes the sheet to pull the powder away from the plate, and when you peel the sheet off, you peel it off with the powder image on it," Carlson explained. The method eliminated the need for sticky paper and proved to be more effective at transferring the powdered resin—which the scientists referred to as "toner"—producing darker copies and leaving less resin on the plate to be cleaned off later.

The third major improvement discovered at Battelle in 1945 involved the method of applying the toner to the photoreceptor. Carlson and Kornei had used lycopodium powder as the toner in their early experiments, and they had applied it by shaking it from a container with a perforated top. The lycopodium spores (which were very small, very dry, and very round) flowed smoothly over the plate, stuck mostly where they were supposed to stick, and were easy to clean off after a print had been made. They were too light in color to make clear images, however, and they couldn't be fused to ordinary paper, because they wouldn't melt. Carlson and Kornei had both known that a different toner would be needed for any working machine, but so far no one had turned up a likely possibility. The natural resins that Kornei had tried had been too temperamental. They tended to form clumps (which scattered unevenly and smeared) and to stick to the background areas of the plate (which were supposed to remain blank).

A major step toward solving this problem was made by a Battelle engineer named Edward Wise, who found that the application of almost any toner particle could be improved through the addition of a so-called carrier, small beads made of glass or other materials, which became coated with the much smaller toner particles and then dispensed them evenly as the beads bounced and rolled around on the photoreceptor surface. "The powder stuck to the beads electrostatically, and when the beads rolled over the plate they would drop powder on the image but not on the background area," Carlson explained. (It was Carlson himself who developed Haloid's first successful carrier: ordinary sand glazed with a yellow substance that imparted a negative charge to the toner particles.) The cascading carrier beads also created cleaner prints, by picking up stray toner particles from background areas.

Many serious problems remained to be addressed, but Battelle's scientists, in a little over a year's worth of effort, had turned up nothing to convince them that Carlson's idea was unworkable. Schaffert's initial belief that the project was worth pursuing had been based in part on his confidence that fatal flaws, if any, would become apparent quickly. None had emerged thus far. Still, more than a few of Battelle's scientists were deeply skeptical. "Of those who knew about it," Dayton said later, "at least fifty percent thought it was a stupid idea and that Battelle should never have gotten into it. It just goes to prove that if you've got something unique, you don't take a poll."

EARLY IN 1944, before Carlson had begun to negotiate his deal with Battelle, a New York City patent attorney named Nicholas Langer came across a copy of one of Carlson's first patents. Langer had been born in Hungary and had come to the United States in the 1920s to promote (unsuccessfully) an invention of his own: an electronic organ. He now supplemented the income he earned from patent work by writing freelance articles about technology, and he thought Carlson's copying idea might make a good story. He sent Carlson a letter, interviewed him at length, and wrote a laudatory article, which was published during the summer of 1944 in a technical supplement to a magazine called *Radio News*.*

The supplement, which wasn't included in newsstand copies of the magazine, was aimed at radio scientists and engineers. It attracted no notice at all, insofar as Carlson was aware. Eight months later, though, a condensed version appeared in a monthly technical bulletin published by Eastman Kodak. The bulletin—which contained abstracts of articles from a variety of scientific publications—was intended to keep Kodak employees informed about developments in fields related to photography, but its readers included non-Kodak scientists as well. Among those non-Kodak scientists was John Dessauer, who was the chief of research at the Haloid Company, a competing photographic-paper manufacturer,

---

*Carlson was impressed by Langer, and hired him to work in the patent department at Mallory. When Carlson later left the company, in 1945, Langer took his place as the head of the department. *Radio News* became *Radio & TV News* in 1948 and *Electronics World* in 1959.

whose headquarters, like Kodak's, were situated in Rochester, New York. Haloid was interested in developing a new line of business, in a field that wasn't dominated by a powerful competitor, and Dessauer thought electrophotography might be a candidate.

Haloid had been founded in 1906, the year Chester Carlson was born. It was actually the successor to a defunct photographic-paper manufacturer called the M. F. Kuhn Company, which had been started in 1902 by several former Kodak employees. When Kuhn went out of business, four Rochester businessmen bought its primitive manufacturing facility and resumed production, and they renamed the company after the group of silver compounds on which photography was based.

At first, Haloid's prospects seemed little better than Kuhn's. The company's workforce was tiny, and its factory was so cramped that long runs of freshly coated photographic paper had to be doubled back on themselves before being dried by fans blowing across blocks of ice. "The environment was malodorous and stiflingly hot in summer, and it was freezingly cold in winter," Erik Pell writes. Still, Haloid managed to survive and even to prosper. The company built a new, enlarged factory in 1907 and expanded again in 1912. By 1926, it was turning out ten miles of forty-one-inch-wide photographic paper a day, and its manufacturing plant (according to a self-published brochure celebrating the company's twentieth anniversary) was "the largest factory devoted exclusively to photo paper manufacture in America." Four years later, having noticed the increasing use of Rectigraph and Photostat document-copying machines, Haloid began manufacturing the long rolls of photographic paper that those machines used. This paper was called Haloid Record, and it quickly became a popular product. (The main customers were land record offices, county courthouses, departments of motor vehicles, insurance companies, and other organizations with high-volume record-keeping needs.) The new line

was so successful, in fact, that in 1935 Haloid bought the Rectigraph Company, whose headquarters were also in Rochester—a
city that during the early decades of the twentieth century was a
thriving high-technology industrial center, an optical Silicon Valley. Rochester was the home of more than a dozen companies involved in optics or photography, including Haloid, Rectigraph,
Kodak, Bausch & Lomb, and a number of smaller businesses (many
of them run by German immigrants) that made cameras, lenses,
and photographic emulsions.

Of all these companies, Kodak was by far the biggest. It had
been started in 1880 by a local banker named George Eastman,
who had taken up photography as a hobby two years earlier and,
using his mother's kitchen as a laboratory, had invented a method
of manufacturing glass photographic plates. His revolutionary
product, introduced in 1891, had been a simple box camera, for
which he coined the unusual but extremely catchy name by which
his company came to be known. The camera was sold loaded with
film, and its price, $25, included processing. (The Kodak advertis-
ing slogan, which Eastman also created, was "You Press the Button, We Do the Rest.") By the thirties, Eastman Kodak had
become one of the largest and most profitable industrial companies in America, and all the other optics-related manufacturers in
Rochester, while profiting from the industry Kodak had gone a
long way toward creating, felt as though they existed largely at the
big company's sufferance. Haloid's diversification into the
photographic-copying-paper business and its subsequent purchase
of Rectigraph were both moves intended to reduce its vulnerabil-
ity to Kodak—but at the same time those moves underscored the
weakness of Haloid's position, since Rectigraph's main competitor,
the Photostat Corporation, was essentially a Kodak subsidiary.

Dessauer, the Haloid employee who had noticed the abstract
of Langer's article about electrophotography, understood this ten-

sion very well, because he had worked for Kodak competitors for more than fifteen years. Born in Germany in 1905, Dessauer had emigrated to the United States in 1929, primarily to avoid being drafted into what would become Hitler's army. "He arrived just after the stock market crash," Erik Pell writes, "and he walked the streets of New York for six weeks—perhaps even on the same sidewalks as Chester Carlson, but with the added handicap that John Dessauer spoke English only barely. His letters of recommendation from banks and family proved of no help, and he was short of money. It happened that, to save money, he was sharing a room with an organ builder who had a job with Würlitzer to build an organ for St. Patrick's Church in Binghamton." From the organ builder, Dessauer learned that Agfa, the leading German photographic manufacturer, was building a plant in Binghamton. Dessauer applied for a job and had the good luck to be interviewed by an employee who spoke German. He worked at Agfa for six years, doing photographic research, and then went to work at Rectigraph, where he was hired to help create a line of photographic copying paper that could compete with the paper Kodak made for Photostat. When Haloid bought Rectigraph, a few months later, Dessauer stayed on, and he shared his new coworkers' interest in building a business that Kodak couldn't suddenly extinguish. The article he read in the Kodak bulletin was less than three hundred words long, but it described a process that sounded both technologically promising and emotionally appealing. He showed the abstract to Haloid's president, Joseph C. Wilson.

Less than two decades later, Wilson would be regarded as one of the most farseeing executives in the history of American capitalism. In 1945, though, he was a corporate novice. He was thirty-six years old, had only recently been named president of the company, and felt a powerful desire to distinguish both Haloid and himself. "Joe exhorted his staff to come up with new products," Pell writes. "Seismic recording was tried and diazo papers were considered. While Wilson felt that Haloid needed to keep up-to-date with photography, he was concerned that they would be unable to grow in Kodak's shadow." One of Haloid's four founders had been Wilson's grandfather, a former pawnbroker and beloved longtime mayor of Rochester, whose interest in starting Haloid had been mainly to provide a job for Wilson's father, who was now Haloid's chairman and therefore Wilson's boss. As Wilson brooded about the company's future, he felt not only the suffocating presence of Kodak but also the weight of the Wilson family's entire male line of descent: like Gordon Battelle, he yearned to prove that he hadn't simply been born into his office. (At a Haloid company picnic in the fifties, the children of employees were given T-shirts that said MY DADDY WORKS AT HALOID; Wilson, the CEO, received one, too.)

When Wilson read Langer's description of Carlson's idea, he was interested immediately. Haloid, through its Rectigraph division, already built document-copying machines, so the move would be a logical extension of part of its existing business. The best thing about Carlson's idea, though, had to do with what it wasn't. If Haloid could turn electrophotography into a viable product, the company would have a chance to establish itself in an industry that wasn't already dominated by the neighborhood giant. Best of all, Wilson would have a chance to prove himself in a business that hadn't been handed to him by his family.

Haloid's commercial partners at that time included a New York City company called Microtronics Laboratory, which manufactured microfilm equipment and whose president, George Cameron, was a friend of Wilson's. Wilson asked Cameron, as a favor, to contact Carlson and make a report. Cameron and his chief engineer, Ernest Taubes, did so in the fall of 1945, without mentioning their connection with Haloid. Carlson said later, "I met with them and explained it. I also told them that my invention was in the hands of Battelle and that they should go to Columbus, Ohio, to see what Battelle was doing." Cameron told Wilson that Carlson, in their conversation, had made electrophotography seem very promising indeed and that the idea, in fact, "might well be worth half a million dollars"—the first of many earnest but retrospectively laughable underestimates of the commercial value of Carlson's invention.

Not long afterward, Wilson and Dessauer took a train to Columbus, along with Taubes, to see the process for themselves. "This was no ordinary demonstration," Dessauer wrote in 1971, in a memoir called *My Years With Xerox: The Billions Nobody Wanted.* "Joe and I took off our jackets, rolled up our sleeves, and worked with the Battelle engineers. The institute had assigned some very good men to assist Dr. Schaffert, men who eventually made significant contributions to xerography: George Richard, Ed Wise, C. David Oughton, and a few others. We spent most of our time with these scientists and engineers, and when we left, Joe Wilson was as enthusiastic about the prospects of the invention as I was."

IN DECEMBER 1946, AFTER MORE trips to Battelle and at least one meeting with Carlson, Wilson traveled back to Columbus to sign a deal, this time accompanied by his best friend, Sol M. Linowitz, a young Rochester lawyer and recently discharged navy lieutenant. Wilson asked Linowitz to represent Haloid in the negotiation, and the trip turned out to be memorable. "It was abominable," Linowitz wrote in 1985 in a memoir of his own, called *The Making of a Public Man.* "We shared a compartment on a sleeper. Everything was dirty. The beds were bumpy and the roadbed worse, the heat didn't work and the train was bitterly cold, there was no dining car and we had to do without breakfast. We were stuck several hours in the snow, shivering in our overcoats and staring out the filthy windows. And what we found when we got to Battelle did not make me particularly cheerful or optimistic about the prospects for electrophotography." When the Battelle engineers performed the now standard demonstration, Linowitz was incredulous: *"That's it?"* (Recalling the trip years later, Linowitz said, "We went to Columbus to see a piece of metal rubbed with cat's fur.")

Nevertheless, the two parties eventually came to a formal agreement, through which Haloid acquired a nonexclusive license to manufacture electrophotography-based copying machines intended to produce fewer than twenty copies of an original. This agreement was tightly circumscribed. "For our initial $10,000," Linowitz wrote later, "Battelle wished to give us only six months; we insisted on, and got, a year, with options to renew for $12,500 in 1948, $20,000 in 1949, $25,000 in 1950, and $35,000 in 1951. Battelle would spend this money for research on the fundamental process, and Haloid would do its own research on treated papers to improve the process; the two research staffs would work together in their respective areas of responsibility. Haloid would pay Battelle a royalty of 8 percent on any sales of products embodying the patented principles, once a certain sales volume had been reached." The dollar figures in the agreement seem almost hilariously small in retrospect, but at the time they represented a major investment for Haloid, whose earnings from all operations in 1945 amounted to just $100,000.

Although Battelle and Carlson had been seeking licensees without success for a long time, they did not view the Haloid deal as a tremendous victory. Haloid's license did convert Battelle's electrophotography research program into a more familiar form, since the institute's work would now be funded mainly by an outside entity—its standard operating arrangement. But Haloid was far smaller and less well known than the other potential partners Battelle and Carlson had approached, and in Columbus expectations for the deal were restrained. The Battelle representatives who met with Wilson had been impressed by his enthusiasm—a reaction they hadn't encountered elsewhere—but were skeptical about his company's ability to build a serious product. Battelle still hoped that bigger licensees would follow, in areas that Battelle considered to be more significant than simple office copying—such as the production of machines intended to make twenty or more copies (in effect, duplicators) and the manufacture of electrophotography-based toys.

Haloid had its own reasons for hesitation. While the licensing deal was being negotiated, Battelle had given Haloid a lengthy report on the research it had performed up to that point. Page 142 of the report was an electrophotographed copy—a clever demonstration of the potential of the process. Joe Wilson was deeply impressed and, after signing the agreement, asked for more copies of page 142 so that he could distribute them to skeptics on his board. Battelle was happy to comply—but then discovered a problem. "We tried and tried and tried but were unable to reproduce the initial results," Roland Schaffert said later. Battelle's scientists and engineers were baffled, and their inability to supply the copies led to serious misgivings at Haloid: had the first page 142 been faked? There were angry telephone conversations and exchanges of letters, and Dessauer hypothesized that perhaps Battelle's engineers had produced the first, clean copy by carefully vacuuming excess toner from the background areas. The crisis didn't pass until six months later, when Battelle—having determined that the problem lay with a defect in a photoreceptor plate—at last succeeded in making acceptable samples.

Linowitz and others at Haloid also became concerned when they realized that Haloid's eagerness to enter the electrophotography business was apparently unique. Nearly a year into the relationship with Battelle, Linowitz wrote to a friend of his, a trademark expert in Washington, D.C., seeking "information relating to companies and persons who may have from time to time made inquiry or an investigation in connection with [Carlson's] patents." Linowitz, in other words, wanted to know if any other companies had ever shown an interest in electrophotography. The friend made inquiries, Linowitz wrote, and "replied that he could not find any evidence that anyone had ever inquired, which squared with what Battelle and Carlson had told us." Haloid knew that several very large companies—among them Kodak, 3M, and IBM—were almost certainly working on office copiers of their own, using techniques unrelated to electrophotography. Why had all those companies ignored Carlson's idea? Did they know something that Haloid didn't?

Any excitement that Carlson himself may have felt over the Haloid licensing agreement dissipated as well. He left his job as the head of Mallory's patent department late in 1945, roughly a year after signing his agency agreement with Battelle, thinking his circumstances were about to change. But progress at Battelle was slow, and he had to support himself with freelance patent work for nearly a year. Finally, in 1946, he went back to patent work full-time, at a firm that he himself founded. He traveled to Columbus whenever he could, to look in on the research at Battelle and offer suggestions, but he never felt particularly welcome there. He was encouraged by Wilson's enthusiasm for electrophotography, but Haloid's small size and thin capitalization made him nervous. Haloid had never been on any of Carlson's or Battelle's original lists of potential licensing partners; it's possible that Carlson had never heard of the company before he learned of its contact with Battelle. During all of 1947 and 1948, the first two years of the licensing agreement, Haloid did no electrophotography research of its own. In fact, Haloid didn't hire its first physicist until 1949, and it did so then only because scientists at Battelle had complained that no one at the company could understand what they were talking about. (Dessauer's training was in chemistry.) This delay may have been fortunate; if Wilson in 1947 had truly understood the scientific challenges posed by electrophotography, or if he himself had been a physicist, he might never have dared to become involved.

As the months went by, Carlson became more and more deeply discouraged, worrying that his principal patent, which had been issued 1942, might expire before Haloid and Battelle could bring a solid product to market. Patent law gives an inventor seventeen years in which to develop and market an invention, but in return for that protection it requires disclosure of the ideas behind the invention, so that everyone else can see and understand them. Carlson worried that if Battelle and Haloid didn't act fast, companies that were bigger and more aggressive might find clues in his disclosures which would enable them to discover a similar but noninfringing copying process of their own.

Perhaps stimulated by these anxieties, Carlson agreed in 1947 to let his old roommate Larry Dumond write a freelance article about him and electrophotography. Dumond hadn't flourished as a journalist; he was working at *The New York Times*, but in the sales promotion department, not as a reporter. (His wife was a society page editor at the *Daily News*.) He thought that a story about Carlson might be something he could sell to a magazine, thereby providing a professional boost for both him and his friend. He spent roughly thirty hours interviewing Carlson, worked on his notes for months, and, in 1948, wrote a rough draft of what he hoped would become the beginning section of a much longer article. Electrophotography, the draft said, "is photography without chemicals, without a darkroom, without sensitized paper. It is a printing press that prints without pressure and without fluid ink. Like a clothespin, it is simple, cheap and quick. It is nothing but a simple plate or paper film that takes a coating of static electricity and shapes the electrons in the image of a picture upon exposure to light." With guidance from Carlson, Dumond described many possible applications, including several exotic ones that Carlson hadn't mentioned in his patents. One idea was for an electrophotographic equivalent of videotape (which wouldn't be invented until the fifties): "A bank can install a camera with a film on a revolving endless tape and make a picture of every person coming through the door. The film would be wiped clean and exposed over and over again unless there was a hold-up, in which case the latent picture would be developed."

Dumond wrote a cover letter on *New York Times* stationery, submitted his draft to *Collier's* as a proposal—under the title "A Genie in His Hall Closet"—and included a summary of the ideas that he intended to develop more fully in a final article. In response, he received a terse, unsigned rejection letter. "Thank you for sending us the accompanying manuscript," the (lithographically duplicated) form letter said. "We have read it carefully and regret that it does not meet the present needs of Collier's." In coming months, Dumond pitched the idea to other publications, among them the *Times*, but without success.

THE ONE ENCOURAGING PART OF Carlson's life at that time was his second marriage. In the fall of 1945, either shortly before or shortly after his divorce from Elsa von Mallon became final, he met Dorris Helen Hudgins at the home of a mutual friend. (The second *r* in her first name had been added by her mother to encourage people to broaden the *o*, avoiding an exact rhyme with "Boris.") She was forty-one years old, two years older than he, and had been divorced for sixteen years. She had married her first husband, a floorwalker at a Manhattan department store, when she was just twenty; had taken courses at Union Theological Seminary; and had worked mainly as a secretary—for the minister at a church in her neighborhood, for an executive at a sugar company, for the manager of a hotel. She also taught Sunday school. Carlson had been content as a bachelor and had believed he would never remarry, but he was attracted immediately. He wrote in 1963, "I felt, and still feel, that she supplemented me in many ways in background and interests, and made up for some of my lack in social graces. She came from a Portsmouth, Virginia, family in comfortable but modest circumstances, had two sisters and a brother. She was the oldest child and is something of a natural leader." When they met, she was living with her father and one of her sisters in an apartment in Woodside, Queens. Her father worked as a tugboat captain for a company that operated oceangoing coal steamers, and was called Cap; he was separated from Dorris's mother, who still lived in Virginia.

Not the least of Dorris's charms, in Carlson's eyes, was her terrifically fast typing speed, an attainment he had always admired; she, in turn, was impressed by the orderliness of his bachelor apartment. Their courtship lasted just a few months and consisted mainly of getting together for meals—almost always at restaurants that he had tried out beforehand by himself. Carlson "had a very nice little habit of bringing three-by-five cards, which he carried in his pocket, with notes on them for us to talk about," she recalled later. On their first date, Carlson made her suspicious by telling her he had an interesting collection of classical records in his apartment—but it turned out that he really did have an interesting collection of classical records in his apartment and that he was a gentleman. All their evenings ended early. "This was because it would take me time to get to bed and asleep and I am a daytime person, not a nighttime one," she explained. Carlson always offered to accompany her back to Queens in her taxi, but she insisted on going alone, the sooner to get to bed. Carlson once told a friend, "I had to marry Dorris so that I could have a date that lasted longer than nine p.m."

Carlson's marriage proposal was characteristic. "One Sunday early in January, when Chet had invited me to have luncheon with him in New York," Dorris recalled, "he asked me to take a walk over to the East River, where there were benches near the water, and where people went for a little quiet looking at the river. It was while sitting there that he asked me to marry him. And gave reasons!" He took her to Tiffany's to buy a diamond ring, but she rebelled at the extravagance and asked to wear his mother's simple wedding band instead. ("I have not liked anything that made me feel decorated," she said later.) For their honeymoon, they spent a few days in Washington, D.C.—not the most conventionally romantic of travel destinations, but the home of the U.S. Patent and Trademark Office, which Carlson liked to visit whenever possible. When they returned, they moved in with her father and sister (who never liked Carlson), and Dorris became a secretary at Carlson's law firm, where she found patent work to be "the most boring in my life." They took a course in semantics at the New School, went to plays, circumnavigated Manhattan on the Circle Line, enjoyed foreign films, and took walks on Fifth Avenue. Naturally, Dorris heard about her husband's invention, and about his agreement with Battelle, but she paid little attention. "I just thought, Ah, well, another man with a mousetrap," she said. "I figured he'd eventually get over it."

6

THE OX BOX

IN 1948, FUNDING FOR ELECTROPHOTOGRAPHY research appeared from an unexpected source. Haloid, through its Rectigraph division, had sold photographic-copying equipment and supplies to the U.S. military during World War II. That lucrative business had wound down now, but Joe Wilson still had close friends in the Signal Corps. He told them about Carlson's idea and, at their request, arranged a demonstration at Battelle in 1947. The Signal Corps representatives were impressed, and a month later Wilson, Dessauer, Linowitz, and a scientist from Battelle traveled to Fort Monmouth, New Jersey, to talk about a deal.

After a long negotiation, the Signal Corps agreed to invest $100,000 in electrophotography—an amount that would eventually be doubled.* Military planners, three years after Hiroshima, had decided that battlefields in the future were likely to be contaminated

---

*Carlson had actually pitched his idea to the Signal Corps several years before—but without success, because "their needs at that time were for something fully developed and ready to put into actual use," he told Dumond in 1947.

by thermonuclear radiation, and that current reconnaissance techniques, which depended on conventional photography, would
therefore be useless, since silver halide emulsions respond to radiation in the same way they respond to light: in a radioactive environment, ordinary film would fog. What the Signal Corps wanted was
an A-bomb-proof substitute. The new research led to a device nick-
named "Two-Minute Minnie" and, later, to additional military research contracts. These contracts gave Battelle and Haloid the
funds they needed to address technological issues that affected civil-
ian applications as well, including the sensitivity of photoconductors, the rendering of continuous tones (rather than just black or
white), and more efficient development of images. Well into the
fifties, more than half of the money that Battelle spent on electrophotography research came from government contracts.

And it was at Battelle that almost all the important early advances in electrophotography were made. Many at the institute
were still skeptical about Carlson's idea, but the number of scientists committed to the project was gradually increasing. "For a
while we didn't have a single PhD in our group," Roland Schaffert
said later. "What happened, however, was this: Battelle would hire
PhDs in chemistry or physics for some other projects. Sooner or
later these men would have to pass our lab. Curiosity made them
come in to see what we were doing. Or else they'd hear of our
work across lunch tables. Once they knew what we were trying to
accomplish, a good many of them became intrigued."

One such scientist was William Bixby, a physicist, who joined
Battelle in 1946 and became interested in difficulties the graphic
arts division was having with photoreceptors. In early 1947, he was
deeply involved in the occasionally frantic effort to reproduce the
notorious page 142, sometimes with after-hours help from his
wife. While struggling with that problem, he also made a discov-

ery that turned out to be an essential step in the development of a viable copying machine.

In its early experiments with electrophotography, Battelle had relied on the same photoconductive materials that Carlson and Kornei had used in Queens: sulfur and anthracene. Kornei, during the brief period in which he worked for Carlson, had devised a method of coating plates by evaporation—by heating white flakes of anthracene in a glass dish and allowing the vapors to condense on a plate held above it—but his results had been inconsistent. Battelle scientists quickly improved this process by doing the evaporation in a vacuum chamber, a technique that worked with sulfur, too.

A major problem remained, however. Anthracene made better plates than sulfur did, but both materials, when used to make copies, required long exposure times and produced mediocre prints, and the scientists at Battelle realized that they would have to find something better. One theoretically promising material was selenium, a gunmetal-colored crystalline element, which appears directly below sulfur on the periodic table.* Carlson knew about selenium's photoconductive properties—selenium had been used in photoelectric cells for decades—and Kornei had coated a few plates with it. But Kornei's layers had come out rough and uneven, and the selenium wouldn't hold a charge. "The experiments will be continued," Kornei wrote in his lab notebook near the end of his six-month employment period, although he made no further progress. Carlson later tried combining selenium and sulfur, but his results were disappointing as well.

---

*The list of historically important xerographic photoconductors is oddly similar to the list of active ingredients in popular dandruff shampoos: sulfur, selenium, zinc (oxide), and coal tar (the source of anthracene).

Battelle already had considerable experience with selenium, as a result of an earlier project involving copper smelting, of which selenium is a by-product. Bixby discovered that only one type of selenium—a noncrystalline form known as amorphous selenium—had the desired photoconductive properties, and that adding small amounts of it to sulfur or anthracene improved the results obtained with either material. He also found that he could create good layers by using the vacuum coater and carefully controlling the temperature of his materials. The more selenium he added to the mixture, the better his results became—until the selenium reached a certain concentration, at which point performance turned in the opposite direction, a result he didn't understand. "After several more futile attempts," Jack Kinsella, a former Xerox employee, recalled, "his supervisor urged him to drop selenium and concentrate on other alternatives."

One day, though, it occurred to Bixby that the problem might be ambient light. Perhaps amorphous selenium was such a sensitive photoconductor that even the purposely subdued illumination in his laboratory was bright enough to partially discharge his selenium plates before he could expose them to an image he wanted to copy—a problem that would increase as the concentration of selenium rose. He installed the kind of red safelights used in photography darkrooms, repeated his experiments, and found that image quality improved enormously. In fact, he found that pure selenium was roughly a thousand times more sensitive than sulfur or anthracene and was also more sensitive than any combination of the three materials.

This was a landmark discovery. All the crude electrophotographic prints that Carlson or anyone else had made had been contact prints. That is, copies were made by placing an original document facedown on top of a photoconductive plate (or, in the case of Carlson's nonfunctioning model, wrapping the document around a photoconductive drum) and then shining a very bright light through its back—in effect, casting a shadow of the original image on the plate beneath. This technique worked fairly well but had many limitations. It couldn't be used with book pages or other two-sided originals, for example, and it couldn't be used to reproduce an image that was printed on thick or nontranslucent stock. Bixby's amorphous selenium plates were so sensitive that they could theoretically be used to make copies not just by contact but by projection—that is, by brightly illuminating the surface of an original document and projecting its image onto the photoconductor, in the same way that an opaque projector shines an image onto a screen or a wall. Carlson had anticipated this method, and had described it in his patents, but hadn't been able to accomplish it with his crude experimental materials.

Bixby's discovery made projection theoretically possible, and it therefore represented a major step toward building a marketable machine. It also led directly to a crucial patent, issued in 1955, which gave Haloid (and then Xerox) the exclusive control of selenium as a copying machine photoconductor—a preemptive competitive advantage, it turned out, because no effective substitute for selenium would be discovered for many years.* In an interview with John Brooks in 1967, Harold Clark, who went to work at Haloid in 1949 as the company's first physicist, said, "Think of it. A simple thing like selenium—one of the earth's elements, of which there are hardly more than a hundred altogether, and a common one at that. It turned out to be the key. Once its effectiveness was discovered, we were around the corner, although we didn't know it at the time. We still hold patents covering the use of selenium in xerography—almost a patent on one of the elements.

---

*Today, virtually all xerographic copiers and laser printers use not selenium but so-called organic photoreceptors, which typically consist of a photoconductive compound (such as zinc oxide) suspended in a matrix. If you dissect the cartridge in your laser printer—a very messy project, best done outdoors—that's what you'll find.

Not bad, eh? Nor do we understand exactly *how* selenium works, even now. We're mystified, for example, by the fact that it has no memory effects—no traces of previous copies are left on the selenium-coated drum—and that it seems to be theoretically capable of lasting indefinitely. In the lab, a selenium-coated drum will last through a million processes, and we don't understand why it wears out even then. So, you see, the development of xerography was largely empirical. We were trained scientists, not Yankee tinkers, but we struck a balance between Yankee tinkering and scientific inquiry."

HALOID'S AGREEMENT WITH BATTELLE required Haloid to help find additional licensing partners, who were supposed to develop other applications. Officials at both Battelle and Haloid initially believed that the Signal Corps contract would make finding such partners easy, since the deal represented, in effect, an endorsement from the U.S. government. But the contract turned out to make no difference at all, except with other government agencies. Few companies were interested in talking to Haloid or Battelle, and Joe Wilson and others at Haloid gradually realized that if they were going to make a truly major commitment to electrophotography, they were probably going to have to do it on their own. This prospect was encouraging in one way, since exclusivity would give Haloid a competitive advantage. But it was also daunting. Developing the machine was almost certainly going to require Wilson to put the company's continued existence at risk.

Wilson's determination to go ahead came at least in part from Chester Carlson. The two men had met in 1946 and liked each other very much. Wilson was far more outgoing than Carlson, but both men were thoughtful, slow to anger, and deeply sensitive to the feelings of others. Wilson also had an intuitive faith in electrophotography which Carlson not only agreed with but found personally reassuring. One day, Carlson stopped in Rochester on his way back to New York after a visit to Columbus. He told Wilson that he was worried that Battelle wasn't working hard enough to develop his idea, and he reiterated his concern that time was slipping away on his principal patent, which now had just ten more years to run. "Quiet as was Carlson's nature," Erik Pell writes, "he could be aggressive when he became frustrated and when so much seemed at stake—but not aggressive enough to eliminate his own frustration. A continuing issue was that Carlson wished to see more effort toward a salable product (he needed income from his invention), while Battelle wished to sell development rather than a product and tended to emphasize process understanding rather than hardware."

Wilson sympathized. He responded by offering to retain Carlson as a consultant, at a fee of $1,000 a month. Carlson accepted the offer, and, not long afterward, he resigned from the patent law firm he had founded. Then he and Dorris loaded up their aging Studebaker sedan and moved to the Rochester area, where they rented a very modest house in Canandaigua, a small town about thirty miles southeast of the city.

At Haloid, Carlson quietly but relentlessly lobbied for electrophotography. He strengthened Wilson's commitment to the idea by constantly reminding him that the process had potentially lucrative applications in addition to office copying. And he continued to make direct contributions as well, in his capacity as a consultant. Dessauer and others later suggested that Carlson's productive involvement in the development of xerography ended when he signed his agreement with Battelle, but that is not the case. He was so inconspicuous and unassuming that he was easy to overlook, but he tinkered with parts of the process for most of the rest of his life, and he eventually received thirty-six additional xerography-related patents beyond the original four he had held when he made his deal with Battelle.

For those at Haloid who understood his temperament, he was a valuable colleague. Frederick A. Schwertz, a physicist, who went to work at the company in 1955 and became one of the most significant contributors to the development of xerography, said later, "They gave me a couple of helpers and I was supposed to look at special applications of xerography: Could it be used to etch printed circuits on copper-clad plastics? Things like that. It was in that job that I had my first experiences at reinventing things that Chet Carlson had already invented." Schwertz's lab at Haloid was situated a few blocks from Carlson's, and when Schwertz made what he felt was an important discovery, he would sometimes go to Carlson's building to let him know. "I would rush excitedly to Chet and tell him about it," he continued, "and he would say, 'Oh, yes, I filed a patent on that idea. It's number so-and-so.' That kind of thing happened all the time with Chet. You would tell him something you had been thinking about, and he would say, 'Oh, yes . . . let me think now . . .' Then he would tell you all about the idea you had just 'discovered.' Always in a mild way, ever so gently. You kept finding out he had been there years before."

Outside of work, Carlson kept even more to himself. He didn't play golf, as most of the key men at the company did, and he and Dorris seldom went to parties. Compounding his instinct for solitude was his financial condition during the late forties. Dessauer wrote later that "in those days Chet was much poorer than any of us realized." One day, Carlson was invited to lunch by a Haloid employee named Ken Dennis. Carlson declined, saying he'd brought his lunch that day, but then admitted, when Dennis pressed him, that the real reason was that he couldn't afford to reciprocate. Carlson ended up going to lunch regardless, but only on condition that he be allowed to take Dennis to lunch one day when he could—a bargain that Carlson later kept in "regal" fashion, according to a colleague.

The main reason Carlson's finances were strained during that period was that he was gathering every dollar he could to send to Battelle. Carlson's agency agreement with the institute had originally entitled him to 40 percent of all its revenues from his invention. Once Battelle's total research expenditure reached $10,000, though, Carlson's royalty rate fell by one percentage point for each additional $1,000 that Battelle spent, until the rate had reached the contractual minimum of 25 percent, below which it could not fall. The agreement gave Carlson the option of restoring his original royalty rate, however, by reimbursing Battelle, within five years, for half of its spending beyond the original $10,000. That five-year period was now drawing to a close, and Battelle so far had spent $40,000—meaning that Carlson could restore his 40 percent royalty for $15,000, or $1,000 for each percentage point. This would ultimately turn out to be an extraordinarily lucrative investment, since by the mid-1960s each point would be worth millions of dollars. In 1948, though, putting more money into electrophotography seemed recklessly speculative to almost everyone but Carlson—who had just received his first royalty payment ever, a check for $2,500, representing a quarter of Haloid's first payment to Battelle. He sent that money back to the institute and, to raise the rest, exhausted his own savings and sold $100 shares in an "Electrophotography Participation Fund" to thirteen relatives, including several of his in-laws—all of whom would become millionaires as a result.*

Carlson's consolidation of his financial relationship with Battelle was paralleled by a similar process at Haloid. Wilson, Linowitz, and others had come to realize that Haloid needed to

---

*Dorris believed, very possibly correctly, that Carlson didn't need help from his relatives—or hers—but created the participation fund to help them all financially without embarrassing them. She said that her sisters and her brother-in-law were never grateful for their windfall but viewed their investments in the fund as *"their* cleverness"—a sore point with her, though not with her husband.

renegotiate with Battelle before it could proceed with full-scale product development. "If we were going to make major investments of our own funds in this process," Linowitz wrote later, "we had to have an exclusive license, an assurance that nobody could sneak up behind us with greater resources and overwhelm us with faster and bigger exploitation of the same patents. We needed relief from the provision in the license that we restrict ourselves to machines that would make no more than twenty copies (once we sold a machine, after all, there was no way we could restrain the purchaser from making more than twenty copies). Partly because of our growing contacts with Chet, and partly because we were caught up in a vision for the future of xerography, Joe and I were already making speeches about the use of xerography as a means of communication with beings on other planets. We had become increasingly convinced that the Carlson patents opened the door to something much larger than the mere improvement of photocopying, and we wanted to be in on that."

Battelle's attitude toward Haloid had warmed considerably over the past few years—primarily because all its efforts to find additional licensees had failed. Haloid was small and poor, but no other company seemed interested, and Battelle agreed to renegotiate. The new deal made Haloid the exclusive licensee for everything except "toy kits, fingerprint reproduction and electron-microscope shadowgraphs"—applications that Battelle believed to be promising and wanted to retain. The agreement also required Haloid to find three sublicensees—major companies that would defray development costs by investing additional money in related research—a strategy that Linowitz called "latching onto the laboratories of the great companies." Haloid did eventually manage to make a few small deals, although none of them ever amounted to much. For the most part, Haloid simply recapitulated Carlson's old experience with solicitations. "When we did appointments," Linowitz

wrote later, "Joe and I went calling, and waited anxious and inse-
cure in the anterooms of the large companies in the hope that we
might get a meeting with some vice-president—and we were
grateful if we got a polite reception."

DESPITE CARLSON'S ANXIETY ABOUT HIS INVENTION, real technological progress was finally being made. Most of that progress
was still being made at Battelle, but Haloid was beginning to increase its direct involvement as well. By 1948, Wilson realized that
the company was going to have to make a public announcement of
some kind, both to establish its claim on the idea and to satisfy its
legal obligation not to withhold material information from its
shareholders—a major consideration now that Haloid was essentially betting its future on Carlson's idea.

One of the first tasks was to find a more publicity-friendly name
than "electrophotography," a word that was awkward to say and that
made the idea sound like nothing more than a (possibly Kodak-
related) refinement of an existing imaging process. Haloid employees suggested "Kleen Kopy," "Dry Duplicator," and "Magic
Printer," among many others. The solution came from a public relations employee at Battelle, who described Carlson's invention to a
classics professor at Ohio State University and asked for ideas. The
professor suggested "xerography"—from the Greek words *xeros*
(meaning "dry") and *graphein* (meaning "writing"). Carlson didn't
like the name—"I think the original name [his own coinage, elec-
trophotography] is more technically accurate and fits better in technical parlance," he said later—but Wilson did like it, and Haloid's
board adopted it. The company's patent department (which at that
point would have been mainly Carlson and Linowitz) wanted to
trademark "xerography," but John Hartnett, the head of sales and
advertising, said, "Don't do *that*. We want people to *use* the word."

The new term did inspire Haloid's first xerographic trademark, though, by suggesting the word that would eventually be adopted as the name of the entire company. It was Wilson and Linowitz who came up with it. They did so while taking a walk one Sunday when Wilson's wife and children were at church, something the two men did routinely. Wilson had always liked the name *Kodak*, with its nearly palindromic rat-a-tat of *k*'s; *Xerox* seemed similar without being obviously derivative. Some in the company were concerned that the name sounded too much like "zero;" others worried that customers wouldn't know how to pronounce it; and for a time all of Haloid's brochures, manuals, and advertising materials included a parenthetical guide. (The official pronunciation in the early years—"Zee-rox"—was daintier and more tentative than it would later become.) A few, including Hartnett, pushed for the perfectly bidirectional "Xerex," but that name had the fatal disadvantage of sounding like the name of a popular brand of automotive antifreeze (which is spelled with an initial *Z).*

A bigger issue was settling on an appropriate form and forum for a public announcement. Someone noticed that the Optical Society of America would be holding its annual meeting in Detroit on October 24, 1948, two days after the tenth anniversary of Carlson and Kornei's pioneering experiment in Astoria. Haloid and Battelle arranged to present a paper at the meeting and budgeted $25,000 for their presentation—an impressive sum, given the finances of the two organizations—with two-thirds to be paid by Battelle. The goal for the meeting was modest: to make a single copy of a single document in a minute or less. Nevertheless, this was something that neither Battelle nor Haloid had yet accomplished.

"The job to be done was prodigious," Dessauer wrote later. "To make the introduction of the Carlson process as impressive as possible, we decided that the various manual manipulations dry copying then required would be demonstrated in separate red 'boxes.' Such containers, if one may call them by so inappropriate a name, had yet to be designed and constructed. We had to be sure they would be not only attractive but geared to maximum efficiency of operation. Each box had to win the approval of engineers, of designers, and, naturally of top management." According to Schaffert, "This took a lot of planning, a lot of designing, a lot of instructions, a lot of experimentation, a lot of after-hours work, and a lot of worries."

Because physicists and engineers aren't known for their showmanship, Battelle hired a professor from the Speech Department of Ohio State to coach its presenters in public speaking. "On a dark stage spotlights blazed upon each speaker in turn as he explained one phase of the new process," Dessauer wrote. "Then a circle of light played on the red box which, in less than sixty seconds, gave forth a triumphant sheet of paper. Joe Wilson himself ended the performance with a prophetic view of what the future might hold." The presentation went smoothly—as had a similar one conducted for reporters in New York City a few weeks before.

Still, the public impact of these performances was minimal. Although refining xerographic technology for the shows had required a major, months-long effort by physicists and engineers at both Haloid and Battelle, the end result was just a single sheet of paper with a slightly blurry black image printed on one side. The red boxes in the spotlights didn't constitute a "copying machine" in anything like the modern sense; they were merely fancy packages concealing what was really just the same crude demonstration that Carlson had first performed in 1938. Everything worked better than it had a decade earlier, but no part of the process had been automated. The selenium photoreceptor wasn't a drum, as in much later machines: it was a flat, heavy plate. After exposure, that plate had to be hoisted from the first box to the second box so that toner could be cascaded manually over its surface, and the single sheet of paper onto which the developed image was then transferred had to be peeled from the plate by hand and slid into a toasterlike oven for fusing. And even that cumbersome series of procedures was essentially an illusion. Making a second copy, if anyone in the audience had thought to ask for one, would have taken much longer than a minute, since the technicians would have had to clean the selenium plate and set up the boxes again before going through all the awkward steps once more.

Nevertheless, the demonstration did receive some good press, and Carlson was deeply pleased to see tangible progress at last. "The trip to Detroit was perfect from beginning to end," he wrote to Wilson, "and I can truthfully say—you thought of everything. The more I see of you and your associates at The Haloid Company the happier I am to be associated with you rather than with any other group of persons with whom I am familiar."

Carlson's happiness could not have been complete, however. Although the presentations in New York and Detroit—and a third held in Rochester the following month—had the look and feel of a new-product introduction, no new product had actually been introduced. When Haloid and Battelle went to Detroit in the fall of 1948, they had nothing to sell beyond the outline of an idea. Turning the red boxes into a marketable machine would take most of the next year, and that machine, when it finally appeared, would turn out to be a failure in every respect but one.

THAT NEW MACHINE WAS CALLED the XeroX Model A Copier. Within the company, it was usually referred to as the Ox Box, a nickname that borrowed the last two letter's of Haloid's newest trademark and also suggested the lumbering clumsiness of the

Chester Carlson's parents, Olof and Ellen, grew up on neighboring farms in Grove City, Minnesota, a tiny Swedish farming community about seventy-five miles west of Minneapolis. This photograph was taken in Seattle around 1900, either shortly before or shortly after they were married.

1

2

In 1909, when Chester was three and a half, the Carlsons moved to Kingsburg, California, where one of Olof's brothers owned a vineyard. Olof hoped the mild climate would help his tuberculosis and his arthritis. It did not. He next tried a tent in Arizona, then an adobe hut in Mexico, before returning to California on a rusting freighter late in 1910. At sea on Christmas morning, the freighter's captain, feeling sorry for his youngest passenger, gave Chester the only present he would receive that day: a chocolate bar.

3

The Carlsons moved from Los Angeles to San Bernardino in 1912, when Chester was six. Their decrepit house, which they could barely afford, rented for $12 a month.

4

Chester knew his father only as an invalid, never as a provider. Ellen did her best to support the family, by taking in sewing and doing other odd jobs. Here Ellen is chopping wood behind the family's house in San Bernardino.

5

In 1915, Olof moved the family to the village of Crestline, in the mountains outside of San Bernardino, because he thought cold weather might help his lungs. The Carlsons spent the winter in a shed that had been built as a warehouse for cement. The snows that year were three and four feet deep, and each morning Ellen used a hand mirror to signal to a storekeeper in the valley below that the family had survived another night.

Chester began working odd jobs for money when he was eight. By the time he was twelve or thirteen, he was rising each morning at four o'clock so that he could work for two or three hours before school. He sold soda water, pulled weeds, picked fruit, harvested potatoes, swept sidewalks, washed store windows, sold fish, and raised guinea pigs for a research laboratory. By the time he was in high school, he had become his family's principal provider.

Chester's cousin Roy (left) was an important figure in his life. This photograph was taken in 1918, when Roy was seventeen and Chester was twelve. Chester told Roy that year that he was going to invent something big someday, and Roy took his ambition seriously. Roy found Chester's company so stimulating that when he was in college he used to ride his bike eleven miles to visit him on weekends.

Chester graduated from high school in 1924. His mother had died the year before, and he and his father had been reduced to living in a former chicken coop, whose single room had a bare concrete floor. Chester— hoping to muffle the sound of his father's coughing and to lessen his own chance of contracting the disease that had killed his mother—slept on the ground outside.

Chester worked his way through Riverside Junior College, earning an associate's degree in physics in 1928. He commuted by bicycle to a nearby cement plant, where he sometimes worked three shifts in a row.

Chester and Olof Carlson in Riverside in 1926, shortly after Chester's twentieth birthday. Olof was fifty-six years old but looked considerably older. The year before, he had squandered Chester's minimal savings on an ill-considered health food business—an episode that Chester later described in a journal simply as "Pa gone crazy 1924-5."

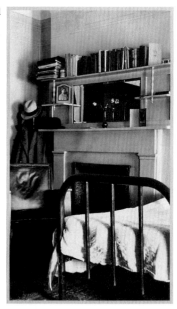

After graduating from Caltech in 1930, Chester went to work as a lab assistant at Bell Telephone Laboratories in New York. He lived in the Brooklyn Central YMCA for nearly a year, then spent six months in this rooming house on Henry Street, where the rent was less than a dollar a day. He had a roommate, who slept in a bed next to this one, just out of the picture on the right. A photograph of Chester's mother stood on the left side of the mantel.

Carlson and a hired assistant, Otto Kornei, made the world's first xerographic copy on October 22, 1938, in a rented room next to a beauty parlor on the second floor of this building, at 32-05 Thirty-seventh Street in Astoria, Queens. The room had previously been used as a janitor's closet. Its single window is visible just behind the large ventilation duct rising along the outside of the building.

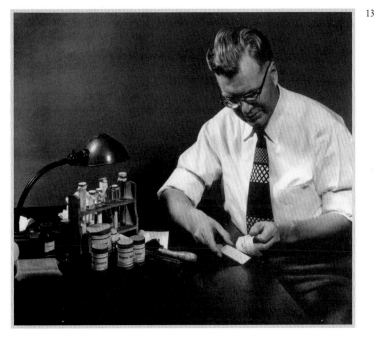

In 1962, two years after the phenomenally successful introduction of the Xerox 914 Office Copier, Carlson reenacted his original Astoria experiment. The jars and test tubes on the table contain some of the substances that he and Kornei worked with in 1938 and 1939, among them crystalline sulfur, lycopodium powder, and a natural resin known as dragon's blood.

Elsa von Mallon gave Carlson her telephone number after dancing with him to Duke Ellington records at a party at the YWCA in 1934, and they married soon afterward. Elsa said later, "I don't know what to do or say— he's so much smarter." They divorced in 1945.

In 1946, Carlson married Dorris Helen Hudgins, who was two years older and had been divorced for sixteen years. During their courtship, Carlson "had a very nice little habit of bringing three-by-five cards, which he carried in his pocket, with notes on them for us to talk about," Dorris said later. They spent their honeymoon in Washington, D.C., in part so that Carlson could visit the U.S. Patent and Trademark Office, something he liked to do whenever he had the chance.

During the summer of 1948, Carlson quit his job as a patent attorney and became a consultant to the Haloid Company, which was struggling to turn his invention into a marketable product. The Carlsons loaded up their aging Studebaker sedan and moved into this rented house in Canandaigua, about thirty miles southeast of Rochester, New York.

John Dessauer, Chester Carlson, and Haloid president Joseph Wilson with Battelle's experimental Xeroprinter, in 1948. Battelle's scientists sometimes allowed the device's toilet-paper-size output to cascade through an open fourth-floor window, to prevent the unfused toner from smudging.

Haloid's first xerographic copier was the Model A—known within the company as the "Ox Box"—which was introduced in 1949. "Awkward in its lack of co-ordinated design, it required more than a dozen manual operations before it would produce a copy," the company's chief of research wrote later. Shown here are two prototypes—with cabinets made of wood—and an early production model. All three of these machines were able to make only contact exposures, by shining a bright light through the back of an original.

Joseph Wilson (center) felt not only the suffocating presence of Eastman Kodak, a Rochester neighbor, but also the weight of the Wilson family's entire male line of descent: Haloid had been founded by his grandfather, and his father, a xerography skeptic, was the current chairman. At a company picnic in 1951, Wilson was given a large version of a T-shirt that had been produced for the children of employees.

Haloid's embryonic physics department was situated not in a modern laboratory but in this cramped old house on Hollenbeck Street. Bob Gundlach, who would eventually hold 155 xerography-related patents, worked in the attic, in a room whose sloping ceiling made standing difficult. During breaks, the physicists would climb onto the roof of the one-story structure in back of the house and pick cherries from an overhanging tree.

23

Four stars from Haloid's physics department in the early fifties. From left: *George Mott, Fred Hudson, department head Harold Clark, and Bob Gundlach. The men are in Clark's office, on the second floor of the house on Hollenbeck Street, and they are working on a vapor fuser, which used trichloroethylene fumes rather than heat to bind toner to paper.* "We must have been preparing to show some important visitors a demo," *Gundlach says today,* "because you won't find many other pictures in which I'm wearing a necktie."

24

Assembling a Copyflo was an adventure. John F. Klizas, who was in charge of producing the machines, once said, "It took from four to eight weeks to produce each one, depending on who was assembling it. But that was understandable, because the assemblers worked from very gross instructions: 'Install feeder rolls.' 'Install optics.' His first day on the job, one of these young men would say, 'I'll never be able to do it.' My response would be 'Give it a try.'"

During the early years, some of Haloid's scientists and engineers worked in a bleak, tenement-like brick building on Lake Avenue whose ground-floor storefront was occupied by the Crosby Frisian Fur Co.—whose original specialty, in the early twentieth century, had been taxidermy. Early Xerox copiers contained fur cleaning brushes that were hand-sewn by the father of the owner of the shop.

By 1952, the Model A Copier had evolved into the Model D Processor, which was used exclusively for making masters for offset lithographic printing presses. An accessory called a Camera No. 4, at the left end of the table, enabled a user to make exposures by projection rather than contact; the toaster-oven-like accessory at the far right is the fuser. An ensemble like this was known as Xerox Standard Master-Making Equipment.

The earliest 914 prototype was an engineering breadboard—a perforated metal panel, like an industrial-strength Peg-Board, on which the machine's continually evolving components were mounted, modified, tweaked, replaced, and rearranged. The breadboard device looked more like a science fair project than an office machine. It could make copies, but only in the dark. One version stood nearly twelve feet tall.

The first 914s were assembled on the third floor of this forlorn-looking former box factory on Orchard Street. "Do not ask where the restrooms were," Horace Becker says today, "because for a while I am sure we were in violation of the labor laws." On the day the company moved into the building, one employee had to shovel coal from an old bin on the ground floor so that the space could be used as an inspection station for arriving parts.

In December 1959, shortly before production of the 914 began, the company held a modest pep rally for employees and suppliers in the factory on Orchard Street. Horace Becker—shown here demonstrating one of the first machines at that party—said later, "Everybody was keyed up. The union people temporarily forgot their grievances, and the bosses forgot their performance ratings."

The first 914 ordered by a paying customer left Orchard Street in March 1960. Despite what the sign in the photograph says, it was shipped to King of Prussia, Pennsylvania. It had to be delivered on a tilting dolly so that its L-shaped, 648-pound bulk could be angled through doors.

"*Our company was unknown, our advertising budget was small,*" *the company's head of marketing said in a speech at Harvard Business School.* "*So we decided to limit our campaigns to the business publications and to use only those ads having the unique and fresh approach that we wanted to be characteristic of our project.*"

To show how easy the 914 was to operate, the company aired a television commercial in which a chimpanzee successfully copied a business letter. The next day, secretaries all over America found bananas on their desks, then had to deal with coworkers who scratched their armpits and made ape sounds when they wanted something copied. The salesmen were horrified, and the commercial was quickly withdrawn.

At a 1960 trade show in Washington, D.C., one of the three 914s in the Haloid Xerox booth caught on fire, but no potential customers noticed. Having several machines on hand increased the likelihood that at least one of them would be working.

Advertising for the 914 couldn't begin until the factory on Orchard Street was producing more than five machines a month. Shortly after the first ads finally appeared, in late 1960, Haloid Xerox and its advertising agency realized that they needed to tone down some of their claims—not because the claims were false, but because people assumed that no machine could actually do what the 914 did.

35

Chester and Dorris Carlson in the backyard of their modest home in 1965. "His real wealth seemed to be composed of the number of things he could easily do without," Dorris said of her husband after his death. People who knew him casually seldom suspected that he was rich or even well-to-do; when one acquaintance asked him what he did for a living and he said he worked at Xerox, the acquaintance assumed he was a factory worker and asked if he belonged to a union.

machine's operation. The machine itself was a slightly streamlined version of the Detroit demonstration model—instead of four boxes the size of window air conditioners, there were one and a half—but it functioned in essentially the same way, with a multitude of fussy steps. "Awkward in its lack of co-ordinated design it required more than a dozen manual operations before it would produce a copy," Dessauer wrote later.

Remarkably, that was an understatement: four dozen manual operations was more like it. Xerox's historical archives contain a lengthy set of typed "Temporary Instructions"—the original draft of the first Ox Box operating manual, which was given to the users of several test models. "Hold plate with left hand on wooden frame and simultaneously move charging bars ½-inch forward (with right hand) while pushing plate into charging chamber," the instructions recommended. Charging was then accomplished by "moving bar over plate, i.e., push black knob forward and return in approximately <u>15</u> seconds." On the copy in the archives, the "15" has been crossed out by hand, and "10" has been written above it in blue ink. Exposure was made by contact, by placing the selenium plate on top of the (one-sided) original document and turning on a bright light that shone up through the original from underneath. That meant the machine couldn't be used to copy double-sided pages—since the type on both sides would have cast shadows on the plate—or images printed on opaque stock.

Even in its final, public form, the operating manual for the Model A was filled with dire instructions: "Dry the plate surface by striking it lightly and briskly with a clean, dry, UN-TOUCHED portion of cotton. . . . With a spoon, carefully spread one-fourth of a teaspoon of XeroX Toner over the developer. . . . When mounted in the process tray, the four tabs of the electrode should protrude no more than approximately ¼4" above the level of the side gaskets, nor should they go below the side gasket." While doing all this, the operator had to be careful not to scratch, nick, dent, mar, smudge, abrade, or get fingerprints on the dark, shiny surface of the plate, which sold for $100 and, with careful handling, was expected to produce "several hundred copies" before becoming unusable. Other promotional publications and brochures assured potential customers that the machine was "easy to operate" and that "your office girls can follow the simple processing shown here." With practice, Haloid promised, a skilled operator could hope to make a copy every three minutes or so, with a break after fifty copies to clean the plate with XeroX solvent (sold separately) and allow it to dry thoroughly.

One of the trickiest parts of the process was peeling the finished copy away from the selenium plate. The operator had to do so without touching the delicate selenium surface and without smudging the unfused toner on the paper. (Unfused toner is the black powder that gets all over your hands when you clear a paper jam from a xerographic copier or a laser printer.) The image was made permanent by turning over this piece of paper, placing it image side up on a metal tray, and sliding the tray into the second box, which contained a radiant heater. "The hot plate is to be up to temperature before fusing prints," the Temporary Instructions warned. "This requires approximately 15 minutes. Fusing time is approximately two seconds. Excessive fusing will char paper." In subsequent models, the temperature in the fuser was reduced and the fusing time was lengthened to ten seconds, but a copy could still burn if the telephone rang while it was baking or the operator was distracted by a colleague.

The first Ox Boxes were literally boxes: the cabinets, and more than a few of the other parts, were made of wood, some of which was painted silver to make it look like metal. "They were crude,"

Dessauer recalled later. "Yet when the first Xerox Model A Copier was ready we gathered around it as if we were celebrating the birth of a baby. Joe Wilson ran a hand over its surface, clearly enjoying the very touch of the thing. Somebody behind me said, 'Now do you believe in miracles?' "

These ecstasies were premature. Haloid shipped Ox Boxes to several large companies for field testing before full production began. All the machines were returned promptly. "Too complicated" was the verdict. Haloid had pitched xerography as a replacement for carbon paper, among other things, but the testers found that a skilled secretary could actually retype a typical business letter in less time than it took to reproduce it on a Model A. And using the machine to make multiple copies was a greater nuisance, since all the steps had to be repeated for every copy. In addition, the quality of the copies was poor. Using the Model A required more practice, dexterity, and patience than any of the field testers were willing to invest. "Staring at the rejected machines, we were appalled," Dessauer wrote later. "Even Joe Wilson was stunned into silence."

THE MODEL A MIGHT HAVE DISAPPEARED and taken Haloid with it had it not been useful at doing something other than making copies. That something was creating paper masters for offset lithographic printing presses. This sounds like a more exotic use today than it was at the time; back in the pre-Xerox era, every company of any size owned at least one lithographic duplicator, which it used whenever it had to run off a large number of copies of an announcement, a bulletin, a companywide memo, or any other widely distributed document. The most popular such machine was the Multilith Offset Duplicator, which was made by

Addressograph-Multigraph Corporation. The XeroX Model A was almost perfectly suited to creating inexpensive masters for it, and that application saved the machine.

A Multilith duplicator was a serious piece of business equipment: a top-of-the-line model could print duplicates at a rate of thousands per hour. It employed the same lithographic principle that Alois Senefelder discovered back in 1795 (see chapter 2), except that in a Multilith machine the master, or printing plate, was made of heavy paper instead of limestone, and during printing the

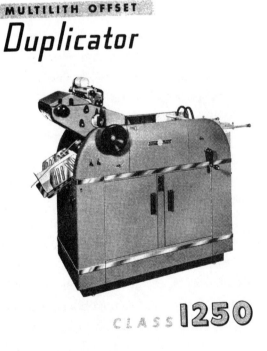

Offset lithographic duplicator, 1957.

master was wrapped around a rotating cylinder rather than pressed flat against each sheet of paper. As in all lithography, the process depended on the fact that oil and water don't mix: the text or image to be duplicated was inscribed on the paper master using a greasy, water-repellent substance; the master was wrapped, image side out, around a cylindrical drum and wetted; an oil-based ink, which stuck to the water-repellent image but not to the wet paper, was applied to the master; the printing drum was rotated, and, as it turned, the ink on its surface was transferred to a second drum, which was covered with rubber; this rubber-covered drum, in turn, rolled the ink onto sheets of regular paper. This and similar printing processes are called "offset" because the image isn't transferred directly from the master to the final sheets of paper (as was the case with Senefelder's lithographic printing press) but is first rolled, or offset, onto a second drum, which then does the actual printing. The second drum is useful not only because its relatively soft rubber surface works better as a printing plate, especially with textured papers, but also because transferring the master image reverses it, so that it will appear in the proper orientation after being reversed again, as it is when it is rolled onto the sheets of paper.*

Before the Model A came along, there had been only two methods of making a paper lithographic master: by typing with wax-coated carbon paper on a master similar to the ones used with Ditto machines, and photographically, using a metal plate coated with a modified silver halide emulsion. Typed masters took a long time to

---

*Offset printing was invented, accidentally, in 1906, the year Chester Carlson was born, by Ira A. Rubel, an American paper manufacturer. A paper misfeed in a lithographic press that Rubel was operating caused an inked image to be applied to a rubber-coated paper-handling roller rather than to a sheet of paper, and the rubber roller then transferred that image to the back of another sheet. This accidental image was sharper and more saturated than the press's usual output, and Rubel realized that the rubber must be responsible.

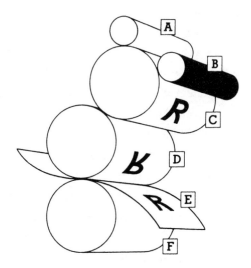

How offset printing works.

create, were hard to correct, and couldn't be used to reproduce documents that already existed; photographic masters could duplicate
existing documents, but they were slow and expensive to create,
and they required messy chemical developers and fixers. The
Model A made both techniques unnecessary. XeroX toner was
manufactured from a resin that repelled water and attracted oil-
based inks; that meant a Multilith operator could create a printing
plate simply by using a Model A to xerographically copy any image
or typed or printed document onto a blank paper master.

"If you had a good operator, and if you got your half-tones
done right," a Haloid executive said later, "you'd come up with
good reproductions." Although the Model A seemed slow and
awkward to anyone who thought of it as an office copier, it looked
like lightning to a Multilith operator. It reduced the cost of making a lithographic master from more than three dollars to less than

forty cents, and it cut the time required to just a few minutes. Given the amount of offset duplicating that most companies did in those days, the savings could be substantial. Ford Motor Company was so impressed by the Ox Box that it mentioned its duplicating windfall in an annual report.

Dessauer wrote later (and was subsequently quoted by others, including Linowitz) that the Model A's usefulness in lithography had been unanticipated and might have gone unnoticed if Lewis E. Walkup, an electrical engineer at Battelle, hadn't called Joe Wilson one day "in the midst of our emotional turbulence" about the failure of the Ox Box field tests and asked, "Say, do you fellows know what you've got up there?"

This makes for a good, dramatic story but can't be true. The association between xerography and offset duplicating would not have surprised anyone at Haloid in 1949. In fact, Carlson and Harold Clark both printed their Christmas cards that year on an offset press in the Haloid lab using masters they had made on an Ox Box.

More to the point, Carlson had always viewed lithographic master making as the most promising secondary use of his invention, and Otto Kornei, working in Carlson's Astoria laboratory, had actually succeeded in making a lithographic master on an anthracene-coated metal plate in 1939. Later that same year, Carlson devoted a lengthy section of his main xerographic patent to lithography, and pointed out that most of the dusting resins he had tried so far could be used to make lithographic plates, too. He also described how the resins could be customized for lithography (by adding "a small amount of lithographic crayon material," for example) and stated specifically that his method would work with "the newly-developed paper or parchment-like lithographic sheets" that were sold "for use on the 'Multilith' machines." This was eleven years before Walkup's "discovery." In addition, Carlson said that the process could be used with metal lithographic plates, which were more common than paper masters in the late thirties—a trickier application, which Haloid would also develop commercially, although not until a few years later.

It is true that Haloid (and Carlson) had been interested from the start in building a true office copier—a machine that would prompt secretaries to give up carbon paper and cancel their Photostat accounts. But lithography had never been far from anyone's plans regarding Carlson's invention. Battelle, in fact, had focused on lithography during its original negotiations with Carlson, in 1944, and had developed its xerographic toners with lithography in mind. The Model A's usefulness to lithographers may have been fortunate, but it wasn't a surprise.

No matter where the idea came from, though, the Multilith application truly did save the Model A. One version of the Ox Box was even renamed the Lith-Master and was marketed directly to users of offset printers. "We contracted with Todd Equipment Company, a Rochester manufacturer, to build the machines," Linowitz wrote later. "By 1953 the revenues from the sale and lease of the Lith-Master, and the sale of the special papers, toners, and plates it required, had passed the $2 million mark." That money kept Haloid profitable during a difficult period and financed the research that would lead, nearly a decade later, to the introduction of the 914. If the Ox Box had failed entirely, Haloid would have been forced to scale back its xerography development program, or perhaps to abandon it.

To SELL THE MODEL A and its immediate successors, Haloid hired fifteen new salesmen, all of them young men—primarily because the company's existing sales force, most of whom had been selling photographic paper and Rectigraph supplies for years, if not decades, were suspicious of the new technology. "Each got $50 a week plus a 3 percent commission," John Hartnett said later. The entire sales operation had an improvised feel. Hartnett did his hiring in a shabby office, where he used an upturned orange crate as a bookcase and as a place to keep his lunch pail. Early in 1950, as the first production models of the new copier were becoming available, he took his new salesmen to Philadelphia for a month-long single-market test. To save money and simplify nighttime supervision of his (mostly unmarried) sales force, he booked the group into the local YMCA, where rooms cost $1.50 a night.

"I guess the boys were not too charmed when they saw their quarters," he said in the 1970s. "A room was just wide enough for a bed and a dresser, and you had to walk about a block to get to the toilet. Anyway, when I got to *my* room I found they had all stuffed their bags in there—all fifteen of them—bags stacked right up to the ceiling." Hartnett relented eventually, under continued pressure from the new salesmen, and moved the group to the Adelphia Hotel, where, in the meantime, he had managed to negotiate the same room rate.

While in Philadelphia, the Haloid crew, in conjunction with representatives from Addressograph-Multigraph, held a series of Model A demonstrations, to which Hartnett had nearly three thousand local businesspeople. The shows were held two or three times a day for a week and attracted eight hundred visitors. Many complications arose. The machines had a tendency to stop working suddenly, especially when cool weather drove down the humidity. Even under ideal conditions, the results were inconsistent. Most of the training the new salesmen received during the trip was in maintenance and repair. And even when the machines were working, selling them was arduous.

"These were the days when one fellow would have a territory that included San Francisco plus all of Oregon, Washington, Montana, and Idaho," Hartnett recalled. "He lived in his car. I mean literally. He would place one of those units in an office someplace, and then he would have to see that it kept on working. The poor guy would beat his brains out. Winter would come along, the box would stop working. Then he would have to tell his customer: 'Stick with us for a little while. We're working on that problem. We'll lick it.' Of course, he had no idea whether we could ever solve the problem, but he just had to have faith that our scientists and engineers would find a way out."

Completing a sale sometimes required a high level of determination on the part of the customer. Haloid's branch office in Boston was situated in a run-down building in an unattractive part of town. The office was illuminated by a single bare light bulb, and most of the furniture was broken. Because floor space was limited, the machine's components were kept in separate rooms, and a prospective customer who wanted to watch a complete demonstration had to follow the branch manager through a maze of stacked boxes as he carried the selenium plate from one room to the next. Equally worrisome was the reaction of many of Haloid's oldest and most reliable customers. They viewed the Model A as unwanted competition for their Photostats, Rectigraphs, and blueprinting machines, all of which used sensitized papers manufactured by Haloid. Joe Wilson had to promise these customers that they would be given the first opportunity to lease or purchase Lith-Master equipment in their own territories.

These difficulties and others were extraordinarily stressful for Haloid's executives. Hartnett and Wilson both suffered heart attacks in 1953—Hartnett at age fifty, Wilson at forty-three. Wilson had to bear the skepticism of many of his customers and employ-ees, as well as that of his father, the company's chairman, who had more than once described xerography as "tomfoolery" and was in the habit of asking the company's scientists and engineers if they really believed that it would work.

7

THE HOUSE
ON HOLLENBECK STREET

"THE MORE YOU UNDERSTAND ABOUT XEROGRAPHY," Bob
Gundlach told me once, "the more you are amazed that it works."
Gundlach must be more amazed than anybody, because no one
understands the process better than he does. He accumulated 155
xerography-related patents during a Xerox career that began in
1952 and ended officially in 1995—although he occasionally still
plays a (usually ceremonial) role at Xerox. He also still tinkers with
xerography, mostly as a consultant to other companies.

When I first met Gundlach, at the 914's induction into the
Smithsonian Institution, in 1985, he was dressed like an absent-
minded inventor: light-blue pants, a light blue plaid jacket, a light
blue striped shirt, and a light blue tie with a large bird painted on
it. When I saw him more recently, at his home in a suburb of
Rochester, he was dressed like a regular retired guy, in jeans, a
plaid workshirt, and running shoes. He is tall and thin and physically fit. He gets up at five-thirty or six, runs a mile and a half, and
does seven pull-ups—a program he has maintained for decades—

and when he moves quickly around his basement workshop he is as light on his feet as a marionette.

Gundlach was born in 1926 in a tiny town a few miles outside Buffalo. "I worked on a farm across the street, pulling onions, weeding, at a dollar a day for an eight-hour day—twelve and a half cents an hour," he told me. "One of my friends worked on another farm, and he got ten cents an hour, so he had to work ten hours to make his dollar." Gundlach's grandfather was a minister in the German Reformed Church, which had many small strongholds in upstate New York, and he preached in German. Gundlach's father, whose name was Emanuel, was a chemist. Among Emanuel's inventions were menthol cigarettes—although he never patented or developed the idea—and Wildroot Cream-Oil, a hair preparation. When he made his first batch of Cream-Oil, he put it in a tube, anticipating Brylcreem by many years. Executives at Wildroot, where he worked, didn't like his invention, though; they thought it looked like toothpaste. Then World War II depleted the nation's supply of alcohol, the principal ingredient of Wildroot's bottled hair tonic. Emanuel's invention was alcohol-free. He added more water to it, so that it, too, could be poured from a bottle, and resubmitted it. This time the executives loved it. Reminiscing in his office more than forty years later, his son began to sing (to a tune cowritten by Woody Herman): "You'd better get Wildroot Cream-Oil, Charlie, start using it today, something, something Cream-Oil, Charlie, keeping all the girls away." As a teenager, Bob Gundlach spent one summer standing over a large vat in Buffalo, mixing all the Wildroot Cream-Oil in the world.

The German Reformed Church didn't appeal to Emanuel, and he and his family became involved instead with the Quakers and with a Quaker-like pacifist organization called the Fellowship of Reconciliation. Bob was drafted just after the end of World War II, following his freshman year at the University of Buffalo, and spent a year in conscientious objector camps in New York and Tennessee. When he returned, he graduated from Buffalo with a degree in physics (after switching from chemistry, as Chester Carlson had also done) and spent two years in graduate school, although he never completed his PhD. He had trouble finding a job at first, because the companies he approached weren't interested in physicists who refused to do war work.

"One day, I was driving home from a job interview and I was running out of gas, and I almost coasted in to this gas station," he told me. "I looked across the street and I saw a sign that said 'Durez Plastics and Chemicals,' and I asked the gas station attendant, 'Do you suppose they hire physicists over there?' He said, 'What's a physicist?' " Gundlach walked across the street, got hired, and drove home.

At Durez, he worked in the physical testing laboratory. In 1952, he learned from Ernest Lehmann, an old University of Buffalo classmate of his, that a small, interesting company in Rochester, called Haloid, was hiring. He applied, and was interviewed by Harold Clark, the company's chief physicist. Clark was notorious within Haloid for grilling applicants in unusual ways. (He asked one to estimate the number of hairs on the head of an average New Yorker.) Clark gave Gundlach a written physics test, on which he did extraordinarily well, and offered him a job. Gundlach accepted after Joe Wilson, Haloid's president, promised that he would never be required to work on military projects. Wilson also gave him an extra two weeks off that first year to take a troop of underprivileged Boy Scouts to summer camp. "After that," Gundlach told me, "I would have done *anything* to make that company thrive."

Shortly after Gundlach went to work at Haloid, he and his wife, Audrey, bought a building lot in Spencerport, a Rochester suburb, and built a house. "The house cost $2,600," he told me, "and twelve men put it up in one day." Gundlach did all the plumbing and interior finish work himself, and he installed the furnace. "I enjoy working with my hands," he continued. "In fact, I believe that there is a hand-mind synergy and that you can do a lot of good science with Scotch tape, string, and rubber bands. A lot of people think it's not science unless you use a $200,000 spectrophotometer—but, no, science is the design of the experiment, posing the right question, and then pursuing an answer in ways that are open to lucky accidents."

WHEN GUNDLACH WENT TO WORK AT Haloid, he discovered, happily, that much of the company's xerographic research was essentially accident based. The embryonic physics department was situated not in a modern laboratory but in a cramped old house on Hollenbeck Street, adjacent to the less ancient but more decrepit Rectigraph plant, in what is today an inner-city wasteland but was then a fairly lively working-class neighborhood.

"You had to park about a block away and walk," Gundlach said. "They put Ernie Lehmann and me up in the attic, in a room that had a ceiling that sloped so that you couldn't stand up except in the middle of the room. There was a group working on powder cloud development, which involved making a fog of submicron carbon particles. Every once in a while, we would have to vent the developing device, because it would become clogged with carbon dust, and we had to learn not to do that on Tuesdays, because that was when the lady next door hung out her white linens." At lunchtime, the physicists often ate in the cheap, dreadful restaurant at the Arch Hotel, across the street, or snuck into the employee cafeteria at Kodak, where Kodak scientists would sometimes help them with problems they'd encountered. (One future Haloid employee was actually interviewed for his Haloid job over lunch in the Kodak cafeteria.) During breaks back at the house, they climbed through a window onto the roof of an annex in the back, picked cherries from an overhanging tree, and talked about the scientific problems they were struggling with. There were few titles and very little organizational structure. "We didn't really have objectives, in the usual sense," one of them said later. "I don't even remember seeing a budget, for many, many years. On the other hand, we knew what we had to do: the number one thing was that we were going to succeed."

Gundlach's first patent was for an invention that solved a problem which Otto Kornei had first noticed, back during those pioneering experiments in Astoria, and which adversely affected the quality of prints made by the Model A and its first successors. Xerography was good at reproducing thin lines and printed characters, but it did a poor job of reproducing large, solid black areas, which came out looking washed-out everywhere except at the edges. The reason was that the xerographic effect depended on the difference in electric potential between exposed and unexposed surface areas on a photoreceptor. Along the edge of an image, that difference was very large—the difference between the 700-volt electrostatic charge of the (undischarged) image area and the zero-volt electrostatic charge of the (discharged) background. Between any two points within the interior of a large, solid image area, though, the difference was very small—the difference between 700 volts and 700 volts. "It's like, a ball won't roll off a flat table unless you put the ball right at the edge," Gundlach explained. "In the center of the table, there are no unbalanced forces acting on the ball. But at the edges of the table, there's an unbalanced force acting on it, and it can roll off." Typewritten characters, handwriting, and line drawings reproduced well because the figures were so thin that they were essentially all edge, but large solid-black areas usually didn't.

The solution, Gundlach decided, was to place a grounded metal plate directly above, and very close to, the photoreceptor during development—thereby creating a seven-hundred-volt difference between that grounded plate and every part of every image. (To extend Gundlach's ball-rolling analogy, this was a little like turning the table on its side.) Gundlach's invention was called the Tone Tray. When the company decided to build it, the engineer in charge said, "We're putting about $10,000 worth of tooling costs in this, so I hope you know what you're doing." Gundlach said, "Well, I don't know what it's going to do in the field, but it works in the lab." It ended up working in the field, too. "A Tone Tray cost $23 to manufacture," Gundlach told me, "and Haloid rented it for $10 a month, so the company got its money back on each one in less than two and a half months, and two thousand of them were rented the first year. I never did the math, but a few years ago somebody told me, 'Do you realize what that did? It paid all the salaries in the physics department'—which at the time added up to something like a quarter of a million dollars a year. That wouldn't cover one vice president's salary for one year today, but in those days it paid all the scientists."

GUNDLACH HAS A SMALL OFFICE in his basement. It is dominated by file cabinets; tilting piles of papers and scientific journals; a desk; a computer; a chair for Gundlach; a chair for the cat; a mysterious contraption that Gundlach fabricated from paper towel tubing, coat hanger parts, plastic grass, and plywood; and several parts of a self-invented system with which Gundlach heats and cools his house for approximately $600 a year. (The system's most important elements are a heat pump and three thousand feet of subterranean piping.) The heating and cooling system is just one of his many nonxerographic inventions; he also holds patents for a snowmaking process, a shadowless sundial, an unusually comfortable backpack, and an inexpensive twenty-thousand-volt electrostatic generator, among other things. Next to the office is a storage room in which Gundlach's papers are archived according to a scheme that is thoroughly though inadvertently secure from corporate espionage: the labels on most of the folders and envelopes bear no relation to their contents.

In the main room of Gundlach's basement, surrounded by cross-country skis and lawn mower parts, is an old Model D Processor—a direct descendant of the Ox Box—which was introduced in 1953.* Gundlach moved some binoculars and a carton of empty pill bottles from the top of one of its components, in preparation for giving me a demonstration. Before my arrival, he had found (after digging to the bottom of a pile of bulging manila folders in another room) a forty-five-year-old selenium plate in what he felt was reasonable condition. "I couldn't find a better one," he said, holding it up so that I could examine it: a dark, heavy, wood-framed rectangular panel slightly larger than a legal pad, roughly similar in appearance to a small blackboard or a shallow cocktail tray. The selenium surface was shinier than slate but duller than steel. "See how it's been chipped?" he asked. "It's pretty delicate, and if you touch it with your fingers, it crystallizes. The crystals are pink. You can clean it with Brasso, but I couldn't find any—just some copper polish, which I think would be too abrasive."

To charge the plate, he slid it into a slot near the bottom of the Model D's main unit—like inserting a huge floppy disk into a disk

---

*Between the Model A Copier and the Model D Processor came the Model B (an improved but never marketed version of the Model A) and the Model C (which had oversize plates, for copying engineering drawings). The Model D was called a processor rather than a copier because by 1953 Haloid had realized that almost no one was using the machines for anything other than producing lithographic masters. The Model D and its accessory devices came to be known collectively as Xerox Standard Master-Making Equipment—or, for short, the Standard Equipment.

drive—and flipped a toggle switch, producing a sound like that made by a hardware store paint can shaker. After ten seconds, he flipped the toggle switch back and pushed a black light-blocking panel into a groove in the top of the plate's wooden frame, to shield the selenium surface from the basement's fluorescent ceiling fixture (which would have discharged the plate). He then inserted the covered plate into another machine, the Camera No. 1—an Ox Box accessory, introduced in 1950, that enabled the Model A and its successors to make noncontact exposures and, therefore, to be used with two-sided originals. The Camera No. 1 was as large as a modern desktop copier but had only one function: to shine a bright light onto the original document and project its image onto the surface of the selenium plate. (Gundlach also has a Camera No. 4, which was able to make enlargements and reductions, and could be used with oversize originals. It looks like a supersize version of the bellows view cameras that Mathew Brady photographed the Civil War with.) I placed my business card upside down in the middle of the Camera No. 1's glass platen, closed the lid, and—with guidance from Gundlach—pulled the light shield back out of its slot in the frame of the selenium plate. Then I pressed a button, which caused a timed light to expose the plate for ten seconds, and slid the shield back into position. The plate was now ready for development.

Getting this far had taken us three or four minutes and a fair bit of discussion, and we weren't halfway to our copy yet. I could easily see why the Ox Box's original field testers had been exasperated. Still, there was a certain fascination.

"Now, this is an awkward operation," Gundlach said. He had to remove the light shield while simultaneously clamping the selenium plate upside down to the top of the development tray, which looked like a shallow cake pan and contained a thin layer of developer—as the mixture of carrier beads and toner particles is called—

but he had to do it without creating gaps that light might be able to sneak through. Secretaries in the fifties found that performing this operation successfully required both hands, at least one elbow, and possibly the chin. Gundlach managed by pressing a forearm across the top of the plate, then carefully removing the light shield with one hand while using his other hand to successively fasten four spring-loaded clips along the edges of the plate's wooden frame. The clips were tightly tensioned; they snapped like mousetraps when he clicked them into position. Gundlach, with his upper body practically resting on the top of the tray, looked like a cartoon character attempting to close an overstuffed suitcase.

"Was that technique an officially recommended procedure?" I asked.

He laughed. "More or less," he said. "You got used to it. People's expectations were different then. And I've done this thousands of times."

When the plate was firmly attached to the tray, Gundlach allowed me to develop the image myself, by manually rocking the tray in its metal frame, which was mounted in a teeter-totter-style pivoting mechanism.

"We found that four passes works best," he said.

Forward, back, forward, back. The rocking caused unseen toner-covered carrier beads to cascade across the surface of the selenium, first in one direction, then in the other, depositing toner particles on the charged image and leaving the rest of the plate blank. The beads, as they slid around inside the tray, sounded like sand on a cookie sheet. After I had completed the four passes, Gundlach leaned back onto the top of the plate and released the spring-loaded clips one by one. He then removed the plate and turned it over. And there, in the center of the selenium surface, was a perfect, reversed image of my business card, written in black dust.

I looked at it closely, trying not to breathe on it and not to jostle the plate. The toner was so fine and the lines so sharp that the image looked almost as though it had been printed with ink.

"Now we'll transfer it," Gundlach said. He handed me a sheet of white paper, and I placed it on top of the image. "Hold that edge down tight, so it doesn't slip," he said—a delicate operation, which the Model A's 1950 instruction manual described this way: "Place end of a sheet of Copy Paper on paper guide. Avoid smudging image by shifting paper. Using index finger, press and hold end of sheet onto paper guide lip. Carefully lower paper over developed image, while still pressing paper against edge of paper guide. After paper has settled over developed image, remove finger from paper guide." With the paper in place, I removed my finger and used it to press the charging button while carefully (with my other hand) sliding the tray back into the charging slot in the machine.

"See, when you developed the plate, the negatively charged toner was attracted to the positive latent image on the plate," Gundlach said. "So now you're putting positive ions on the back of the paper, and they're pulling the toner up to the paper from the plate and making it stay there. O.K., it's all done."

I pulled the tray back out. I carefully lifted one edge and peeled the sheet away from the plate. The image of my business card, now in the middle of the paper, revealed itself.

"If you had turned off the lights and let your eyes get dark adapted for five minutes before peeling the paper away," Gundlach said, "you actually would have seen a line of light as you pulled, because the charges holding the toner would have ionized the air as you separated the two surfaces."

I admired my copy. It wasn't as bold as the copies I make on my Xerox machine at home—a result of the age of the plate, Gundlach said—but it was legible. Gundlach looked almost proud, making it clear that after half a century he still gets a kick out of Carlson's invention—a reaction I could easily understand. Even if you think of making copies as office drudgery, xerography at this very basic and unadorned level seems like something from another dimension. How could those grumpy IBM executives not have been intrigued by Carlson's demonstrations, even if his materials were hopelessly crude?

The image of my business card was unfused—it was just black dust arranged neatly on the surface of the paper. Worried that the toner might slide to the floor if I let the paper tip, I handled the sheet as delicately as if it were a platter of ball bearings. Gundlach took the paper from my hand and waved it through the air, to show me that my anxiety was unnecessary.

"The electrostatic forces holding the toner to the paper are two thousand times the weight of the toner," he said. "And for particles that size, the sticky forces, the van der Waals forces, are stronger than the electrostatic forces." Van der Waals forces are electron-related attractive forces that, to oversimplify, cause very small things to stick tightly to one another and to other things. (The dust on a TV screen is held there mainly by van der Waals forces; the dirt in dirty clothes is secured mainly by van der Waals forces—without which you would be able to clean your clothes simply by shaking them; one method of "weaponizing" anthrax spores is to coat them with silica dust, which prevents van der Waals forces from causing the spores to clump together and causes the spores to disperse through the air and into victims' lungs.) Van der Waals forces were named for their discoverer, a Dutch scientist named Johannes Diderik van der Waals, who won the Nobel Prize in physics in 1910. Van der Waals named his only son Johannes Diderik Jr. and named one of his three daughters Johanna Diderica.

Gundlach handed me back my copy. Then he disappeared into

his office and returned with a balloon, which he blew up. He rubbed the balloon against his shirt, giving it an electrostatic charge, and touched the balloon to the ceiling. It stuck.

"See, it holds its own weight," he said. "The electrostatic force holding the balloon to the ceiling is stronger than the force of gravity pulling the balloon toward the floor. And a balloon is at least twenty thousand times bigger than a toner particle, and the mass varies as the cube of the volume while the surface area varies as the square, so the forces holding a ten-micron particle to a sheet of paper are much, much stronger than the forces holding the balloon. In fact, you can drop a developed selenium plate to the floor edgewise and not dislodge the toner."

With intentional carelessness, therefore, I placed my copy on the tray of the fuser, which we had already warmed up, and slid the tray into the glowing interior. Ten seconds later, I pulled the tray back out. My copy was warm to the touch, slightly scalloped at the edges, and fully fused. I ran a finger over the image of my business card. The toner stayed put.

Model D users were also able to fuse copies without heat, by using an accessory called a vapor fuser (in whose development Carlson participated). Ox Box toner, in addition to melting when heated, dissolved in certain solvents. If an unfused copy was exposed to the vapors from such a solvent, the toner would liquefy like ink and sink into the paper—a process that made offices smell terrible, and possibly also caused mild neurological damage among secretaries, but produced terrific prints. "The vapor fuser makes every little toner particle turn from a golf ball shape into a pancake shape, so it really enhances the image density," Gundlach said. He showed me an old vapor fuser, which he was currently storing near the top of a large pile of firewood and old athletic equipment. He couldn't demonstrate it, though, because he didn't have any solvent. "Paint thinner doesn't work," he explained.

"And gasoline doesn't work. I know because I've tried. Acetone works, but I don't have any." Early machines used trichloroethylene. The solubility of xerographic toners in certain hydrocarbons explains why a xerographic copy will sometimes leave a ghostly image of itself on something like a plastic page protector or the underside of a see-through desk pad: plasticizers escaping from the plastic act like the vapors in a vapor fuser and dissolve some of the toner in the copy, causing it to stick.

Now we had to clean the selenium plate—every secretary's least favorite part of the job. "You transfer 90 percent of the toner when you make a copy," Gundlach said, "but the other 10 percent stays stuck to the plate, and you have to get rid of it for the next time." To do so, we had to overcome all those forces that he had just explained. In the Model A, this cleaning was accomplished by rocking the plate back and forth in a so-called cleaning tray, which looked like a development tray but was filled with a mildly abrasive granular substance rather than developer. Haloid tried several such substances—coffee grounds, soybean meal, flaxseed, cornmeal—but quickly discovered that all attracted vermin. (Being startled by a fat, panicky mouse leaping out of a cleaning tray was an occupational hazard for early Model A users.) Soybean meal, furthermore, covered plates with an oily residue that quickly destroyed the plates.* Diatomaceous earth—a pale, claylike powder composed of the remains of tiny aquatic organisms, and a common ingredient of cat litter—worked better but not perfectly. Then someone discovered that a seemingly unrelated invention of Gundlach's worked best of all. It was an electric switch that reversed the polarity of the machine's corona charging wire; Gundlach had conceived of it as part of a (too complicated to explain)

---

*Haloid discovered this by using soybean meal to clean test images from an entire batch of brand-new plates, all of which were ruined—a major disaster at the time.

method of making multiple copies from a single exposure. The multiple-copy feature attracted few users—who weren't using the machines to make copies, after all—but another Haloid scientist guessed correctly that running a dirty selenium plate under a reversed polarity corona wire would cause the residual toner to magically unstick itself from the selenium surface: problem solved.

"The early machines are a great tool for xerography experiments," Gundlach told me a little later. "They let you work separately on the different steps of xerography: charging, exposure, development, transfer, cleaning, fusing. Today, all those processes are combined in one machine, and they happen very quickly. With a flat-plate machine like the Model D, you can tinker with them one at a time."

Gundlach, still tinkering, then used his Model D to show me a nonxerographic method of making a print. He took an index-card-size piece of white paper and covered it with a rulerlike plastic alphabet stencil—the kind a kid might use as a guide for printing neat, uniform letters. Then he inserted the paper and stencil into the charging slot on the Model D. He pressed the charging button, causing the corona wire to spray ions onto the stencil and onto the uncovered parts of the paper, including the areas directly beneath the stencil's letter-shaped cutouts. Then he pulled the tray back out of the slot and showed me the paper. It looked—well, it looked exactly the same as it had before, of course: you can't see electrostatic charges.

"Now we're going to develop the latent image, but in a different way," he said. He picked up a jar of what looked like royal blue talcum powder and unscrewed the lid. Attached to the underside of the lid was a brush, roughly the size and shape of a rabbit's foot, whose bristles were thickly coated with blue powder. "Sweep this across the paper," he said. I did—and a perfect image of the stencil letters appeared, exactly as though I had sprinkled blue dust very carefully through the holes in the ruler.

"Wow," I said.

"This isn't xerography," he said. "It's called 'ionography.' Nothing much came of it, except for a couple of medical-imaging applications, but it's interesting. The paper isn't photoconducting, and it has no other light-related properties, so it doesn't need to be kept in the dark. It's coated with an insulating material—lacquer, I think—and the electrostatic charges just sit on it, the way they did on that balloon." He slid the paper into the heat fuser. A few seconds later, he pulled out a perfect, permanent image, in bright blue, of the stencil letters.

"Now feel the brush," he said. I swept it down the length of my index finger. The bristles felt as soft as baby hair. "It's not actually a brush," he continued. "There's a magnet in the middle, and the 'bristles' are really chains of iron filings. Magnetic attraction makes the filings hang together like little hairs, and the toner sticks to them electrostatically until it's pulled away by the oppositely charged areas on the paper. It's pretty ingenious." The brush, like Battelle and Haloid's carrier beads, also cleaned up after itself, by depositing toner particles only on the electrostatically charged latent image and picking up strays.

MAGNETIC BRUSH DEVELOPMENT WAS INVENTED not by Gundlach or anyone else at Haloid but by a pair of scientists at RCA, which in 1953 exacerbated the already precarious cardiovascular health of Haloid's top executives by informing them that it had invented a small, moderately priced office machine that made copies xerographically but—according to RCA's lawyers—didn't infringe on any patents issued to Carlson, Haloid, or Battelle. RCA called the new copying process Electrofax. Sol Linowitz, who by then had gone to work full-time at Haloid, as a vice president, later described RCA's announcement as "a bombshell."

Two years before, RCA had taken two xerographic licenses from Battelle, including one for a xerographic computer printer— a more obscure and limited application at the time than it sounds like today—and Wilson, Dessauer, and others at Haloid had been hopeful that these deals would grow into a productive ongoing research partnership. (A major element of Wilson's strategy for developing xerography was to leverage Haloid's tiny budget by entering into licensing agreements and joint ventures with companies that were richer and smarter—and few technology companies in those days were richer or smarter than RCA, whose research division was on a level with Bell Labs.) Now, though, it appeared that RCA had used its xerography licenses, along with the considerable information disclosed in Carlson's patents, which were public documents, to develop a device it had initially claimed not to care about: an office copier. RCA offered to pay $50,000 for an unrestricted license, while making it clear that it felt its offer was legally unnecessary. RCA also informed Haloid and Battelle that it intended to license its invention to other manufacturers.

Wilson was devastated. Linowitz wrote later, "In a memo he wrote to himself for a meeting at RCA in April 1953, he pointed out that Haloid over the previous five years had spent some nine hundred thousand dollars—20 percent of its total profits—for research in xerography; a comparable portion of the RCA profits would have been $62 million." Carlson, equally appalled, felt that RCA was attempting to appropriate "90 percent of the present strength of our patent position."

The consternation in Rochester and Columbus was exacerbated by the fact that RCA's copying process was technologically dazzling. The two scientists who devised it—H. G. Greig and

C. J. Young—had found a way of making xerographic copies while apparently sidestepping all the major existing xerographic patents. The photoconductor they used was not selenium but crystalline zinc oxide—a bright white powder that is also a common ingredient in paint and sunscreen, among other things. (RCA had extensive experience with photoconductors, which were also used in television screens.) Greig and Young applied their photoconductor not to a heavy plate, as in the Model A, but to the copying paper itself, in the form of a thin, slightly glossy coating. This was a drawback in one sense, since Electrofax, unlike the Ox Box, wouldn't work with plain paper (and the coated stock it required was expensive and felt slick), but it was an advantage in another sense, because it eliminated the necessity of transferring a developed image from one surface to another—one of the trickiest steps in xerography, and the main one that ultimately defeated Carlson's attempts at model building. And because each sheet of Electrofax paper functioned as its own photoreceptor, there was no delicate, costly selenium surface to be meticulously maintained, cleaned with a reversed polarity corona wire, rubbed with solvent-soaked balls of cotton, or polished with Brasso.

"I didn't foresee the Electrofax application, where the photoconductor is applied to the paper and the final print still is on the photoconductor to eliminate the transfer," Carlson said in an interview a dozen years later. "While I realized that a copy could be made on coated paper, I didn't know of any good photoconductor that would be both good and cheap enough so that it needn't be used again. I figured that probably the photoconductor would be an expensive element and that the only way to use it economically would be in a reusable process. This is the way Xerox uses it. Then RCA discovered zinc oxide that provided a cheap coating which is commercially competitive to some extent."

Greig and Young's most impressive invention, though, was

their magnetic brush development system, which was unlike any technology described in existing xerographic patents. There were no cascading mechanisms, and there were no carrier beads. The brush was a tube with magnets inside it and toner-covered iron filings clinging to the outside. The brush rotated just beneath the paper path, allowing the electrostatic charges on the surface of each photoconductive sheet to pull toner particles from the filings, while gravity and the brush itself handled postdevelopment cleanup. (Many later Electrofax-type copiers used a liquid development system, in which the charged toner particles were suspended in a kerosenelike fluid.) All these innovations added up to a system that was far more streamlined—and therefore more compact and less expensive to manufacture—than any machine Haloid had built or conceived up until that point.

Carlson and others at Haloid, after studying the process closely and brooding about its implications, eventually decided (correctly, it would turn out) that Electrofax's dependence on coated paper was a fatal flaw—although Carlson always called Electrofax "the second best way to do copying." In the meantime, nevertheless, the vexation at Haloid was intense. There were strained negotiations with RCA, menacing letters from lawyers, a major lawsuit, and other distractions. Gundlach said later that xerographic process development at Haloid was set back by six months, as the physicists on Hollenbeck Street were redeployed to figure out what RCA was up to. Dessauer was so traumatized by Electrofax that he didn't mention it in his autobiography, and he referred to it only once and only in passing in a major technical work on xerography that he and Harold Clark edited more than a decade later. For many years, in fact, he forbade Xerox scientists to experiment with magnetic brushes—a ban that probably harmed the company, since the technology later became widely used in some kinds of xerographic machines, including, years later, several that Xerox itself manufactured.

Dessauer's reaction to what he and Linowitz both viewed as RCA's betrayal of an honorable licensing agreement was emotional and probably counterproductive, but it was also understandable. Electrofax had evolved directly from ideas conceived by Carlson, Battelle, and Haloid, yet Haloid was still years away from being able to manufacture a copier that could come close to competing with it on speed or price. Particularly worrisome was RCA's plan to license Electrofax technology to as many manufacturers as possible, creating a potential galaxy of low-cost Haloid competitors. Many at Haloid worried initially that the game was over before it had begun and that the company had lost its big gamble without having had a chance to place the bet. A few years later, Linowitz argued that Xerox should protect itself by manufacturing an Electrofax machine of its own—an idea that might have changed the course of copying history had Wilson and others not overruled it.

TECHNOLOGY DOESN'T EVOLVE STEADILY AND continuously. New ideas often arrive in clusters, having been generated by cumulative cultural forces whose origin and exact nature aren't always obvious at the time, or even later. Duplication technology changed relatively little at the fundamental level during the three and a half centuries following the publication of the Gutenberg Bible. Then, within a few years on either side of the turn of the nineteenth century, the world received the polygraph, the copying press, lithography, and the first generation of carbon paper. Those and other innovations emerged and flourished because they met a need for improved record keeping which the industrialization of Europe had created, and then their existence stimulated further demand, accelerated the pace of industrialization, and inspired additional innovation—a self-sustaining technological feedback loop. A similar threshold occurred half a century later, when stencil duplicating, spirit duplicating, blueprinting, photography, the typewriter, and the second generation of carbon paper all created large, growing markets for themselves within a relatively short period of time.

And the same thing happened yet again during the decade following the end of World War II, as the major Western economies rebuilt themselves and entered an extended period of growth and prosperity. The Ox Box was just one of several new copying and duplicating machines introduced around 1950, a period that constituted a virtual Cambrian Explosion of document replication technology. No one understood yet what office copying really was or how big the market for it would ultimately be, but all the major manufacturers of office machines were building or developing or licensing copiers of one kind or another.

While Haloid was selling the Ox Box as a producer of lithographic masters, other companies were addressing the copying problem directly, with varying degrees of success. In 1950, for example, 3M introduced a machine called Thermo-Fax, which used infrared light to make blurry copies on thin, rubbery, translucent copy paper that had been coated with heat-sensitive chemicals. The Thermo-Fax principle had been conceived in the early forties by a 3M scientist named Carl Miller, who, like Chester Carlson, was motivated by the drudgery of taking notes by hand. Miller thought of thermography after noticing a dark leaf that, by radiating heat it had absorbed from the sun, was sinking into a snowbank by melting the snow directly beneath it. According to an account on 3M's corporate Web site, "He took the cellophane wrap from a box of candy sent to him by his mother, coated it with a heat-sensitive, mercury-based salt, and then stretched the coated cellophane over an image. When this assemblage was placed beneath an infrared light, the darker portions of the underlying image were registered onto the coated cellophane." Developing

Thermo-Fax took a decade, but the machines became a major financial success for 3M.

There were other processes as well. In 1952, American Photocopy began selling the Dial-A-Matic Autostat, which employed a photographylike silver halide process called diffusion transfer—as did similar machines sold by Agfa, Apeco, Copease, Cormac, A. B. Dick, Gevaert, Remington Rand, and Smith Corona. All produced an intermediate negative copy, called a matrix, which had to be run through the machine a second time to produce a dark, malodorous, impermanent, and expensive positive copy. In 1953, Kodak introduced Verifax, which was based on a variant of a color photographic process called dye transfer. During roughly the same period, diazo copiers, which used ammonia fumes to develop images on coated paper—a method similar to the blueprint process—were sold by Bruning, Ditto, Copymation, and others. And copiers based on RCA's Electrofax idea were sold under such names as Copytron, Electro-Stat, and Keuffel & Esser.

Most of these devices were small and inexpensive, and all of them both answered and amplified the growing demand for copies among resurgent American businesses. Carlson, Wilson, and many others at Haloid believed that these competing machines would eventually be seen as technological dead ends because they required expensive supplies and, for the most part, made curling, smog-colored copies that were hard to read, unpleasant to touch, and almost impossible to file. But all the machines, however imperfect, existed in the marketplace, while Haloid's plain-paper office copier did not. There were many times when the challenges Haloid faced seemed insurmountable. Carlson told Harold Clark one day that if xerography turned out to be too cumbersome to work in a small machine, they could at least take consolation in knowing that their work had constituted a "catalyst" for 3M and Kodak, by accelerating the development of Thermo-Fax and Verifax. Clark said later that Carlson had made this comment not in despair but "rather philosophically."

Today, of course, we can easily see that all of those competing processes really were doomed: none of those machines are manufactured today. If you conducted a door-to-door search of the nation's businesses, in fact, you would be likely to find just one of them, Thermo-Fax, still in service—and only in tattoo parlors, where the machines are sometimes used to make rub-on tattoo patterns.* In the early fifties, though, Electrofax, Thermo-Fax, and the others were genuine threats. None of them could do what Carlson, Wilson, and the scientific staff at Haloid were convinced that xerography could do, but each of them made copies, and you could buy any of them that afternoon. Flawed or not, they were functioning machines. And there were more threats to come.

---

*A tattoo design is copied onto Thermo-Fax paper, then transferred to skin by rubbing the copy with K-Y jelly or roll-on deodorant. The relationship between copying and tattooing is even older than Thermo-Fax: Samuel F. O'Reilly, who in the early 1890s invented the tattoo artist's principal tool, the electric reciprocating needle, was directly inspired by Thomas Edison's Electric Pen (see chapter 2).

8

AMERICAN XEROGRAPHY CORP.

WHEN CARLSON BECAME A HALOID CONSULTANT IN 1948, his duties were undefined. Among other things, he helped Linowitz look after the company's patent work and manage its intermittently difficult relationship with Battelle. Haloid had no real scientific staff yet—the main function of Dessauer's "research department" was to perform routine quality tests on photographic papers—and almost all the development work on xerography was still being handled in Columbus. Carlson dedicated himself to improving the toners and carriers that Battelle's scientists were using, but he had to do his experiments in his basement at home because Haloid had no xerography lab. (Dessauer worried that xerographic raw materials might contaminate sensitive photographic emulsions in the confined workspaces at Haloid—a reasonable concern.) Carlson brought his toner samples to work each morning in soda-pop bottles with improvised aluminum foil caps, prompting an in-house joke that xerography had a secret formula known only to its inventor.

The situation improved somewhat in 1949, when Haloid hired

Harold Clark, the company's first physicist, and rented an old gro-
cery store warehouse to use as a research lab for the small staff that
Clark was charged with assembling. The following year, in response to steady, stubborn urging by Carlson, Haloid hired an additional patent attorney and began to build a real patent
department—which would grow during the following decade,
though never rapidly enough to keep up with the discoveries of
Clark's scientists and others—and Carlson was able to spend still
more time on experimentation. In 1953, the company gave him a
lab of his own and assigned a young physicist, Harold Bogdonoff,
to be his assistant. The two men shared a small, gloomy space in a
back corner on the ground floor of the Rectigraph factory, which
was situated near the house on Hollenbeck Street, where Clark's
department had now moved. There was a large photographic
darkroom directly above Carlson and Bogdonoff's work area, and
spilled liquids would occasionally drip through the ceiling.

"Mr. Carlson was unpretentious, not an extrovert, not
grandiose—a quiet man, who never used profanity," Bogdonoff recalled in 1980. He also said, "I really can't remember him getting
mad about anything. He was very mild mannered and even toned. I
can't recall ever hearing him swear. I think the strongest thing I
ever heard him say was a 'damn.' Occasionally in our experimental
work we would get shocked from the high-voltage power supplies
or something of that sort, and that was about the only time he
would say 'damn,' but I never recall profanity from him."

Carlson had a thick three-ring binder in which he jotted down
ideas—his habit since childhood. When Bogdonoff arrived for
work in the morning, Carlson would open the binder and say,
"Well, let's see what we have got for today." He would flip through
the pages, each of which contained a brief note or a few lines of his
careful script. "All right, we will do this one," he would say. Carlson was friendly, considerate, and easy to get along with—he

would have been the ideal college roommate—but there was little small talk between the two men. Bogdonoff recalled, "I can remember days when I would say, 'Good morning, Chet,' when I came in, and, 'Good night, Chet,' when I left, and we wouldn't exchange six words in between."

Bogdonoff loved working with Carlson, whose unconventional way of thinking and intensity of focus distinguished him from other researchers.* "I got more out of the two years I spent with Chet, probably, than I got from my first ten years with the company," Bogdonoff said later. "I got an exposure and an education and a maturing that I never would have got otherwise, and I got encouragement and support." Carlson was also generous in sharing credit for inventions, and he listed Bogdonoff on patents for joint discoveries that other senior researchers, Bogdonoff felt, would have claimed solely for themselves.

"His approach to things in terms of the inventive process—if that's the term—is something that I have tried to carry around with me," Bogdonoff also said. "He always had a sheer delight in what he came up with. In many cases he acted surprised when something worked. There was a keen delight in finding new things. Occasionally he would run into an obstacle or total failure on something. He would shake his head and couldn't understand why it didn't work—and then it was pretty much 'back to the drawing boards.' " Bogdonoff once cut out an advertisement from *The Wall Street Journal* whose text (a quotation from Calvin Coolidge) he felt provided an apt description of Carlson's nature.

---

*Harold Clark later recalled what he felt was a simple but telling example of the way Carlson's mind worked. One day, the two men and one or two other scientists were talking in an office at Haloid when a bee flew into the room. "We tried to shoo him out but weren't able to do it," Clark said. "Then Chet got up, said nothing, and turned off the fluorescent light, which had attracted the bee, and it flew out the window."

He recalled, "The ad read: 'Press on. Nothing in the world can take the place of persistence. Talent will not; nothing is more common than unsuccessful men with talent. Genius will not; unrewarded genius is almost a proverb. Education alone will not; the world is full of educated derelicts. Persistence and determination alone are omnipotent.' There's no question that Chet had substantial measures of each of those."

Carlson sometimes accompanied Bogdonoff and the other scientists when they went to lunch at the Arch Hotel or the Kodak cafeteria. He seldom talked much, unless the topic was a scientific question that engaged him, in which case he could be forceful and animated. He was not a gossip. Many who knew him well remarked later that they had never heard him speak disparagingly of another person. (In all the years after xerography became a success, he never publicly named any of the companies that had turned him down.) He had a dry sense of humor and a logician's love of puns. His favorite joke, which he included regularly in speeches and skillfully spun out to tremendous length, concerned a human cannonball who had decided to retire from the circus but was asked to stay on by his boss, who explained, "I'll never find another man of your caliber." After his death, his widow, Dorris, once said, "He did have a keen sense of humor, but it was turned on at rare times. He certainly didn't seem to be a person who walked around with a grin on his face, or a smile, but his face always looked to me as though he were about to smile, that it would be very easy for him to."

During the two years that Carlson and Bogdonoff worked together, they had the usual assortment of hits and misses: a number of their ideas were incorporated into production machines, and many others weren't, including an idea of Carlson's for a xerography-based system of printing for the blind. Carlson's most important contributions to xerography during this period were probably at the corporate level. He continually pressed Wilson, Linowitz, and Dessauer to invest more money in research, to be assiduous about patenting the research department's discoveries, and to make an unambiguous commitment to building a marketable machine. Wilson shared Carlson's faith in the future of xerography, but his father and many members of his board were skeptical about the new technology, and many of the company's veteran executives and other employees felt that Wilson was diverting resources from a reliably profitable enterprise. Even those who believed in xerography were anxious about its future. Dessauer's hopes for the process were so high that he mortgaged his house to buy more Haloid stock, but at the same time he was consumed by fears of what would happen if he failed. "My neck was way out," he told John Brooks in 1967. "My feeling was that if it didn't work Wilson and I would be business failures but as far as I was concerned I'd also be a technical failure. Nobody would ever give me a job again. I'd have to give up science and sell insurance or something."

Carlson's steady pressure helped to keep Wilson committed. "What Bell is to the telephone—or, more aptly, what Eastman is to photography—Haloid could be to xerography," he told Wilson in a letter in 1953. Most of the discussions between the two men, and the ones between Wilson and the board, took place in private, but rumors circulated. Harold Clark said later, "I think the great issue between the Haloid Company and Chester Carlson was one in which Chet's judgments were better than those of Haloid management." That issue, Clark felt, had to do with the level of Haloid's commitment to xerographic development. Carlson was always civil when discussing these questions with Wilson and others; in his own mind, though, he came close to despair. His patents were ticking toward expiration, and Haloid, to him, seemed paralyzed. In his journal in 1953 and 1954, he recorded a few characteristically terse notes on his frustrations: "May leave

Battelle & Haloid. . . . Haloid has an asset which is slipping thru its fingers. . . . Battelle never shown awareness. . . . Heartbreaking to me."

One major source of concern was Haloid's relationship with IBM—a company that Carlson had viewed with irritation ever since his unpleasant and unsuccessful attempt, back in the early forties, to interest its research department in investing in his discovery. ("IBM treated him like a little boy with a toy," his wife said many years later.) IBM's interest in xerography had been revived in 1949, when Thomas Watson Jr., who was one of the company's vice presidents (and who, like his friend Joe Wilson, was a tortured corporate son on the way to surpassing the achievements of a powerful father who was also his boss), saw and was captivated by a television report about Haloid and Battelle's presentation at the Optical Society meeting in Detroit. Nothing came of Watson's initial interest, but in 1951, after continued urging by Linowitz and Wilson, IBM took licenses for two relatively obscure xerographic applications, involving punch cards and mailing labels.

Then, in 1954, IBM made a request that in some ways seemed as ominous as RCA's Electrofax announcement the year before. The company wanted an exclusive license to manufacture a xerographic office copier or to distribute such a machine if Haloid was already building one. Linowitz later wrote, "To Dessauer's distress, they showed a sketch of what they had in mind, which was virtually identical to the machine we were trying to develop ourselves; indeed, Dessauer maintained that they had simply followed the ideas we had discussed with them in previous meetings."

A second corporate giant had now spotted the prize that Haloid had been clutching since 1947, and Wilson's first, cautious impulse was to capitulate. A licensing deal with IBM, in combination with Haloid's agreement to manufacture photoconductive paper for the Electrofax, would create a steady stream of cash that would keep Haloid profitable indefinitely. Was there any point in resisting?

After a period of deep anxiety and reflection, Wilson countered by offering IBM a nonexclusive copier license, including an agreement that Haloid itself would not manufacture a closely similar machine. IBM curtly rejected the offer, holding out for exclusivity and a promise that Haloid would never manufacture an office copier at all. And that, finally, was a demand that Wilson knew he had to turn down.

IN 1954, as Kodak's Verifax was beginning to find a market, Haloid introduced a new copier of its own. It was called Copyflo 11, and it made decent prints on plain paper xerographically at the rate of nearly thirty pages per minute. Still, Copyflo wasn't an office copier in any ordinary sense. In contrast with Verifax, which was small enough to sit on one corner of a secretary's desk and sold for as little as $100, Copyflo was roughly the size of a mail truck, required 220-volt current and a reinforced floor, made its copies only from microfilm and only onto continuous rolls of paper, and had a retail price (in some later models) of $130,000.*

Of course, Copyflo wasn't really a Verifax competitor. Haloid sold it not to regular businesses or individuals but to large companies and organizations that kept lots of records. The machine was a modified, commercial version of a microfilm printer that Haloid and Battelle had developed for the navy, and it was the direct descendant of a primitive experimental device called the Xeroprinter, which Roland Schaffert of Battelle had pieced together

---

*Few Copyflos were actually sold for that or any other amount; almost all customers leased them and paid fees based on usage. But Copyflo was still by far the most expensive copying machine on the market. A standard Thermo-Fax, for example, sold for about $300.

from odd parts in 1948 and which also did its printing on continuous rolls. (Battelle's scientists had sometimes allowed the Xeroprinter's toilet-paper-size output to cascade through an open
fourth-story window, to prevent the unfused toner from smudging.) In 1956, Haloid introduced a second Copyflo model, which
made copies from opaque page-size originals—a feature that made
it capable of reproducing ordinary documents. But all the Copyflo
models were too huge and too expensive for applications that
weren't bleakly bureaucratic. "Our early products were all mon-
sters," Harold Clark said later. "We could make big, fast, steadily
running machines, but that was all we could make."

Copyflo nevertheless represented an important step in the evo-
lution of a true plain-paper office copier, because it was fully automatic and its selenium-coated photoreceptor was a rotating drum
rather than a flat, heavy plate, as in the Ox Box. Still, the machine's

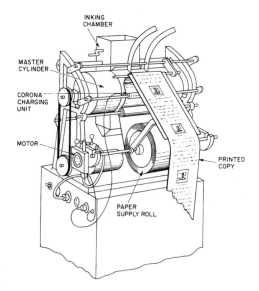

Schematic drawing of Battelle's Xeroprinter, 1948.
XEROX CORP.

ungainliness and frequently perplexing behavior hinted at the problems Haloid still had to solve. Copyflo was enormous because it had to contain and isolate all the complex suboperations that xerography comprised: charging, exposure, development, transfer, fusing, cleaning. Turning Copyflo into an ordinary office copier would mean shrinking it to less than half its size without allowing any internal operation to interfere with any other, and finding a way to make it handle cut sheets rather than continuous paper—a huge challenge.

Even when Copyflo was working properly, there were complications. At a sales presentation in 1958, for example, no one remembered to attach the machine's paper roll to the take-up spool, and when the machine was turned on, its printed output spewed into a curling pile on the floor. Wilson, who was helping with the demonstration, had the presence of mind to ask an engineer to grab the stream of paper and walk it out into the room. "We want you all to have a close look at the quality of the copies," Wilson, improvising, told the audience. This turned out to be such an effective selling tactic that Haloid's sales force adopted it.

Another gnawing concern had to do with Copyflo's impact on the sales of Haloid's nonxerographic products. Later Copyflo models—the ones that made prints from opaque originals—competed directly with the company's photographic-copying equipment, including a relatively new, Rectigraph-like system called Foto-Flo. That cannibalization of existing business infuriated the sales force and created consternation among the xerography doubters on Haloid's board. At one point, Haloid learned that International Harvester, a Copyflo customer, had used its machine to establish a commercial copy shop that competed directly with a shop owned by Haloid. The only reason such conflicts didn't become a bigger crisis was that the market for Copyflo was very, very small.

• • •

YET THE MARKET FOR COPYFLO was not nonexistent. Although
just five hundred of the machines were ever built, the customers
who used them tended to use them a lot and, therefore, to buy
costly supplies at an encouraging clip. Xerox Standard Equipment
and its supplies—the company's flat-plate lithographic-master-
making system—also sold steadily, and by 1956 xerography-related
products were contributing almost 40 percent of Haloid's revenues.
That percentage was increasing steadily, although the revenues had
been won at considerable cost, and Wilson continually worried
that Kodak, IBM, RCA, or General Electric, among others, could
suddenly darken Haloid's future. (At the annual shareholder meeting in 1954, he announced that a large competitor might put the
company out of business *that afternoon.*) But Wilson and a significant number of others increasingly believed that the company's future, for better or worse, really was going to depend on xerography
and that the time had come to make a serious commitment.

In the spring of 1955—two years after Copyflo's introduction,
and during the period when Wilson was fretting about how to respond to IBM's request for an exclusive license to build xerographic office copiers—Dessauer assembled an internal group,
called the "small copier committee," to study the entire office
copier issue and to make a recommendation about how (or
whether) the company should proceed. He asked Carlson to serve
as the committee's chairman. The committee didn't have much
firsthand data to extrapolate from, since the first of Haloid's two
commercial xerographic machines wasn't a copier and the second
wasn't small. And a common opinion within the company at that
time was that a xerographic office copier would be economical
only for users who needed to make as many as a hundred copies a
day—a number that seemed so absurdly large "that we didn't quite
see how the whole thing could be pulled off," Harold Clark, who

served on the committee, said later. Still, the group concluded, in a report that Carlson delivered to Dessauer six months later, that Haloid should continue with its efforts to develop a small copier, even though the smallest possible small copier would most likely not be very small. The committee estimated, in fact, that the most compact production machine possible might weigh six hundred pounds, have a manufacturing cost of $1,800, and be as large a four-drawer file cabinet—guesses that would turn out to be reasonably prescient.

A few months before the small copier committee could complete its report, IBM, which for some time had been Haloid's only significant suitor, walked away from its licensing negotiations. This left Haloid with no choice but to proceed on its own (assuming that it was going to proceed at all). But the report, when it finally arrived, did strengthen Wilson's resolve. One of his first steps was to seek to clarify Haloid's claims on its technology. Carlson had no agreement with Haloid itself; he had sold his patent rights to Battelle, and the first of his most important patents was due to expire in 1959. Haloid's agreement was also with Battelle, to which it was required to pay a hefty royalty on every xerography-related dollar it received. As Haloid's revenues from the flat-plate machines and Copyflo had increased, the royalty payments had become a major drain, limiting Haloid's ability to invest in additional research. In addition, determining exactly which Haloid revenues were subject to royalties had become a contentious matter now that Haloid was doing more of its own research and manufacturing. In 1955 and 1956, Linowitz negotiated a new deal, whereby Haloid acquired all of Battelle's xerographic rights in exchange for 53,000 shares of Haloid stock to be issued over a period of three years, plus a 3 percent royalty until 1965—a mutually beneficial arrangement that secured for Haloid the cash stream it needed to finance new machines, gave Battelle an endowment that within a decade would make it one of the richest research organizations in the world, and made Carlson a very wealthy man. (There was no direct agreement between Haloid and Carlson, but Carlson's agreement with Battelle entitled him to 40 percent of the institute's revenues from xerography, including the stock.)

Now that Haloid was moving semiconfidently in a new direction, Wilson was convinced that the company also needed a new name. He had first floated this idea among his top executives in 1954 and been surprised when it met firm, unanimous resistance: the Haloid name was half a century old, and changing it would be expensive and inconvenient, and "Xerox" was a confusing word that people didn't know how to pronounce, and so on. Wilson kept trying, though, and in 1955 he circulated a lengthy memo in which he restated his case. "Granting all the objections which you have made," he wrote (as reprinted by Dessauer), "there is no time like the present to start building a trademark strength." He added that making the correct choice was important because "the Company's name is going to appear millions of times, literally, on checks, stationery, financial articles, over-the-counter listings, maybe in the [New York] Stock Exchange listings sometime, and if each one of those times the word Xerox appears as well as the word Haloid, ten years from now Xerox will be a stronger name than it is if it's omitted; and nobody can deny me this point." Wilson liked "Xerox" just fine as a corporate name; at one point, he offered "Haloid & Xerox" as a compromise. Linowitz was in favor of preserving "Haloid" as the company's name but establishing a wholly owned subsidiary called "Xerox, Incorporated." A consultant suggested "American Xerography Corporation" and "National Xerographic, Inc." In the end, the board, with reservations, agreed to "Haloid Xerox"; the shareholders approved the change in 1958.

If the company was going to step perforce into the copier business, it was also going to need new facilities. Throughout the fifties, Haloid's employees worked in a miscellaneous and far-flung assortment of dilapidated structures situated in a variety of unpleasant Rochester neighborhoods. There was the physics department in the old house on Hollenbeck Street, and the drafty, depressing Rectigraph plant behind it. There was the company's modest corporate headquarters, which was filled with tatty furniture and cracked linoleum and which the company ended up giving to the city of Rochester in the early sixties after being unable to find a buyer. There was the research facility on Lake Avenue which looked like, and actually was, a former toy shop. And there were half a dozen other locations, equally unprepossessing.

This geographical dispersion fostered a playful atmosphere at Haloid during the early years, since it allowed most employees to operate without close supervision by dour corporate vice presidents. Jack Kinsella later recalled an extracurricular research project conceived by a scientist named Ed Van Wagner during the early days of the U.S. space race with the Soviet Union. "He put some acetone in a cardboard milk bottle and lit it," Kinsella wrote. "Much to our delight, the box shot across the whole length of the lab. After a few repeats of this, Ed decided this was too tame, so he replaced the milk carton with an empty five-gallon glass chemical storage jug. When this was ignited, it blew up with a tremendous roar, sending glass shards all over the lab." The casual atmosphere was conducive to scientifically valuable risk taking as well; Bob Gundlach often said that he made all his best discoveries when his boss was out of town.

Still, the separation of departments made internal communication erratic, and in 1955 Wilson, looking to the future, went shopping for real estate in Rochester and its suburbs. He ended up buying a large parcel in Webster, New York, a mostly agricultural area ten miles northeast of downtown Rochester and five miles south of Lake Ontario. The Webster parcel would become a bustling research-and-manufacturing campus, but the company couldn't afford to do much with it at first. The only structure Haloid built there in the fifties was a one-story factory in which it manufactured selenium photoreceptor plates for the Model D.

Although the Battelle buyout, the name change, the land purchase, and other initiatives demonstrated that Wilson and his company were moving with some determination in what would turn out to be the right direction, progress during this period was still erratic, uncertain, and easily derailed. In 1957—four years after the introduction of Copyflo and seven years after the commercial introduction of the Ox Box—Linowitz sent letters to 126 technology and business equipment manufacturers, saying, "If your company is interested in discussing with Haloid a license of the application of xerography to your field, we would welcome your inquiry," and received essentially the same response that Carlson had received to similar mailings fifteen years before. The company was mentioned in the press occasionally, but to most business reporters xerography seemed too esoteric to merit extended consideration. The same year that Linowitz mailed his 126 letters, the editors of *Forbes* invited Wilson to visit the magazine's offices and make a presentation about Haloid and its products. The meeting went very well, *Forbes* recounted in an editorial— which it published eight years later, in 1965:

> The *Forbes* men were impressed. The president was a sincere, enthusiastic, extremely articulate man. He believed in what they were doing. He had the facts and figures right at his fingertips. He understood finance and he understood technology. The president handled all our questions beautifully, professionally. And what did *Forbes* do with the story? Nothing. For one thing, the company only had assets of $19 million, and that was well

below the size we had set for a company before it could be grist for our editorial mills. There was something else. One editor who was present at the meeting recalls saying later: "It's a great company. But 40 times earnings! That stock has discounted all the possible good news for the next ten years."

THIS WAS THE EMOTIONAL, economic, and physical landscape within which Wilson and his company, in the mid-1950s, began their final push to build the world's first plain-paper office copier, which didn't have a name yet but would eventually be known as the 914 (because it was capable of handling originals that were nine inches wide and fourteen inches long). A successful outcome was by no means inevitable when the process began, and the defeats along the way came close to outnumbering the victories. At the final moment, when the last screws were being tightened in the first production machines, there were still many reasons to worry that the entire enterprise might simply collapse. The project sometimes seemed to be sustained by nothing more than its own inexplicably gathering momentum, which somehow enabled all involved to overcome setbacks and disappointments. "It is hard to believe our utter naïveté in electrostatics when we started this thing," Lewis Walkup of Battelle said later. "Xerography went through many stages in its development at which any sane management committee would have been justified in turning it down. There always had to be something *extralogical* about continuing."

9

THE 914

Hiring at Haloid accelerated in the mid-1950s, as the 914 project got under way. Among the new employees was John Rutkus, who joined the company in 1955. He had served in the navy in World War II, and had worked for IBM for several years in connection with that company's effort, under a license from Battelle, to produce mailing labels xerographically. Rutkus met Dessauer during the IBM project, and Dessauer was impressed by him and offered him a job. When he arrived at Haloid for his first day of work, he discovered that the company, which was still organized about as formally as a college fraternity house, didn't have a desk for him. Rutkus was an engineer. He found an old drafting table and a hammer, and nailed a wood brace under the table's slanting top, causing it to lie flat. Then he went looking for a chair.

Rutkus's next assignment was to work with Dessauer, Clark, and others in blocking out a rough design for a desktop copier. The men soon realized that this goal was unrealistic. The copier that began to take shape in Rutkus's drawings was more nearly the size of a desk. And not a small desk, either.

In designing the 914, Rutkus and the others began by studying
Haloid's existing machines, looking for technology they could borrow, adapt, or scale down. They started with the Copyflo 11. That
machine's photoreceptor drum had a diameter of fifteen inches and
therefore a circumference of just under four feet—dimensions that
created plenty of workspace for the closely choreographed succession of operations that had to take place on its surface, but that
made the drum too large to fit into a machine even the size of a
desk. Haloid and Battelle had recently worked with Kodak on a xerographic microfilm printer for the navy which was similar to
Copyflo but somewhat smaller. That machine used an eight-inch
drum—as small as the Haloid scientists felt they could go at the
time. Rutkus added an eight-inch drum to the design.

Deciding on the drum's dimensions was one thing; fabricating
functioning photoreceptors was another. Haloid had little money
to spend on parts, so in the early days Rutkus and his colleagues
had to improvise. The engineers tried bending sheets of metal
into cylinders, welding the ends together, and coating the outside
surfaces with selenium, but they couldn't get the selenium to stick
to the welds. They considered creating a timing mechanism that
would prevent a drum's weld from ever ending up in the field of an
image—something like the synchronization gear that enabled
World War II fighter pilots to fire machine guns through turning
propellers. But this solution and others seemed to create more
problems than they solved. One day, one of the engineers was
rummaging through a pile of old car parts at a junkyard on Clin-
ton Avenue, where he and his colleagues often went to scrounge
for bolts and springs, when he found a length of discarded aluminum pipe. The pipe had been extruded and therefore didn't
have a seam. He took out his tape measure and checked the outside diameter: eight and a half inches. He bought ten feet, carried

it to a small machine shop in the same neighborhood, and asked the brothers who owned the shop to tool it down. Back at Haloid, another engineer cut the pipe into short lengths, then used the company's vacuum coater to deposit a thin layer of selenium on each length's outside surface: photoreceptors on the cheap.

As new parts were found or fabricated, Rutkus and the others installed them in various prototypes, the earliest and crudest of which was an engineering breadboard—a perforated metal panel, like an industrial-strength Peg-Board, on which the 914's continually evolving components were mounted, modified, tweaked, replaced, and rearranged while the engineers tried to figure out how to make them work together. The breadboard device was able to make copies—though only in a darkened room, since it had no exterior cabinet to prevent the room's lights from discharging the drum and ruining the images—but it looked more like a science fair project than an office machine. One version stood nearly twelve feet tall.

Donald Shepardson, an engineer who had come to work at Haloid the same year Rutkus did, said later, "Every element of the total system had to be relatively simple, even when we knew how to do things in more sophisticated ways. For example, we knew about reliability techniques that were coming out of space age technology in the late 1950s. If we had been able to use such techniques, our first copying machines would have worked a lot better than they did. They would have been more reliable, for one thing. But we could not go in that direction for a very simple reason: money. We had to keep the cost of each individual piece of hardware to a minimum because—you have to remember—the revolution we were later to see with the 914 had not yet occurred. For all we knew, we were building a new product that people would use only a few times a day."

• • •

IN ALMOST ANY AUTOMATED MACHINE that uses paper, one of the most vexing engineering problems is keeping the paper from becoming torn, crumpled, snarled, ripped, snagged, or stuck as it moves from one end of the machine to the other. There are many potential dangers: rubber rollers harden and shrink, frictional surfaces wear smooth, springs are pulled and twisted out of shape— and paper itself has an almost limitless number of variable physical qualities, any one of which can suddenly induce mechanical mayhem, either by acting alone or by conspiring with one of the other factors. The engineers knew that the 914 was going to have to handle everything from card stock to paper as thin as onionskin, and it was going to have to work in all climates and humidities. Paper in New Orleans is soggier than paper in Cincinnati, and it behaves differently in a machine. Different kinds of paper curl in different ways when they're stressed, and any curl added in one part of the process had to be subtracted in another. The way paper is cut during manufacturing puts a burr on the edges, and the burr can cause one sheet to stick to another. And so on.

Paper handling hadn't been a (mechanical) problem with the Ox Box, because each sheet used by that machine was moved manually by a human operator. And paper handling hadn't been a (big) problem with Copyflo, because it used continuous rolls rather than cut sheets. (Continuous paper is vastly easier to move through a copier, because it can be kept under tension and spooled from one end to the other—just as continuous audiotape is vastly easier to move through a tape recorder than a succession of inchlong audiotape segments would be.) But paper handling was a big problem with the 914 and its prototypes. The copier's paper path was long, and it twisted and turned from one xerographic step to the next, and it exposed each page to numerous malevolent forces, including heat, gravity, and static electricity.

"I had a friend who took physics with me," Bob Gundlach told me. "Every time we went into an exam, he said, 'Force equals mass times acceleration and you can't push a rope—that's all you need to know about physics.' " You also can't push a piece of paper through a Xerox machine; you have to pull it. An early idea was to use a pair of dime-size mechanical grippers to grab each sheet at the beginning of the process and drag it all the way to the end, but the engineers decided that the grippers might harm the selenium drum as they lifted each page away from the photoreceptor and, furthermore, that they would obscure part of every copy. A vacuum system was also considered but was rejected because the engineers felt it would be too expensive, too power-hungry, and too likely to disturb unfused toner. Their solution, finally, was to use the electrostatic charges inherent in xerography to tack the paper to the system's moving surfaces—like sticking a balloon to the ceiling. This idea entailed many complications. To cause a sheet to properly attach itself to the selenium drum, for example, the engineers had to prevent the sheet from skidding on the drum's surface as it first became engaged—something it tended to do because at that point the charge sticking the paper to the drum and the charge sticking the paper to the belt were pulling the paper in opposite directions. The engineers, after several false starts, solved the problem by using a clutch to briefly reverse the paper's direction as it reached the drum, then pushing the sheet forward against a restraint, causing it to form a small buckle near its leading edge.

One danger in using electrostatics for paper handling was that charges tended to accumulate in ungrounded parts of the machine (or, conversely, to accidentally drain away before they could perform such necessary functions as holding developed images to sheets of paper). The engineers, by trial and error, managed to eliminate most of these problems, but they still encountered surprises. "Not long after the 914 came out," Gundlach told me, "there was a

very cold winter in Chicago, with extremely low humidity, and secretaries there were complaining that they were getting sparks about
four inches long as they went to pick up a stack of paper. They would
get these huge voltages, which accumulated page by page by page,
and when they reached over to pick up their copies, they would get
a shock. Some of them complained that it was killing the nerves in
their arms. So we had a brainstorming session, and we thought
about making them reach through a chain of beads or putting little
grounded needles where the paper comes through, to make it discharge to those." They ended up using Christmas tinsel.

Almost every solution created additional problems. The engineers had a blackboard on which they listed the principal issues
that remained to be addressed, and every time they were able to
erase one, it seemed, they had to add three or four new ones.
George Mott—a scientist who had been hired the same year
Gundlach was, and who had ended up working on xerography at
Haloid rather than on high-energy physics at MIT primarily because he had contracted polio while completing his PhD at the
University of Rochester—said later, "After many painful experiences, we learned you cannot set out to improve any one step in-
dependently; you must work within the total system, with all the
steps of the process at once." The fact that a new idea didn't work
immediately in the breadboard device or in subsequent prototypes
didn't necessarily mean that it was worthless; modifying one or
two other components might suddenly make the new idea work
and thereby improve the entire process. As a result, nearly everyone involved in developing the 914 spent a great deal of time tinkering with machines, staring into space, and not paying attention
to their surroundings. One of the scientists explained to his colleagues that he was lucky to be present that morning, because the
solution to a vexing problem had suddenly come to him as he was
on his way to work and he had nearly driven off the road.

• • •

ONCE THE ENGINEERS HAD FIGURED OUT how to make a moving sheet of paper stick itself to a moving selenium drum, they had to find a way to get it unstuck again, so that they could transport it to the fuser. Grippers and vacuums had already been rejected. Electrostatics alone wouldn't work, because a voltage strong enough to lift the paper from the drum would also be strong enough to lift the toner from the paper. What was left? Rutkus hit upon the solution one day while he was working in his garage.

"I was pumping air into a child's bicycle tire when I thought of it," he told me in 1985. "I placed a piece of paper on the hood of my car and used the pump to blow it off." He tried the same thing in his lab with a tank of compressed air and an array of hypodermic needles, then designed a device that fired short puffs of air at an angle toward the leading edge of each new copy, disengaging it from the drum. George Mott explained, "Then we placed a transport device right at that point—right where the edge of the paper was puffed away from the drum. Now the electrostatic charge on the sheet of paper caused the paper to stick to the transport device instead of sticking to the drum, and away the paper would go. It peeled off the rotating drum and moved along to the next step of the process." Rutkus's puffer was one of the innovations that made the 914 possible, and it became legendary at Haloid. (And Rutkus ended up with more patented inventions in the 914 than anyone else at the company, including Gundlach.)

As brilliant as the puffer seemed, though, it didn't always work: a puffed piece of paper sometimes flapped back against the photoreceptor drum rather than attaching itself to the moving belt, for reasons no one understood. The engineers cleaned the nozzles and repositioned the belts, but the problem kept recurring, sometimes for days in a row.

Among those who discovered the solution was Horace Becker,

an engineer who had joined the company in early 1958. Before coming to Haloid, Becker had worked for the Davidson Printing Press, a division of Mergenthaler Linotype—a company that played an important role in the early history of xerography, since Roland Schaffert of Battelle had worked there, and a colleague of Becker's named Paul Catan had been hired from there just a few months before. Becker was from Brooklyn and had served on B-26s during World War II. He had attended the Drexel Institute of Technology on the GI Bill, earned a degree in engineering in 1948, and worked in the printing business for a decade. At Mergenthaler, his specialty had been offset printing using cut sheets of paper. At Haloid, his job was to take 914 into production—a huge task, which he accomplished with the help of what John Brooks described in 1967 as a talent for "eloquent anguish."

"I won't tell you how many hours we spent screaming and shouting at one another until we figured out why the paper was sticking back to the drum," Becker told me one day not long ago, in a conference room at Rochester's Jewish Community Center, where he had suggested we meet. He was a few days away from turning eighty, but he still gave off flashes of the emotional intensity that Brooks had noticed thirty-five years before. Several times during our conversation, in fact, small tears formed in the corners of his eyes as he told me about fraught or emotional moments in the development of the 914.

The sticking problem, he said, turned out to be caused by the grain of the paper the engineers had been using. All paper is made of fibers, which tend to line up predominantly in one direction or the other. (See chapter 2.) If the general arrangement of the fibers is parallel to the length of the sheet, the paper is called "long-grain"; if the fibers run perpendicular, the paper is called "short-grain." One way to determine the grain's direction is to tear the sheet: all paper rips more readily and neatly in the direction of its grain, a phenomenon you may have noticed when tearing something out of a newspaper. Another way to determine the grain's direction is to observe the way a sheet of paper droops when it's supported by just one of its edges: a sheet of long-grained paper droops less from end to end than from side to side, because the fibers act like cantilevers, and a sheet of short-grained paper does the opposite. A sheet of paper's resistance to drooping—its rigidity—is known as its beam strength.

What Becker and the other engineers eventually realized was that they had been using both long-grained and short-grained paper in the prototypes, and that the short-grained paper didn't have enough longitudinal beam strength to prevent it from flopping back against the photoreceptor once Rutkus's puffer had lifted its leading edge. The resulting paper jams were referred to by the engineers as "mispuffs"—and they were a grave concern, because mispuffed sheets tended to bunch up against the hot exterior of the fuser and catch on fire.

One way to eliminate mispuffs would have been to reduce the diameter of the photoreceptor. (If you want to remove a single mailing label from a sheet of labels, you bend the sheet into a curve near one of the label's edges and keep bending until the beam strength of the label exceeds the adhesive force holding the label to the sheet—same idea.) But the engineers had already made the photoreceptor as small as they felt they could. The only practical solution, they concluded reluctantly, was to specify that only long-grained paper be used in the machines. This solution annoyed the marketing department, because it undercut one of xerography's main selling points: that it made copies on "plain paper." But there was no good alternative.

Becker—who had spent part of his career working for a paper manufacturer—helped to solve another major paper problem as well. For reasons that initially mystified the engineers, toner sometimes failed to fuse completely: a copy would look normal, but if you scraped your thumbnail across a line of print, entire characters would chip off. At first, the engineers had worried that this phenomenon, which they called "crust fusing," might be caused by the toner, but Becker correctly deduced that the problem was actually in the paper—or, rather, in water that the paper contained.

Water is an ingredient in all paper, and has been since the Egyptians first made papyrus. Most of the water in paper is squeezed out during production, but some of it inevitably remains. Manufacturers have an incentive to preserve this moisture, because paper at the wholesale level is sold by weight, and water is both heavier and cheaper than plant fiber. The engineers obtained a device called a sword hygrometer—which looks like a letter opener with a pocket calculator attached to its handle and which people in the paper business use to measure moisture content— and discovered that if a batch of paper contained more than a certain percentage of water, melted toner wouldn't stay stuck to it. Harold Clark explained that heat from the fuser must be vaporizing some of the moisture in the paper, causing a pillow of steam to form beneath each character and preventing the liquefied toner from soaking into the paper's fibers.

Now they needed a solution. One possibility was to install a heater in the paper storage tray, to drive moisture from the sheets before they entered the paper path. Another was to buy a paper mill and manufacture low-moisture paper under the Xerox brand. Both possibilities were unappealing, expensive, and likely to be filled with hidden complications. In the end, the company decided to add another caveat to its "plain paper" promise and to work with paper manufacturers to create a list of approved varieties, whose moisture content (and grain direction) made them compatible with the 914.

After the mispuff problem had been solved, fires caused by paper jams were still an occasional problem with the 914 prototypes. Copyflo had been equipped with a safety device known in-house as "bomb-bay doors"—a pair of hinged steel panels that snapped shut over the fuser if the paper web broke or became stuck. Installing a similar device in a 914 was considered but rejected, mostly because it was too bulky to fit. (There was scarcely enough room for the fuser, which was large to begin with and then had to be insulated heavily to keep it from destroying the photoreceptor.) Haloid's engineers, unable to design a way around the danger, wanted to equip each machine with a small carbon dioxide fire extinguisher—another idea that appalled the marketing department. In the end, a compromise was reached: if the threat of fire couldn't be eliminated, it would be renamed. Fire extinguishers were installed (on the outside of the cabinet, close to the fuser), but they were called "scorch eliminators."

As I learned in Bob Gundlach's basement, a certain amount of toner remains stuck to the photoreceptor after a xerographically reproduced image has been transferred to paper, and this residue must be cleaned away before another copy can be made. In the Ox Box, the cleaning had at first been done mechanically, with diatomaceous earth and other mild abrasives, and then electrostatically, with the corona charger. (See chapter 7.) In Copyflo, the cleaning had been done by a pair of rotating fur brushes, which swept the drum as soon as each print was peeled away—and which were themselves cleaned, in turn, by a bladelike paddle called a flicker bar.

That Haloid thought of using fur may have had more to do with real estate than with science: some of the company's scientists and engineers in those days worked in a bleak, tenementlike brick building on Lake Avenue whose ground-floor storefront was occupied by the Crosby Frisian Fur Co.* Every morning on their way to work, the men would see the sign in the window that said FUR & CLOTH COAT STORAGE, and when the time came to think about drum cleaning, one of them must have suddenly thought, Hey! They tried and rejected beaver and raccoon, then determined that the back fur of Australian rabbits worked just about right. Rabbit fur, in addition, was attractively inexpensive.

A fur brush, to clean a drum properly, had to just graze the surface of the photoreceptor. If the fur was too short, it wouldn't clean the drum; if it was too long, it would damage the selenium. The brushes also had to be uniformly sized and interchangeable, so that installers and repairmen wouldn't have to waste time adjusting them. Becker told me, "In the breadboard we would move each brush in and out by hand until we got the proper engagement for that particular piece of fur. We'd sort of rotate it and nudge it and look at it and move it a little more before tightening the nuts, meanwhile eyeballing it from the side to be sure it was perfectly parallel to the drum. We had a couple of guys who could adjust a fur brush pretty well in no more than an hour and a half. But once we go into production we have a different situation."

Becker went to see the shop's owner, whose name was Adams, and asked him if he could cut rabbit fur to the exact dimensions the 914 required, give or take a sixty-fourth of an inch. Adams was used to doing his fur trimming with an enormous pair of shears. He asked, "What's a sixty-fourther?"

---

*Crosby Frisian was an old Rochester company, founded by men named Crosby and Frisian. Its original specialties included big-game taxidermy—commissioned by Theodore Roosevelt, among others—and its 1919 catalog contained photographs of an elephant hide being tanned. By the fifties, little of the old company remained except the name.

Becker took the tape measure from around Adams's neck, stretched it taut between his hands, then gave it a gentle extra tug. "There," he said. "I just moved it more than a sixty-fourth." Adams was appalled. He said, "I don't even know what you're talking about." But he told Becker that Haloid might be able to find what it needed two hundred miles east of Rochester, in Gloversville, New York, which happened to be the glove-making capital of the United States.* Adams explained that the fur lining in leather gloves has to be trimmed precisely, because fur won't keep you warm if it's too short but will block your fingers if it's too long. If trimming rabbit fur to a sixty-fourther is possible, he said, the people in Gloversville will know how to do it. An engineer named Robert Benson was sent to find out.

When Benson returned to Rochester, a week later, he helped his colleagues build a replica of a fur-trimming machine he had studied in one of Gloversville's factories. The machine had a horizontal spindle mounted parallel to what looked like the blades of a reel lawn mower. An untrimmed fur brush was slid onto the spindle and rotated at high speed, like a centrifuge, so that the hairs stood out straight. Then the lawn mower blades, which were very

---

*Gloversville was named after gloves, of course—but it was known as Stump City until 1828, because its founders, who settled there shortly after the end of the Revolutionary War, made room for their settlement by leveling a forest. By the outbreak of the Civil War, there were so many glovers in Gloversville that residents treated gloves and mittens as legal tender. According to the city's official Web site, "Between the years 1880 and 1950, Gloversville enjoyed a sustained and stable golden age, during which most American leather and nearly all American gloves were manufactured here. The population grew to 25,000 and in 1890 Gloversville became a city. Millions of pairs of gloves were regularly shipped by rail to all parts of the world. This created fabulous wealth for dozens of prominent families, many of whose names are echoed in the titles of several philanthropic foundations today." According to another Web site, the most common names in Gloversville during its early years were Burr, Ward, Giles, Mills, Lindley, Mann, Bedford, Jones, Lord, Heacock, Griswold, Wilson, Crossett, Greig, and Throop.

sharp and were also spinning, were moved slowly toward the brush, until the blades just nipped the tips of the fur. A bright light was aimed down the axis of the brush as it spun, so that a circular shadow of its cross section was projected onto the wall. When the brush's shadow had been reduced to the desired diameter, give or take a sixty-fourth of an inch, the brush was ready.

The brushes themselves were made by hand. Adams's father would cut a rectangular section from the back of a pelt and sew the long edges together, creating a rabbit-skin sheath with the fur on the inside. Then he would turn the sheath inside out, so that the fur was now on the outside, and slide it over a cardboard cylinder that looked like the tube from a roll of paper towels. Each brush was expected to last for a few thousand copies—a very large number, everyone figured at the time. When the 914 actually reached the market, though, and users discovered that they loved making Xerox copies, a typical brush replacement cycle turned out to be weeks or days rather than months. To keep up with the demand, the engineers decided to try using belly fur, too—a possibility they had rejected initially because they worried that the nipples, which were hard, might mar the selenium. But they discovered that they could punch out the nipples and still have plenty of fur for drum cleaning. So now each pelt yielded two brushes instead of one.

By the mid-1960s, when the 914 had been succeeded by faster, higher-volume machines, doubling up was no longer enough, and the company switched from rabbit fur to synthetic alternatives—one of which was invented by Gundlach, who was inspired by a shoeshine cloth he had found in a hotel room in Columbus during a visit to Battelle. The company warned Adams many months in advance that the change was coming, but he didn't believe a synthetic replacement would work. Nor did one of his buyers, in France, who amassed a large inventory of rabbit pelts. When Xerox finally did abandon fur, the French buyer, fearing that he was ruined, committed suicide.

FUR BRUSHES SOLVED ONE PROBLEM in the 914, but they aggravated another. George Mott explained: "What was supposed to happen once a copy had been made was that a fur brush would come along and sweep across the drum's surface, cleaning away all excess toner and readying the photoreceptor for another copy. But the fur brush was not doing a thorough job of cleaning, and consequently the copies coming out of the machine got progressively dirtier the longer the machine ran." What was happening was that the toner particles, which were relatively soft, were sticking to the selenium surface as they cascaded across it, then smearing as the brush tried to sweep them away. "Imagine a particle of plastic toner falling to the surface of the drum," Mott continued, "while immediately behind it comes its carrier, much heavier and falling like a rock. Thousands of times with each new copy, toner fragments were being beaten into the drum's surface. In short order, you had a nasty film of plastic and dirt on the photoreceptor surface." The scientists called this problem "film on the drum."

Film on the drum was partly a consequence of the engineers' own determination to build a machine that could be plugged into a regular electrical outlet—the kind you might find on a regular wall in a regular office. This was a big change from Copyflo, which required a dedicated 220-volt circuit, drew as much current as an electric range, and sometimes caused the lights in entire buildings to dim. The 914's engineers knew they had a limited number of amps to apportion among the machine's components and not many volts to push them around with, so they had to be stingy wherever they could. The most power-hungry component in the 914 was the fuser, which used radiant heat to liquefy the powdered toner and was essentially an electric toaster. To keep it from draw-ing too much current—and to prevent it from frying the other components crammed into the 914's cabinet—the engineers knew they had to make it operate at a relatively low temperature. And that meant they had to have a toner that would operate at a rela-tively low temperature, too.

A xerographic toner has to have many mutually exclusive char-acteristics: it has to melt quickly and completely, but it can't be so soft that it smears on the drum, yet it can't be so hard that it dam-ages the photoreceptor when it strikes it, although it has to be brittle enough to be capable of being ground to a fine powder, but the resulting powder can't be so fine that it fouls the carrier beads, yet the powder nevertheless has to be fine enough to yield sharp, high-resolution images, although the particles can't be so large that the force of impact causes them to shatter. "The problems are self-exacerbating once they begin," Gundlach told me. And meet-ing any of the requirements makes meeting all the others more difficult. An ideal toner, the scientists realized, would have some of the same properties as ice, whose viscosity, as you warm it, doesn't change until the moment it turns into a liquid. Most thermoplas-tic resins, in contrast, pass through a gradient of states between solid and liquid, the way chocolate does. (If you want to gain a vivid appreciation of one part of the toner problem, spread half a teaspoon of cocoa powder on the palm of one hand and gently rub your other palm against it for a while. Then try to blow off the powder.) "What do you do in a situation like that?" Mott asked. "You do not know what the optimum is. There is no way on earth that you can calculate it. All you can do is try."

The engineers couldn't use the same toner they had used in Copyflo—their first idea—because that toner melted only in Copyflo's much hotter, high-amp fuser. (Copyflo's fuser was so po-tent that it sometimes caused certain printed characters, such as *o*'s, to burn right through the paper; the machine's operator controlled the heat with a rheostat, winding it down until the output had stopped smoking.) The viability of the 914 depended on finding a toner that would work at a lower temperature, and when the project began, no one could be certain that the search would succeed. The head of the toner program complained that the engineers kept making impossible demands—and then changing them abruptly— but finding an acceptable formula was a necessity. As Rutkus told me in 1985, "If we hadn't accomplished the lower-melt toner, we wouldn't have had a product." In the meantime, Haloid simply proceeded on the assumption that a suitable toner would be found.

That toner was found, virtually at the last minute, primarily through the efforts of Michael Insalaco, a chemist, who had come to work at Haloid before the war, after studying organic chemistry at the University of Rochester. During the prexerography days, he worked primarily on the dyes used in photographic emulsions. Now, with help from colleagues at Haloid and scientists at Battelle, he tested hundreds of resins and pigments and carrier configurations, until he was finally able to devise a formula that met almost all of the engineers' requirements. His fellow scientists at the company viewed him as one of the true heroes of the 914 project, because the toners that he and his team developed were crucial to the machine's success. Those toners continued to be used in Xerox copiers for nearly twenty years.

HALOID IN THE FIFTIES had had no real manufacturing experience. The Ox Box was built by an outside contractor, and each Copyflo was put together essentially from scratch—as the old Rectigraph machines had been. Representatives from IBM, during their abandoned licensing negotiations, had repeatedly warned Haloid that Haloid didn't have the expertise or the facilities to manufacture a complex machine, and that it faced the possibility of incurring "infinite costs." This was a negotiating tactic, but it was also substantially correct: Haloid truly didn't know what it was getting into.

One of the surest signs of Haloid's manufacturing naïveté was its attitude about parts. When a new shipment of Copyflo bolts arrived, an assembler might discover, say, that all or some of the bolts were too long. Rather than sending the bolts back to be replaced—which would hardly be worth the trouble, since so few of the machines were produced—he would use extra washers when he installed them in a machine, or take them into the shop and cut them shorter, or search his workbench for something he could use instead. As a result, each Copyflo contained shims and patches and work-arounds, and Haloid servicemen had to carry files, mallets, thread taps, and sheet-metal scraps so that they could make adjustments in the field. Replacing a photoreceptor drum—a chore that I accomplish with my own copier in a few seconds, by opening the top and sliding a new cartridge into place—could take more than an hour with a Copyflo, because the technician, after modifying the new drum's mount to make it fit correctly, had to create compensations in other parts of the machine so that interconnected elements would continue to function together.*

---

*Assembling a Copyflo was an adventure. John F. Klizas, who was in charge of producing the machines, once said, "It took from four to eight weeks to produce each one, depending on who was assembling it. But that was understandable, because the assemblers worked from very gross instructions: 'Install feeder rolls.' 'Install optics.' His first day on the job, one of these young men would say, 'I'll never be able to do it.' My response would be 'Give it a try. You'll be surprised what you can do.' A few of them had had prior experience of that kind. But in some ways prior assembly experience was a handicap. One fellow was a shoe salesman before he came to me. Another was a commercial artist. Our recruiter would go down to the YMCA and corral them. They had to have a high school education, and they had to be intelligent, but we were not looking for machinists or model makers or anything as specialized as that."

Haloid's parts suppliers couldn't be blamed for all of their inconsistencies, because the drawings they were given to work from were often inexact. Don Shepardson recalled later that Haloid's own production engineers, who were charged with finding a way to actually manufacture the machines, would look at the early plans and say, "Nobody could manufacture anything out of this. These drawings are terrible." One of the first tasks that Becker, who had had experience with manufacturing at Mergenthaler, assigned to himself and his staff when he began at Haloid was to rework all of the 914's blueprints, in order to make sure that dimensions and tolerances were clearly indicated and that every part, if made to spec, would work with every other.

As new parts began arriving on Haloid's loading dock, Becker did something else the company had never done before: he rejected bad parts and told the purchasing department not to pay for them until they had been replaced with ones that matched the specs. This was standard procedure at almost all manufacturing companies of any size, but it caused consternation at Haloid. Joe Wilson called Becker to his office and explained that the company had relationships with local suppliers which dated back to the days of his grandfather, and that Rochester was a small city, and that some of the men who ran these companies were personal friends of his. But Becker was adamant about the need for precision, and Wilson came around. So, eventually, did most of the suppliers.

Several key suppliers not only agreed to meet Haloid's requirements but also made significant engineering contributions to the machine. "A salesman would visit us, see the possibilities, and he'd knock himself out convincing his main office to make parts for the Haloid Company," an engineer said later. "Those guys got very small commissions for their efforts, because our purchases weren't all that big, but they'd get caught up in our enthusiasm." An example was the lamps used to expose the photoreceptor. Haloid's engi-

neers—in order to save precious amps, reduce waste heat inside
the cabinet, and avoid wavelengths of light to which selenium was
unresponsive—had decided to use fluorescent lamps rather than
incandescent ones. But designing a sufficiently bright fluorescent
lamp with the right wavelength characteristics for xerography was
beyond their capability. A General Electric salesman named
George Oliver, who had seen the breadboard in operation and believed, perhaps more firmly than some Haloid executives did, that
xerography had a lucrative future, persuaded his employer to design and manufacture the tubes, even though the resulting orders
were going to be so small that GE had no chance of earning an immediate return on its investment. The lamp that GE came up with
was a marvel of precision engineering. It had the wavelength characteristics that the 914 required, and the inside of each tube had
an opaque phosphor coating with a narrow slit, which ran the
length of the tube. Each 914 required two lamps, and the pins at
their ends had to be positioned so that the beams of light emitted
from the installed tubes' slits would exactly intersect at the surface
of the platen. Later, both GE and Oliver profited enormously
from their relationship with Xerox, but their early contributions
to the 914 came close to being charitable acts.

Other suppliers were less tractable. When Haloid began
preparing to build real machines rather than prototypes, the engineers could no longer rely on the local junkyard as a source of
photoreceptor drums. Becker called Alcoa, said that he needed to
order some eight-inch aluminum tubing, and asked if Alcoa would
mind sending a salesman to talk to him. The man on the phone
asked, "How much are you going to need?" Becker said, "Oh, at
first, maybe a hundred feet." Alcoa had tubing mills that almost
couldn't be started and stopped fast enough to produce just a hundred feet. The representative told Becker to look for his tubing
somewhere else.

Alcoa had an office in Rochester, so Becker, undeterred, drove over and asked at the front desk if he could see someone from the sales department. "Nobody wanted to talk to me," he told me. "Finally a young lady came out, and she listened to me and said, 'Let me see what I can do.' To make a long story short, she entered a special order for this tubing, which she said they would run on the tail of some other order, and we got what we needed." A decade later, Alcoa threw a big party at the Genesee Valley Club in Rochester to celebrate its long and profitable relationship with the Xerox Corporation, and Becker announced that he wouldn't attend unless Alcoa could track down the woman who had taken that crucial first order. Alcoa did find her, and the two of them sat together at the party.

In 1958, as Haloid Xerox's scientists and engineers were pulling together their design for the 914, the company's negotiations with IBM suddenly resumed. Wilson had become convinced that he owed his shareholders another attempt to spread the risk of production, and IBM had concluded, as a result of its own research under Haloid Xerox licenses, that a xerographic office copier was indeed feasible. IBM had produced a detailed design for a machine that was bigger than a Thermo-Fax but smaller than the projected 914. The company's negotiators urged Haloid Xerox to step aside for its own good and let the big boys take over. "They were far from complimentary about our capacity to build the machine we planned," Linowitz wrote later; "the IBM engineering staff warned that our production run machines would never make copies of the quality they had achieved with their hand tooled models."

While these unpleasant discussions were under way, IBM hired the distinguished old Boston consulting firm Arthur D. Little to assess the potential market for a copier like the 914. Haloid Xerox cooperated with the study and allowed the consultants to speak with its employees. It also shared the specifications for the 914 and for a smaller copier, called the 813, which the company hoped would follow the 914 to market. In addition, the consultants interviewed eighty potential 914 customers, to gain a sense of their copying needs.

The consultants' conclusion, which they presented in a report to IBM in December, was unequivocal. "Model 914," they wrote, "has no future in the office copying market." The nation's businesses already had carbon paper and inexpensive desktop devices like Thermo-Fax and Verifax for ordinary copying, and they had offset printing, spirit duplicating, and other well-tested technologies for high-volume reproduction. Office workers, in field interviews, had expressed little interest in the Haloid Xerox concept and no interest at all in carrying documents to a centralized copying room in order to reproduce them. The 914 didn't exist yet, but the niche it was meant to occupy was already vanishing, the consultants believed, and its projected unit manufacturing cost, roughly $2,000, was frighteningly high. The report concluded that total demand, now and in the future, could be satisfied by a maximum of a few thousand machines—not enough to make production worthwhile. A. D. Little urged IBM to "terminate consideration of the 914 as a new market opportunity." And that's what IBM did.

Overnight, Wilson's feelings about IBM changed from anxious uncertainty to something like panic. A distinguished technology company and its distinguished consulting agency had both concluded, in effect, that Wilson's father was right. Even worse, Bell & Howell, which made movie cameras, movie projectors, and other optical equipment, had also rejected a proposed manufacturing partnership with Haloid Xerox—and not because Bell & Howell thought a (modest) market for copiers didn't exist, but because they thought the 914 wouldn't work.

Bell & Howell's skepticism had to do mainly with the 914's complex optical system. That system had been conceived by Clyde Mayo, the head of Haloid's engineering department, who had realized early in the design process that the key to building a desk-size xerographic copier would be finding a way to "fold" Copyflo's image projection optics so that it could be contained in a smaller space. The 914's system would have to project an image of a flat, stationary document onto the curved surface of a rotating cylinder, and it would have to do so while maintaining a uniform level of illumination and without allowing any part of the image to slip out of focus. Mayo's solution, Erik Pell writes, "was to scan the document at a velocity synchronized to the tangential velocity of the drum surface, through a lens which was itself moving at half of this velocity (since the lens was located at half the distance from drum to document)." A narrow slit above the photoreceptor prevented more than a small strip from being exposed at one time, so that the image wouldn't be "smeared" by the curve of the drum. A pair of fixed mirrors created the required thirty-three-inch separation between the document and the photoreceptor. The lens, which was made by Bausch & Lomb, had a narrow aperture, to give it the deepest possible field of focus while keeping the exposure adequate for the design speed of seven copies per minute, and its motions were precisely timed.

Bell & Howell's engineers were quite familiar with tricky optics, and they concluded that the 914's moving scanner—which had been developed in part in a laboratory situated in the basement of a Masonic temple—was certain to fail. A hand-built prototype might make copies under test conditions, they felt, but a regular production machine was doomed. Somebody would bump a chair against the side of a copier and cause the lens to become misaligned, and the machine would stop working. The 914 was like a movie projector in which the film remained stationary while

the lens and light source skimmed along it and attempted to project a focused image onto a fixed, distant screen—an absurdity.

Shortly after IBM and Bell & Howell had delivered their ver-
dicts, Wilson commissioned a study of his own, from the consulting firm Ernst & Ernst. The traditional role of management
consultants in corporate planning is to find compelling ways of
telling executives what they already think, but Ernst & Ernst
didn't quite do that. Their report was less pessimistic than A. D.
Little's had been, but it was scarcely enthusiastic, and it made the
point that potential customers appeared to be interested only in
very small copiers, not in machines the size of deep freezers. (This
conclusion highlights one of the challenges faced by companies
that try to be "customer driven": customers are much better at describing what they currently do than they are at envisioning what
they might do if circumstances changed.) Wilson, in the end, decided simply to ignore the report's most discouraging sections.
Linowitz wrote later that "this was one of those mountains we got
over by faith."

Yet that faith wasn't entirely blind. While IBM was still delib-
erating, Wilson asked Harold Clark to head an internal study
group similar to the old small copier committee, and that group
had emphatically recommended that Haloid Xerox proceed on its
own. "We said, *Please* don't give automatic xerography to another
company," the physicist Frederick Schwertz recalled later. "We all
felt so strongly about its potential importance that we didn't want
to see another company get hold of it."

Wilson had also received some credible indications that the
914, despite what the consultants said, might lucratively fill a real
business need. John Glavin, who in 1957 became the head of new
product planning, had conducted some informal market research,
and his findings were far more encouraging than A. D. Little's or
Ernst & Ernst's. "We went out and talked to companies around

Rochester, and day by day our eyes began to open," he said in the 1970s. "We found out that people used copiers a lot more than anybody realized." Thermo-Fax, Verifax, and their direct competitors were becoming increasingly common in offices at that time, and secretaries had begun to develop a sense of what they could do. "The absolute number of copies being made in many establishments was higher than anybody dreamed, except for the manufacturers of those machines," Glavin continued. "We also found that people were looking for better ways of making copies"—ways that didn't involve noxious chemicals or coated papers. He noticed as well that although a Thermo-Fax was much smaller than the copier Haloid was developing, a Thermo-Fax invariably sat on a table, along with various copying supplies, and this combination of machine and furniture required about the same floor space as a 914.

Glavin later took half a dozen members of his marketing staff to Baltimore for several weeks, to perform a similar investigation. "We were not what you would call scientific market research people," he said later. "None of us had any training at all." Glavin and his men would interview businesspeople during the day and compare their findings in a hotel room at night. "We were astounded at the amount of copying those firms were doing," he continued, adding, "Kodak knew that. Pico knew it; 3M knew it. But we were just catching on." A. D. Little and Ernst & Ernst had erred by thinking of office copiers as providing a one-to-one replacement for carbon paper; they hadn't anticipated that a change in technology might transform copying itself. The evidence had been apparent, in the steadily increasing output of Thermo-Fax, Verifax, and other coated-paper machines, but the consultants had focused instead on what they already understood.

The members of Glavin's team saw what the consultants had missed. One day, one of them stopped by the Baltimore Social Security office, which had recently purchased a number of coated-paper copying machines.

"How much of that paper do you use?" he asked.

"What do you mean—how many carloads, or what?"

The Haloid man's eyes lit up. *"Carloads?"*

There was also encouraging evidence at Haloid Xerox itself, although no one paid much attention at the time. By early 1959, an engineer who needed copies of a technical drawing wouldn't ask a secretary to send it out to a blueprinter, the way he had in the past; usually he would just copy it on one of the 914 prototypes that he and his colleagues were working on. "Size drawings, documentation drawings, change orders," Shepardson recalled later. "We just ran the wheels off those machines." Other employees noticed, and soon they were making copies on the prototypes, too. In fact, pretty soon it began to seem as though every time an engineer needed to make a copy of something, he had to stand in line.

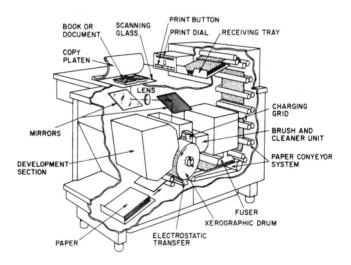

Schematic drawing of Xerox 914, 1960.
XEROX CORP.

Late in 1959, the company conducted a serious field test by installing preproduction 914s at half a dozen local companies and institutions, among them Rochester Gas & Electric, the University of Rochester, Taylor Instruments, and Bausch & Lomb. From users at those locations, the engineers learned (or were reminded) that a stack of paper needed to be fanned before being loaded, that a stray staple or paper clip could bring a machine to a standstill if it made its way inside the cabinet, that paper jams were a perennial problem, and that every company that leased a 914 would need to designate an employee—later known as the "key operator"—to receive training from Haloid Xerox in how to fan paper, remove staples and paper clips, clear paper jams, and so on. By the time the field test ended, the engineers had gathered so much raw data on their machine's shortcomings that they couldn't help feeling deeply disheartened. When they went around to retrieve the prototypes, though, they received an encouraging surprise: None of the testers wanted to give their copier back.

10

NICKELS

By the mid-1950s, Haloid was investing every available dollar in xerographic research and development. Scrounging those dollars was largely the responsibility of Harold Kuhns, the company's controller and a legendary corporate tightwad. In 1957, a young marketing executive named C. Peter McColough—who was Canadian, had served as an airman in the British Royal Navy during World War II, and would succeed Wilson as the company's president in 1966—told Kuhns that the office he'd been assigned in the company's decaying headquarters was so noisy that he had trouble working in it, and he asked if the bare linoleum floor could be carpeted to muffle the sound. Kuhns, after stalling for several weeks, did buy carpet—but only a remnant and only enough to cover the back of McColough's door. Kuhns's parsimony helped the company husband scarce cash during a critical period, although Kuhns could be an impediment to progress as well. When the 914's engineers told him they needed a $200,000 industrial drill press, his reaction was to sputter, "Gee! Gee!" and to resist the purchase for as long as he could.

Much of the developmental engineering work on the 914 took place in a Kuhns-friendly brick building on University Avenue whose ground floor was occupied by a garden-seed-packaging company. The Haloid Xerox engineers worked in the gloomy loft upstairs and came and went by way of a boxcar-size freight elevator. There was only one enclosed office, for Clyde Mayo, the department head. Kuhns viewed individual telephones as an extravagance, so three or four engineers would push their desks together and share. "The switchboard operator sat out in the open," one of them recalled. "We would yell over to her to hook us up." There was no air-conditioning. On hot days, tar from the roof dripped through the ceiling onto desks, prototypes, and engineers.

During the winter of 1959, as Wilson fretted about whether or not to send the 914 into production, Kuhns rented an even grimmer space, an old warehouse on Lyell Avenue, and the company built a few final prototypes there, outside the engineering lab. The engineers then ran those machines continuously, hoping to identify and eliminate the many defects that remained. The building's owner, to save money, turned the furnace down at five o'clock, so the engineers erected a canvas enclosure around each machine, to contain the heat given off by the fuser, and worked inside. "They all wore parkas, but their feet would just freeze in there," Horace Becker said later. "Those guys worked seven nights a week all through that winter, working under the most miserable conditions. After a while, they looked like bums, because they quit shaving."

When an engineer was at home with his family, his mind often drifted back to the warehouse. His wife would be talking, and suddenly he would think of a possible solution to a problem with the fuser or the power supply or the moving lens, and he would be unable to repeat whatever she had just said. He would find an excuse to leave the house, then drive back to Lyell Avenue. "I came down because I was worried," an engineer explained at the time. "I wanted to think about it some more." When Becker came to work at Haloid in 1958, he left his wife and three children at home on Long Island for the first six months and lived alone at the Rochester YMCA. His family moved up to join him after the school year had ended, but his wife sometimes felt she had seen more of him when they were living apart, because then he had at least visited on weekends.

Living at the YMCA and working overtime did not make Haloid Xerox's employees unhappy, however: trying to build a functioning office copier was the most engaging group activity that some of the men had been involved in since the end of the war. Still, at one point Wilson became worried that the 914 development program was overstressing his workers, and he hired a psychological-testing firm to assess the company's mental health. "They came in and gave a questionnaire to all the employees," Frederick Schwertz recalled later, "but then when they examined their results they couldn't believe them." The contentment ratings were so high that the testers thought they must have garbled the data, and they distributed a second set of questionnaires. But the new results came back the same.

LATE IN 1959, after much agonizing, Wilson and the board finally decided to proceed without a manufacturing partner, and Kuhns leased another forlorn-looking structure, on Orchard Street, to serve as a factory for the 914. Railroad tracks ran near the building, which formerly had been used to manufacture paper boxes, and the workers could look down through grimy windows and see loads of pigs rolling by. "You can't imagine the things we had to do there," John Klizas said later. On moving day, Klizas himself shoveled coal from an old bin so that the space could be used as an inspection station for arriving parts. The building's main redeeming feature was its level concrete floors—a major improvement over the sagging wooden floors on Lyell Avenue.

In late December, as production was about to begin, the company held a modest holiday party on the factory floor—a pep rally for the 914, with soft drinks for refreshments. The invitees included Haloid Xerox employees and representatives of the companies that would supply the machine's parts. As a major snowstorm gathered force outside, Wilson explained that for the project to succeed, the company would need the cooperation and forbearance of everyone in the room. And in the coming months, to a remarkable extent, that is what he received.

"Everybody was keyed up," Becker said eight years later. "The union people temporarily forgot their grievances, and the bosses forgot their performance ratings. You couldn't tell an engineer from an assembler in that place. No one could stay away—you'd sneak in on a Sunday, when the assembly line was shut down, and there would be somebody adjusting something or just puttering around and admiring our work."

The 914 assembly line wasn't really a line; each machine was mounted on a wooden dolly and rolled around the floor by hand. Every assembler was directly supervised by an engineer, who sat in a chair beside him as he worked. The engineers called this system "witness assembly"; its purpose was to prevent the assemblers from following their accustomed practice of turning bad parts into acceptable parts by bending them or filing their rough edges or finding other clever ways to make them fit; if parts differed from the specs, the engineers wanted to know. This issue had arisen already with regard to the 914's metal cabinet, the first version of which had been produced by a well-known manufacturer of metal office furniture. The initial shipment of cabinets had looked superb—but then someone accidentally damaged a side panel, and the engineers discovered that the cabinets' main components were not perfectly interchangeable: a panel that fit snugly in one frame would rattle in another. The manufacturer was unrepentant, saying, in effect, That's how we build desks. So Haloid Xerox had to find another supplier in a hurry.

Some improvisation was still necessary. The cooling fans provided for the prototypes had fit perfectly, but the production version of the same fans vibrated violently when the fans were mounted in the machines and turned on. Rather than halting the assembly line so that the part could be redesigned and remanufactured by its supplier, the engineers devised a mounting bracket to dampen the shaking and then worked all night making brackets by hand so that production could resume in the morning.

Every day brought additional problems. "We thought we had everything under control when suddenly the machines all stopped working," George Mott recalled later. "It was the same problem with every one of those machines off the first production line: the machine would make three or four copies, then nothing. It would not make another copy. Every sheet came out blank." The engineers and scientists, feeling frantic, checked everything. Were the photoreceptors charging? Were they discharging? Was the toner being pulled off the paper before the copy got to the fuser? Then someone thought of taking a sample of a malfunctioning machine's developer and testing it on another photoreceptor. It still didn't work. So that meant the problem was in the developer.

"The carrier and the toner are two dissimilar materials," Mott continued, "and for that reason they are attracted to each other. When you put them together, in intimate contact, they automatically exchange charge and cling together. The toner takes on a negative charge, the carrier a positive charge—and when you have the right mix of both carrier and toner, the total mix is electrically neutral." After cascading across a charged photoreceptor, however, that mixture becomes slightly positive, as negatively charged

toner is removed; neutrality is restored, between images, by allowing the developer to come into contact with the grounded metal
parts. "This was known," Mott said. "It was built into the machine. It had always worked fine in the handmade prototypes."

Now it wasn't working. Why? Eventually, a physicist named
Fred Hudson realized that the production models were different
from the prototypes in one significant respect. The metal developer compartments on the production machines had been rust-
proofed by spraying them with a paint that, it turned out, was such
an efficient electrical insulator, it was preventing the developer
from neutralizing itself between copies. The solution? Strip the
paint.

Then it was the fusers. Each fuser's heating element consisted
of a bank of metal rods whose ends were screwed into threaded
holes in a pair of rectangular insulating blocks, which were manufactured by a company in Chattanooga, Tennessee. When the first
batch of blocks arrived, the assemblers discovered that the holes
were too small for the rods. The exact dimensions of the holes had
been specified in the drawings—what had happened? It turned out
that the ceramic material from which the blocks were made shrank
by 15 or 20 percent when it was fired, and the holes, which were
molded into the material before the firing, shrank with it. The
supplier tried to correct the problem by using a drill press to tap
properly sized holes in finished blocks, but the material was too
hard to tool. The delay became a crisis.

"They understood the problem, but they couldn't make the
part," Becker told me. "We were running out of time, so I realized
I had to go to Chattanooga myself." He and Jack Reinhardt, who
worked in Haloid Xerox's purchasing department, took off from
Rochester's tiny airport on a bitterly cold winter morning but got
only as far as Washington, D.C., where they learned that a major
ice storm had just hit Tennessee and their connecting flight had

been canceled. "Our only choice was to take a train," Becker continued. "But the railroad wouldn't accept our Mohawk Airlines tickets, and we hadn't brought enough cash. Suddenly, I remembered that there was a Haloid sales office in Washington. We took a taxi over there, and I went to the girl at the front desk, and explained our problem and asked her how much she had in petty cash. And she said, 'I can't do that.' "

Becker became agitated, and the manager came out of his office. It turned out that he and Becker had corresponded recently, because someone at the White House had heard about the 914 and wanted to order several machines. The manager gave Becker all the cash he had on hand, and Becker and Reinhardt returned to the station.

They arrived in Chattanooga many hours later—and immediately faced another problem: The driver of the only taxi they could find refused to take them to the factory, because, he explained, the roads outside the center of town were still icy. Becker said, "Fella, relax—I'll drive." He took the wheel and, with the cabdriver navigating, drove them (very slowly) to the plant.

The manufacturing problem was too complex to be solved on paper; the only way to approach it was empirically. "I said, 'We're going to have to do things oversize, find out what the percentage of shrinkage is, and ballpark it,' " Becker recalled. "So we made a fixture with dimensions that weren't anything like the ones in the drawing, and then we made another. We had some little templates, and we fired the pieces and measured them, and then we made some more." Every dimension had to be scaled up, including the spacing of the threads in the holes. "By trial and error, we worked our way down to a drilled fixture that had absolutely no relationship to the drawing. But the pieces, when they came out of the furnace, were right."

Becker and Reinhardt stayed in Chattanooga until the factory had produced fifty acceptable sets. They divided the fifty into two packages and returned home by separate routes as a hedge against the weather: Reinhardt took the train while Becker rented a car. The trip was nearly nine hundred miles, but Becker beat Reinhardt, whose train was delayed by another storm. Becker had lived on peanut-butter-and-jelly sandwiches for days, had scarcely slept, and hadn't shaved or changed his clothes, but instead of going home he drove straight to the plant. And Reinhardt did the same thing when he got back to Rochester, a day and a half later. "We were fired up," Becker said.

The first 914s took weeks to assemble—and reassemble. "We were writing engineering changes at a furious rate," Becker told me, "because we were seeing problems in final testing at assembly. We really should have done one more round of prototypes, but we didn't have the time or the money. We were having problems with the paper tray, the flip-flop clutch, the power supply, the main drive motor, the control package, and a few other parts—nothing too bad, just enough to make you throw up each morning after breakfast and then skip lunch because you were so busy. But we couldn't ship yet unless we wanted to ship a tech rep with every machine."

By the end of February 1960, the company had managed to build fifty reasonably functional 914s. Soon, the factory on Orchard Street was turning out five a day. During those first few months, Joe Wilson himself would visit the factory each morning and conduct a brief, convocationlike meeting involving almost everyone connected with the project. "We would bring up problems," Glavin recalled later. "People would get assignments, and they'd come back the next day and report on progress." Wilson was encouraging, cheerful, confident, and charismatic—surprisingly so, given that he was not physically commanding. He was not a stirring public speaker. His voice was not powerful. He wore big glasses and drab suits. But he knew almost every worker by name, and as he walked around the factory floor each morning, he smiled. His unpretentiousness, self-assurance, and evident guilelessness were both comforting and contagious. A number of employees said later that it was Wilson himself who had made the 914 successful, by somehow convincing everyone else that the company's huge gamble was not reckless and by never allowing workers or suppliers to become discouraged.

When a decision was made to increase production from five machines a day to twenty-five, a second large pep rally for employees and vendors was held on the factory floor. Wilson spoke briefly. Then John Hartnett, who was the chairman of the board, stepped up to make a ceremonial copy on one of the machines and said that someone had finally built a copier that he could operate. He placed a document on the platen and pressed the button. A few seconds later, a sheet of paper emerged from a slot next to the control panel—and it was blank. This was an outcome that did not entirely surprise anyone in the room; as Becker would say in 1967, "All in all, at that time the machines had a bad habit, when you pressed the button, of doing nothing." But David Curtin, who was the head of the company's public relations department, lifted the cover from the platen and revealed that Hartnett had placed his original face up. Curtin said, "The machine can't copy it if we don't show it the right side." He turned the original over and pressed the button again. This time a real copy emerged. Everyone applauded and, a little later, went back to work.

EACH 914 COST ROUGHLY $2,000 TO MANUFACTURE—about what the small copier committee had predicted back in 1955. That figure, though frighteningly large, nevertheless included only the cost of parts and labor. By the time the first machine was completed, Haloid Xerox had also spent $12.5 million developing it—

an investment that exceeded the company's total earnings during the entire decade of the fifties. Kodak was selling its smallest Verifax model, which was called the Bantam, for $99.50 retail, a price at which Haloid Xerox would have had trouble turning a profit on fusers. How could the 914 compete without bankrupting its manufacturer?

Haloid Xerox had always suspected that it was going to have to lease 914s to customers rather than selling them—as it already did with most Model Ds and almost all Copyflos.* Leasing entailed tax benefits for Haloid Xerox, which retained ownership of the machines and could therefore depreciate them, and for the customers, who could treat copying as an ordinary expense rather than having to capitalize it. A lease program would also enable Haloid Xerox to continue working on unresolved mechanical problems after the machines had left the factory. But there were drawbacks as well. Under a lease program, Haloid Xerox would have to bear, up front, the entire cost of production—a major consideration now that output was going to be measured in thousands of units rather than dozens and now that the company was essentially living on its credit lines. A lease program would also make Haloid Xerox solely responsible for something it had had no luck with up to now: keeping the copiers working. Another unresolved issue was how to price the leases fairly, since some customers might make only a few hundred copies a month while others might make thousands.

"I can remember the day I came up with the answer," John Glavin said later. "I was sitting in the corner of my office, going over

---

*For customers who insisted on ownership, the manufacturer's suggested retail price for a new 914 was a bit less than $30,000—a figure that was meant to discourage purchases and wasn't even offered until 1963. When the machine was introduced, Wilson said, "The purchase price will be such, I think, that people will rent it."

the market research data and thinking about what we ought to do. Then the concept of *metering* the machine came to me. Why not put a meter on the machine and charge so much for every copy?" Glavin's immediate inspiration was a Pitney-Bowes postage meter that he had noticed in the mailroom not long before. If Pitney-Bowes could accurately track impressions, why not Haloid Xerox? The company had recently begun charging Copyflo customers based on the number of running feet of paper they used, in recognition of the fact that some customers were operating their machines three shifts a day. Glavin hurried downstairs to Wilson's office, one floor below, and explained his idea. Wilson liked it, and told Glavin to sell it to Hartnett and Kuhns. Both men approved. The company settled on a price of $95 a month, plus five cents for every copy after the first two thousand. To tempt customers into taking a chance on an unknown product, the lease included a fifteen-day cancellation clause. "I doubt if any corporation had ever made an offer so completely biased in the customer's favor," John Dessauer wrote later. The leasing plan inspired an early Xerox advertising slogan, which was intended to lure customers away from Thermo-Fax and Verifax: "Don't Buy Their Copier—Borrow Ours."

The first 914 ordered by a paying customer left Orchard Street in March 1960. The customer was Standard Press Steel, a manufacturer of metal fasteners situated in King of Prussia, Pennsylvania. (Today, the company is called SPS Technologies, Inc.) A 914 couldn't simply be mailed to its recipient; it had to be encased in a massive wooden crate, trucked by a freight shipper, uncrated by a carpenter, then delivered on a tilting dolly so that its L-shaped, 648-pound bulk could be angled through doors. When it arrived, an accompanying salesman had to lead the recipients through a lengthy "preinstallation" checklist. The machine was forty-two inches tall, forty-five inches wide, and forty-six inches deep. It required thirty-six square feet of floor space, not including a two-foot gap between the back of the cabinet and the wall (so that waste heat from the fuser could escape before baking the copier's insides), and although it ran on ordinary line voltage, it worked best when connected to a twenty-amp circuit of its own. A key operator and a backup key operator had to be designated, then taught about loading paper, clearing paper jams, checking developer, calling the serviceman, and filling out the copy meter card, which had to be mailed back to Rochester at the end of each month. (Employing meter readers, Haloid Xerox had realized, would be too expensive.)

First-time users had to be introduced not just to the 914 but to the new idea that the machine embodied. "Place the original on the scanning plate," one early summary began. "Close the cover. Anything you want copied, place face down." None of this was intuitive in 1960. Users also needed to be told, in effect, what the machine was for. "You can copy letters, invoices, contracts, graphs, pages from bound volumes, ball point pen signatures, pencil writing, rigid three-dimensional objects," the summary continued. "You can copy colors in sharp black and white, even if there is blue or red in the original. There is no hand feeding of copy paper, no matrix, no rehandling of the original." These last sentences were directed mainly at Thermo-Fax and Verifax users, as were these: "There's no damage to the original regardless of the thickness. Materials to be copied remain stationary on the 914. When 're-load' signal appears, the 914 Copier is ready for a new original. Simply lift the cover, remove your first original and put in another." A couple of hours later, and after some last-minute tweaking, the machine was ready to be put to work.

In the mid-1950s, Chester Carlson and Harold Clark had worried that few businesses might ever need to make as many as a hundred copies a day—the threshold, they felt, at which xerographic office copying would be economical. The 914's lease reflected similar thinking, since its base rate of two thousand copies per month worked out to roughly one hundred copies per business day. During the 914's development, Haloid's marketing department had speculated that very heavy users, at peak periods, might make five times as many as copies, or ten thousand a month, so the machine had been engineered to handle occasional usage at that level. Throughout the company, ten thousand copies a month had been treated as an optimistic upper-limit benchmark.

From the day the first 914 arrived in King of Prussia, the employees of Standard Press Steel used it to make copies at several times the predicted maximum rate. The numbers seemed inconceivable at first, but Standard Press's usage rate remained high, and the same thing happened at other companies. As the first 914 meter cards were returned, Haloid Xerox discovered that customers were using their machines at four and five and ten times the benchmark. At some companies, machines were being run around the clock, with (frequent) breaks only for maintenance and repairs.

Donald Clark,* who had served in the U.S. Army Air Corps during World War II and, at thirty-seven years old, was now responsible for marketing the 914, said later, "The first thing you have to recognize is that copying at that stage of the game was an inherent, unrecognized need. Once you got that 914 in the office, the narcotic effect began." Making a copy on a 914 was seductively easy, since all you had to do was push a button—and the copy itself provided positive reinforcement, since it didn't smell bad, curl up, or turn brown. "The biggest problem our customer had was not with us," Clark continued. "The problem was with their own employees, to stop them from abusing the privilege of having that machine there." Haloid Xerox briefly considered adding a lock to the 914, so that companies could prevent employees from making unauthorized copies, but decided (for the obvious reason) not to.

---

*Not related to Xerox physicist Harold Clark.

When Arthur D. Little and Ernst & Ernst had conducted their field interviews and made their market projections a year or two before, they had focused on the kinds of copying that companies were doing already. Most of that copying consisted of using carbon paper or one of the popular coated-paper machines to reproduce letters, invoices, and other outgoing business documents. No one, including the members of the marketing department at Haloid Xerox, had anticipated that the arrival of xerography might prompt people to begin also making copies of documents traveling in the opposite direction—to take a sales report from another office, for example, and use a 914 to run off a copy for each person in the department, rather than attaching a routing slip to the original and circulating it, the way people had always done in the past. But the 914 was so easy and pleasant to work with that people began using it to satisfy needs they hadn't known they had. Suddenly, agendas for staff meetings didn't have to be written on conference room blackboards; now every participant could be given a xerographically reproduced copy, and if someone unexpectedly showed up late, one of the copies could be copied again. These new, unanticipated capabilities were so beguiling that they converted skeptics quickly. The head librarian at the University of Rochester staunchly resisted the installation of a 914 prototype but became an enthusiast before the end of its first day of operation.

Truly epochal technology shifts are sometimes incomprehensible until after they've occurred. When the first videocassette recorders were introduced, in the 1970s, the Motion Picture Association of America spent millions of dollars complaining to Congress that Hollywood was about to be annihilated. Instead, the VCR revived Hollywood, by generating billions in rental fees and transforming the way movies were financed. No one had guessed ahead of time that the main purpose of VCRs would turn out to be playing rented movies that moviegoers wouldn't have paid to see in a theater. Indeed, the owners of the first VCRs didn't truly know what their machines were for until they found them in their living rooms. As with Xerox machines, the technology itself created the demand that ultimately sustained it. Invention was the mother of necessity.

A couple of years earlier, Glavin had predicted that Haloid Xerox's revenues from xerography might someday reach $30,000 or $40,000 a day—numbers that many of his colleagues had viewed as farcically optimistic. Soon after the 914 began shipping to customers, though, the company's executives realized that Glavin had been far too cautious. Even at just five cents a copy (or four cents or four and a half cents, depending on the year and the terms of the particular lease), the money added up in a hurry. It added up even faster when customers discovered that the 914 could be used as a duplicator, too, and that casually running off a couple of hundred Xerox copies was less bothersome than creating an offset or spirit-duplicating master. The meters whirred. Haloid Xerox's revenues in 1959, the year before the first 914 shipped, had been $32 million. By 1961, they had already nearly doubled. And that was only the beginning. Members of Haloid Xerox's sales and marketing departments commemorated their astonishing success with cuff links made of nickels.

THE IMMEDIATE SUCCESS OF THE 914 also created challenges, the most serious of which had to do with the machine's nearly diabolical unreliability. "As an invention, it was magnificent," Harold Clark said later. "The only problem was that as a product it wasn't any good."

Haloid Xerox's scientists and engineers had always known that the 914, and xerography itself, could be frustratingly temperamental. Now, though, the machines were being used harder than anyone had anticipated, and problems were cascading. Customers were going through toner and fur brushes at an unnerving pace, and they were wearing out selenium drums almost faster than the factory could produce new ones.

When the scale of the 914's popularity became apparent, Haloid Xerox had to assemble a large, well-trained service force in a hurry. Becker told me, "When we started out, we had a goal of getting one preventive maintenance call per five thousand copies, and one emergency call per five thousand copies." That worked out to an average of one call for every 2,500 copies—or roughly one maintenance call per week at the predicted maximum copying rate of ten thousand copies a month. Today, a complex high-speed copier will often make a million copies between service calls, but in 1960 one breakdown per week seemed like a reasonable goal. In reality, though, the 914's service cycle turned out to be more like one emergency call per two thousand copies, and heavy users were exceeding that level daily. Crises were so frequent that Haloid Xerox quickly realized that the scheduled preventive call was unnecessary, since a repairman, responding to an emergency, would almost certainly be on the premises that day anyway. Called in to clear a catastrophic paper jam, the repairman could take a moment to change the worn fur brush, too—or, if he didn't have a new brush in his toolbox, he could make a note to bring one tomorrow or the next day, when he was likely to be called back. At most companies, 914 repairmen soon seemed like family. To attract good servicemen and keep them committed to the company, Haloid Xerox began giving them cars. "We purposely did not do that for our salesmen," one executive said later. "We wanted it to be a special status thing, for service people only."

Haloid Xerox employees got used to being assailed at cocktail parties by people who used the 914 at work. "Let me tell you what your machine did to me today," the people would begin. The list of complaints was long and discouragingly familiar, since customers were now discovering all the problems that Haloid Xerox's physicists and engineers had been struggling with for years— problems with humidity, development, paper handling, fusing, and everything else. However, the complainers had something unexpected in common. No matter how annoyed they felt with their machine, they never said they wanted to give it up, since they had come to believe they couldn't live without it. Rather than angrily canceling their leases, frustrated customers tended to order a second 914, or a third, to increase the likelihood that at least one machine in the building would be working at all times. Haloid Xerox began offering existing customers additional leases for just $25 a month. This was a huge discount from the basic lease, but the program paid for itself by relieving stress on 914 repairmen, since it gave customers a backup copier to use while their original was being serviced. Old Haloid customers hadn't minded sending an ailing Ox Box to the shop for a couple of days or a couple of weeks, but people wanted their 914 back in operation that minute, or at any rate before lunch. According to one of the company's executives, second machine leases "saved our bacon many a time and kept our service costs from going through the roof."

One reason for the relative tolerance among customers was that xerography was so new and unknown that no one yet had a basis for expecting it to work better than it did. The copies themselves, when they appeared successfully, were so much sharper and more pleasant to handle than the copies made by competing technologies that customers were predisposed to forgive. Haloid Xerox also gained from being unknown. One member of the sales force said that customers often felt sorry for this small, obscure manufacturer doing battle with high-technology giants and therefore endured indignities from Haloid Xerox that they would never have tolerated from 3M or Kodak or IBM. Secretaries dutifully filled out and returned meter cards, and they didn't become overly upset when the meters malfunctioned, as they often did.* Users accepted breakdowns as the price of an intoxicating new capability. They happily turned "Xerox" into a trademark-weakening verb.

Office workers, in other words, mentally weighed the costs and benefits, and adapted. "Call key operator" and "Check paper path" became familiar imperatives on a level with "Fasten seat belt" and "Shake well before using." John Brooks, in his (quaintly sexist) 1967 *New Yorker* story about Xerox, wrote, "I spent a couple of afternoons with one 914 and its operator, and observed what seemed to be the closest relationship between a woman and a piece of office equipment that I had ever seen. A girl who uses a typewriter or switchboard has no interest in the equipment, because it holds no mystery, while one who operates a computer is bored with it, because it is utterly incomprehensible. But a 914 has distinct animal traits: it has to be fed and curried; it is intimidating but can be tamed; it is subject to unpredictable bursts of misbehavior; and, generally speaking, it responds in kind to its treatment. 'I was frightened of it at first,' the operator I watched told me. 'The Xerox men say, "If you're frightened of it, it won't work," and that's pretty much right. It's a good scout; I'm fond of it now.' "

---

*Dessauer wrote later, "Unfortunately the metering system was not as simple to achieve as we had supposed. In fact, for a time the meters caused us a good deal of annoyance and expense. The first ones too often failed to register accurately. 'I myself put twenty copies through one machine,' one of our servicemen told me, 'and it registered *two* copies. Then, in another office, every time a copy was made the meter kept ticking away to register maybe ten or more.' "

11

WHICH IS THE ORIGINAL?

IN 1954, JOHN RUTLEDGE WAS A THIRTY-ONE-YEAR-OLD Pennsylvania coal salesman. He had served in the navy during World War II, and had later graduated from Harvard Business School. Now the coal mines were closing, and he knew his job wouldn't last. From a friend he heard about a small, interesting company in upstate New York which was expanding its sales department, and he applied for a job. "I remember the first time they showed me xerography, when I went up to Rochester for the first time," he recalled in the mid-1960s. "They had an old flat-plate thing rigged up in a back room, and one of the fellows ran it for me. I acted like I was impressed, but, frankly, I didn't know what the hell I was looking at."

Within the next few years, however, Rutledge became such a firm believer in Carlson's invention that he borrowed money, cashed in his life insurance, and remortgaged his house to buy as much Haloid stock as he could. (Much of the in-house stock buying at Haloid during the fifties was done by people in sales and marketing, who became convinced fairly early that the machine would profitably fill a thitherto unrecognized commercial and societal need; the scientists and engineers, who truly understood the difficulty of building a functioning office copier, were far less likely to accumulate stock, as were some high-level executives and board members, who were worried that Kodak or IBM might snatch Haloid's market for itself.) Part of Rutledge's job was to help upgrade the company's sales force, which in the late fifties was dominated by slow-moving Rectigraph men, many of whom had been with the company for decades. Those old salesmen, by continuing to push Haloid's photographic papers through the fifties, had "brought in the cash to develop xerography," Rutledge said, but they were generally skeptical of the new technology and couldn't be counted on to be innovative in promoting it.

The new salesmen that Rutledge and his colleagues hired weren't expected to sell 914 leases exclusively. In fact, during the first months of 1960, they were discouraged from selling them at all. The Orchard Street factory was turning out so few units that almost every order was a back order. Rutledge said, "We wanted the guys to sell the stuff we *could* deliver—the photocopy paper, the Ox Box, things like that—so we made the commission contingent on a man's achieving his quotas on those products. After all, that's what paid the rent. So, only if a guy sold 85 percent of his quota in both the paper and the Ox Box would he get a commission for placing a 914—and the monthly commission for placing a 914 was only one dollar, plus maybe a little more if the machine was particularly productive. So that was the way we controlled our salesmen in the early days, and we held to it for a long time."

Once 914 production approached a hundred machines a month, in the second half of 1960, Haloid Xerox began to think more seriously about active selling. This presented a major challenge, however. Xerography was hard to explain to anyone who didn't already know what it was, and the best way to sell machines, therefore, had always been to demonstrate them in person. Doing that was difficult, though, because the 914 was too big and heavy to move around. In 1958, Haloid had promoted another huge machine, Copyflo, with a traveling exhibition called Copyrama. That program, which traveled to eleven cities, had been deemed a success—"Not least of Copyrama's attractions were the exceptionally beautiful young women who supervised the showings," Dessauer wrote later—but the potential market for Copyflo was much smaller than the one Haloid Xerox hoped to build for the 914. The company did hold an ongoing 914 demonstration near the Merrill, Lynch office in Grand Central Terminal, in New York City—with two backup machines for the inevitable mechanical crises—but that program, and similar ones in other cities, had a narrow impact. The company's executives increasingly realized that they were going to have to do something dramatic and expensive, despite the fact that they couldn't really afford to do anything at all. "Our company was unknown, our advertising budget was small," Donald Clark recalled later, in a speech at Harvard Business School. "In fact, our 1960 advertising budget was completely inadequate to enter into a space battle with our major copying competitors. So we decided to limit our campaigns to the business publications and to use only those ads having the unique and fresh approach that we wanted to be characteristic of our project."

The first ad appeared in *Fortune* in September (and in *Business Week* shortly afterward) and was indeed unique: a six-page foldout insert with die-cut openings, which allowed readers to look inside the machine. The ad generated a huge response—not just to the 914 but to the ad itself, which was among the first such inserts ever to run in a magazine. One early 914 advertisement addressed the demonstration issue directly. "A Xerox representative would like to bring a 914 Copier to your office and show it to you," the copy read. "But he can't. The 914 Copier is not a toy; it weighs 648 pounds. That means you'll have to come to *our* offices located in principal U.S. and Canadian cities. (People representing thousands of organizations, from United States Steel to the White House, are glad they made the trip. You will be too.)" Clark later had the idea of affixing an actual (though quite small) Xerox copy to an ad, with a picture of the original underneath.

Many of the earliest 914 print advertisements were memorable, but their impact on sales was less than the company had hoped. Haloid Xerox and its advertising agency soon realized that they needed to tone down some of the claims they had been making for xerography, because people assumed that no machine could make perfectly legible copies on plain paper at the rate of seven per minute. Shortly after one early advertisement ran, the company received an ominous letter from a federal official, who was particularly skeptical about the company's assertion that a 914 could make copies on plain paper—something no other copying machine could do. Linowitz had the official's letter copied onto a paper bag, which was then sent to him without comment.

One of the cleverest ads—which was published in the major business magazines in 1963—challenged readers to tell the difference between a genuine Picasso pen-and-ink drawing of an owl (which someone at the advertising agency had bought in a New York gallery) and, next to it, a Xerox copy of the drawing. "Which is the $2,800 Picasso?" the copy asked. "Which is the 5¢ Xerox 914 copy?" William Hesketh, a Haloid Xerox marketing executive, said later, "It was a great ad, because what they did was take the original and switch the frame: they put the antique frame on the Xerox copy and another frame on the original." Sixteen thousand people responded, with their votes about evenly divided between the two images. (All who responded were mailed the prize that the ad had promised to correct guessers: a Xerox copy of the drawing.) The company later included the two pictures in a travel-

ing xerography exhibition and discovered in St. Louis that the
Haloid Xerox employees traveling with the show had been locking
up the wrong picture each night.

THE MOST SUCCESSFUL OF ALL the 914 marketing efforts were
the ones that enabled people to see the process for themselves, if
only from a distance. Shortly after the print campaigns began, the
company's marketing executives realized that the only way to
reach a truly large audience with a public demonstration would be
through television. This was a depressing thought, because television was more expensive than print advertising, and Haloid Xerox
was already perilously overextended, but there seemed to be no alternative.

The first 914 commercial, which aired in 1961, was created by
Papert, Koenig & Lois, the advertising agency that had created
the print campaigns (and whose thirty-year-old founder, George
Lois, would later make "Think Small" for Volkswagen and "I
Want My MTV" for MTV). The commercial was inspired in part
by Donald Clark's wife, who had made twenty-five rag dolls for
the company's salesmen to use in demonstrating 914s. (The dolls
fit easily under the platen's flexible rubber cover and reproduced
clearly, and potential customers were amazed to see that the machine could copy a three-dimensional object.) The commercial
begins with an exterior shot of a tall office building in a big city,
then cuts to a businessman sitting behind a desk in an abstractly
stylized office.

"Debbie, will you please go make a copy of this?" the man asks
a little girl.

"O.K., Daddy," she says.

"That's my secretary."

Debbie goes skipping off to the 914, which, standing alone

against a plain white background, looks large but not much more intimidating than a washing machine. The control panel, mounted above the broad desktop, has just four moving parts: a dial for selecting up to fifteen copies, a PRINT button, an ON button, and a (red) button with no label, for turning the machine off. Debbie raises the thick rubber flap covering the platen, places her father's letter facedown on the glass, and presses PRINT. A man's voice explains that the 914 makes a first copy in less than a minute (actually, about fifteen seconds) and seven copies a minute after that.* Debbie waits, removes her copy from the output tray, turns, stops—an idea!—and returns to the machine to make a copy of her rag doll. Then she skips back to her father's office.

"Thank you, Debbie," her father says. "That was fast." Then he looks at the two pieces of paper and asks: "Which is the original?"

Debbie scratches her head. "I forget!"

A modern viewer's first reaction to the Debbie spot is likely to be astonishment that people in the sixties were willing to sit through minute-long television commercials. At the time, though, the main reaction was amazement. An angry competitor demanded proof that Debbie wasn't an adult midget; how could a child operate a high-technology office machine? And was it even a machine? Wasn't there another midget, inside the box, pushing paper through the slot? An official of the Federal Trade Commission traveled to Rochester to investigate. Hesketh recalled later, "We said to him, 'Look, we'll show you a picture of our machine and we'll tell you how to operate it. Then you go to the machine and make a copy yourself. If you can do that, will you then believe the 914 is simple to operate?' He thought that would be pretty good

---

*Copier marketing hasn't changed in centuries. Advertisements for James Watt's copying press in the late 1700s claimed that "any person may take an exact copy of a letter or other sheet of paper, written with common ink, in a minute or less."

evidence. So he did it, and we got a clean bill of health. He even interviewed the little girl and her mother."

The Debbie commercial was a hit with customers, and sales rose sharply. A few months later, the agency made a humorous sequel: a scene-by-scene reshoot of the original, but with Debbie's role filled by a trained chimpanzee (whose professed inability, in the final scene, to distinguish the copy from the original was arguably more convincing than Debbie's had been). The FTC monitored the shoot and certified that the chimp—whose name was Skippy but who was called "Sam" in the spot—really did make copies by himself. This time, though, the reaction from viewers was negative. Key operators all over America arrived at work the next day and found bananas on their desks, then had to deal with coworkers who scratched their armpits and made ape sounds when they wanted something copied. The salesmen were horrified. They worried that secretaries would feel humiliated and would stop performing the complex maintenance on which the machines depended, and they demanded that the spot be withdrawn immediately. And it was. "I was sorry," Hesketh said later, because it was a funny commercial. "Don Clark and I even had lunch with the chimp in New York. He ate with a spoon, drank from a glass. We had a lot of fun. Too bad about those bananas." Nevertheless, sales continued to rise. The ten thousandth 914 shipped in late 1962.

Several early Xerox spots remain among the more memorable commercials from a decade notable for clever advertising. One involved a football game being played in pouring rain. Time is running out. The coach of the trailing team scrawls a desperation play on a piece of paper and sends it to the huddle with a player from the bench—who detours through the locker room to make eleven copies. The quarterback sticks his rain-soaked copy to the center's rear end, then reads from it as he calls the signals. The wide receiver carries his copy downfield, consults the diagram, takes a step toward the sideline, looks up, and catches the game-winning touchdown pass. The early commercials ran on *CBS Reports*, NBC documentary specials, and other sophisticated programs, and the company—which in 1961 joyously embraced the success of the 914 by changing its name to Xerox Corporation*—acquired a useful public image as a thoughtful, intelligent, and witty manufacturer of complex machines. "We found out that the people we wanted to talk to were the ones who watched those shows," Clark said later. "After a while, we became known as the company that did really good television shows: well produced, and on subjects that were somewhat controversial. This helped us a great deal—it opened the door for our salesmen."

WITHIN A SHORT TIME, Xerox salesmen needed very little door opening: customers happily came to them. The 914, for all its flaws, was a major commercial success. "I think it was the forerunner of making graphic communications possible," McColough told Gary Jacobson, a reporter for the *Rochester Times-Union*, in an interview more than twenty years later. "It broke through that big logjam. It allowed people to share information inexpensively and easily. The 914 killed carbon paper. And that was good because carbon paper was inefficient."

The 914 didn't really kill carbon paper (although another xerographic machine, the laser printer, eventually did). But the 914 nevertheless transformed the way businesses operated. "The thing that surprised all of us on the 914 and gave us a lot more volume was what happened in making copies of copies," McColough con-

---

*Xerox Corporation's stock was first listed on the New York Stock Exchange on July 11, 1961, under the ticker symbol XRX. Seventy-seven hundred shares traded that day, at an average price per share of a little over $100.

tinued. "No one anticipated that." In 1959, as the 914 was nearing production, Wilson had speculated that the machine might enable Haloid Xerox to double its annual revenues by 1965. The doubling did come, but four years ahead of schedule, and actual sales in 1965 amounted to six times Wilson's prediction, or nearly $400 million. The next year, revenues reached $500 million, and two years later, $1 billion.

In 1959, Haloid Xerox was nothing—a small manufacturer of photographic paper, a maker of equipment that produced economical masters for offset lithographic printing presses, one of the dozen or so largest companies in Rochester, New York. Seven years later, Xerox Corporation was the fifteenth largest publicly owned corporation in America as ranked by market capitalization; it was bigger than RCA, bigger than Bell & Howell, bigger than Chrysler, bigger than U.S. Steel, gaining ground on IBM. Back in the fifties, Haloid Xerox had instituted a stock option program for top employees, primarily because it didn't have enough cash to pay bonuses; now the program had turned dozens into millionaires. The University of Rochester, whose endowment included a large block of old Haloid shares, found itself one of the richest private universities in the world. A $10,000 investment in Haloid Xerox stock in 1960 was worth $1 million by 1972.

The 914's success quickly became global. In 1955, Haloid had cultivated a relationship with the Rank Organisation, a large British corporation that at the time was involved mainly in the production and distribution of motion pictures. Rank's executives were interested in xerography and were especially interested in Haloid's intention to eventually build a small office copier. In 1957, the two companies signed a joint venture agreement whereby a newly formed Rank subsidiary called Rank Xerox acquired the exclusive right to manufacture and sell Haloid xerographic products outside the United States and Canada. This agreement reflected extraordinary foresight on the part of Rank, because Haloid wasn't much of a partner at the time. Years later, Linowitz recalled a 1956 visit to Rochester by John Davis, Rank's managing director. "He kept saying he wanted to see the Haloid factory," Linowitz wrote, "and he wished our schedule of meetings and entertainments at home, at the Genesee Valley Club, and at the Rochester Club could be relaxed to permit a visit of inspection. Finally, he said with wide eyes, 'You know, I don't believe you *have* a factory'—which was quite true, for almost all the parts that went into [Ox Box, Lith-Master, and Copyflo] were made elsewhere, and merely assembled in unfinished loft space we rented for the purpose."

At first, Rank gained little from its faith in xerography, because paper lithographic masters, the main output of early Xerox machines, were not used in the United Kingdom (although Bob Gundlach soon invented a way to use a Model D to make metal masters—the kind preferred throughout Europe). After the 914 had become an established success, the Rank agreement was renegotiated, and new ventures were established in Japan, Latin America, and elsewhere. "The Japanese were marvelously inventive in selling the 914," Linowitz wrote later. "To prove that it made seven copies a minute, they would make Xerox copies of the customer's watch, showing the second hand advancing."

Two hundred thousand 914s were built, if you count the machines called the 720 and the 1000, which were speeded-up and improved versions of the original. Those two hundred thousand copiers accounted for more than six hundred thousand individual placements, since retired copiers were usually refurbished and sent back into the field. The popularity of those machines made the 914 (according to *Fortune*) "the most successful product ever marketed in America" in terms of the company's return on what had once seemed to many to be a colossally irresponsible investment.

(Xerox continued manufacturing 914s until the early seventies and offered service contracts for them until 1985; more than a few of the machines are still in service around the world.) The 914 was followed as well by other successful machines, including two that had been developed alongside it, in the same labs and engineering facilities: the 813, which was the world's first desktop plain-paper copier and was introduced in 1963, and the 2400, which made 2,400 copies an hour and reached the market the following year. Both of those machines arose from development programs that were in many ways as harrowing as the 914's. All three machines generated vast amounts of cash, which financed the company's blink-of-an-eye expansion into a major corporation. Enormous manufacturing buildings rose on the Webster property. In 1963, a third of all Xerox employees had been hired that year.

At a meeting of the Boston Security Analysts Society, Joe Wilson described the huge gamble taken by his company—"a company with meager financial resources, without much research and engineering competence, with a small, thinly spread sales force, and obviously without specialized plants because xerographic products had not been made before by any man anywhere." He continued, "I must confess that if we had fully foreseen the magnitude of the job, the millions for research and new capital, the marketing complexities, the manufacturing problems involved in making new things work right and reliably all over the world in all temperatures and humidities, we probably would not have had the fortitude to go ahead."

What's remarkable about Wilson's speech is that he made it not in 1961, after his company had become an astounding success, but in 1958, when the biggest gamble, the decision to build the 914, still lay ahead. As he spoke, he knew that many at Haloid Xerox still believed the company shouldn't try to build an office copier at all but should concentrate instead on producing an automated version of the Ox Box—a streamlined unit that would create litho-graphic masters faster and more economically and thereby consol-idate the company's domination of a steadily profitable market. Wilson had already succeeded in giving his company an identity and purpose independent of Eastman Kodak's, and he had in-creased Haloid's revenues far beyond what they had been during his father's tenure as chief executive. He could have stopped there and been considered a notably successful corporate executive, and he could have enjoyed the final years of his business career with plenty of money, relatively little personal stress, and lots of time for golf.

Instead, having gambled his company's future once and not been wiped out, he was about to gamble it again. He believed now that his early hesitation to plunge into development of a desktop copier—the typewriter-size machine that IBM had wanted a few years before—had been not only prudent but shrewd. Late in 1953, Carlson, near the low point of his regard for Haloid and Battelle, had written to Wilson to express his unhappiness that the company had produced no device to compete with Thermo-Fax and Verifax, which had just reached the market. Wilson replied (in a letter quoted by Linowitz), "When you say we missed the boat completely, I, of course, believe the opposite. I believe that if we had taken the wrong boat two years ago we would be infinitely worse off now. Now we know what the real competition is. Let's assume it's Thermo-Fax and Verifax. They have shot their wad. . . . Now we know what we have to do. Either we can beat these processes inherently or we cannot."

Carlson and Wilson were useful foils to each other: Haloid's ultimately profitable path through the fifties was partly a product of the tension between their conceptions of the pace at which xe-rography ought to be developed. They agreed more than they disagreed, though, and Wilson could have been speaking for both of them in 1958, when he described to the Boston Security Analysts Society the ultimate source of his interest in Carlson's invention: "The mark of man, the characteristic which distinguishes him most from the beasts, is his ability to communicate with his fellows in the present, and through time by means of recorded history. We build on the treasures of others' minds, present and past. Intellects of other centuries and from other lands contribute to our progress now because we can make use of their ideas; work and thought are not lost when they are recorded."

12

To Die a Poor Man

CHESTER CARLSON BEGAN EARNING ROYALTIES from his invention in 1947, when Battelle sent him a check for $2,500—his share of Haloid's $10,000 initial investment in xerographic research. He was forty-one years old. Four years later, in 1951, Carlson's payments from Battelle amounted to about $15,000, a level at which he and Dorris needed no other income to support their markedly modest lifestyle—their house was small, and they had no children and no extravagant hobbies—although Carlson continued to put in regular hours at Haloid until 1955, and he remained a consultant to the company until he died, in 1968. In 1953, he traded his old Studebaker for a new one. He also bought a six-acre lot southeast of Rochester, in what was then sparsely developed exurban countryside, and built a larger but still unpretentious house—a typical postwar American three-bedroom home, in which he and Dorris lived for the rest of their lives. (Later, he bought an adjoining thirteen-acre parcel, which he allowed neighborhood children to treat as a playground and which was later given to the city for the same purpose.) In 1956, when Haloid purchased Battelle's interest in xerography, Carlson became a very wealthy man, since 40 percent of the stock and cash that Battelle received as a result of that transaction went to him. He distributed roughly a quarter of these payments to the thirteen members of his Electrophotography Participation Fund—the relatives who in 1948 had helped him buy back his original royalty rate from Battelle. He continued to receive royalties for nearly a decade; they amounted to something like a sixteenth of a cent for every Xerox copy made, worldwide, through 1965. In 1968, *Fortune* included him in a list of the wealthiest people in America, and he sent the magazine a terse correction: "Your estimate of my net worth is too high by $150 million. I belong in the 0 to $50 million bracket." The main reason for the discrepancy was that for more than a decade Carlson had been deeply but quietly involved in what might be considered the second great undertaking of his life: giving his fortune away. His one remaining ambition, he had told his wife on several occasions, was "to die a poor man."

Carlson may be unique in the history of high-technology multimillionairedom in that his becoming extraordinarily rich had little impact on the material circumstances of his life. He wore Hickey-Freeman suits, and he enjoyed nice restaurants, and he liked to buy gifts for other people, but he didn't pamper or indulge himself. "His real wealth seemed to be composed of the number of things he could easily do without," Dorris said after his death. People who knew him casually seldom suspected that he was rich or even well-to-do; when one acquaintance asked him what he did for a living and he said he worked at Xerox, the acquaintance assumed he was a factory worker and asked if he belonged to a union. Carlson never bought a second home or a second car, and he and Dorris didn't own a television set until shortly before he died. He told Dorris, who loved good clothes, that she must always buy what she wanted without looking at the price tag, but he seldom spent large sums on himself, and Dorris had to urge him not to buy third-class train tickets when he traveled in Europe. The Carlsons later added a fourth bedroom and a sitting room to their house, to give them more privacy when they had house-guests, but Carlson felt the addition was unnecessary, and he told Dorris that he could be just as happy, or perhaps happier, living in a trailer in the yard. "I think he felt guilty about having a nice, comfortable house," she said later, "and when people would come in and say, 'Oh, this is lovely,' he would say, 'Dorris planned it all.' " She was never certain how truly serious he was about his trailer, but he mentioned it frequently, and she would tease him when he did: "And will you take your thirteen steel filing cabinets with you?"

Despite Carlson's unease with affluence, he loved his house and the large yard behind it. In the summer of 1928, shortly after graduating from Riverside Junior College, he had sketched in his notebook a plan for an idealized country estate—the kind of place he dreamed of building for himself someday. The plan was rectangular, and it encompassed "about 10 or 15 acres." There was an "English Farmhouse," a barn, a lodge, a caretaker's house, a pond for fishing, two orchards, a grove of nut trees, a corral, a "hilly pasture," and areas for chickens and livestock. A low stone wall separated the main yard from one of the orchards, and Carlson made a detailed drawing of the wall's (quite odd) design, which included "white rock *slabs*, granite boulders, and red bricks" held together with "black mortar." His actual estate was far less opulent—if you walked down his old street today, in the Rochester suburb of Pittsford, you would never pick out the house as the residence of a wealthy man—but it embodied a similar yearning for rural tranquillity. The house was built on the side of a slope, so that the basement, where his office was situated, opened into the yard.* He liked to garden, to teach tricks to his cocker spaniel, to walk along the creek at the bottom of the hill, to sit among the trees in a spot that Dorris referred to as his "hideaway," and, occasionally, to fly a kite. He was quiet and observant, and he had what Dorris and others viewed as a preternatural relationship with other living things. He once reported to Dorris that he had spent the morning in "a flirtation with a butterfly," which had settled on his jacket while he was reading his mail in the yard and had accompanied him for two or three hours as he worked in the garden. When a friend noticed a bee on his arm and told him to stand still so that he could swat it before it stung him, Carlson said not to worry, the bee wouldn't sting, and then picked it up with his fingers and released it. Two friends once pointed out that the tulips in his garden were being eaten by rabbits, and he said, "Yes, they are. The ladies"—Dorris and the housekeeper—"are quite upset about this, but I am on the side of the rabbits."

When it became clear that xerography would be a commercial triumph, Carlson felt exuberant, even vindicated. Dorris asked him later if he had known that his invention would be as big a success as it had turned out to be, and he said that he had, although there had been times when he had come close to giving up hope that anyone would actually manufacture it. After some early euphoria, though, Carlson became uneasy. The great ordeal of his life had culminated in almost unimaginable success, and he didn't know what to do next. He was too young to retire. Dorris watched

---

*In 1932, when he thought that literature might be a possible career, he wrote a poem about houses built on hills: "Some houses perch on hilly rise / And rear their walls against the skies / A house ahill should haughty brood, / In self-sufficient solitude, / Or with a regal, breezy flair, / Proclaim itself the king of air."

him moping and worried that he had become disenchanted with her. Finally, she insisted that he tell her what was wrong—something she knew he would never do without firm prompting. He said, "I feel that I'm no longer productive." As a young man, he had sustained himself in an often miserable existence by dreaming of the life he would lead once he had become a rich inventor; now he was a rich inventor, and he had no secondary aspiration. He told his old assistant Hal Bogdonoff, "It came too late, the struggle, the race to achieve success of some sort. By the time the rewards and the recognition came—gee, I haven't time to do all the things I've wanted to do all along."

Time wasn't really the issue; he was just fifty years old. But the personal qualities that had contributed to his professional success—his persistence, his imperviousness to repeated rejection, his emotional self-reliance, his tolerance for solitude, his independence of mind—now combined to prevent him from exploiting his sudden wealth with anything like conventional abandon. If he had been the type of person who could run out and impulsively buy himself an airplane or a yacht or a Van Gogh, he would not also have been the type of person who could endure decades of sustained disappointment—and it was inconceivable that he would be transformed now. In 1958, in a letter to his cousin Roy, he wrote, "I feel somewhat at loose ends at present and uncertain as to just how I should spend my time. As a result I haven't been spending it very efficiently or productively. Still I am not the kind of person to enjoy going out golfing or fishing, or even partying. With a rather fabulous amount of money at my disposal one would think I could find hundreds of things to do and would have the means to carry them out—but right now I feel at sort of a stalemate. I hope it is only a temporarily dry period between periods of purposeful activity." He soon realized, with some reluctance, that his next purposeful activity would most likely be giving his fortune away. In the end, he came to terms with his wealth by systematically divesting himself of most of it.

Carlson's philanthropy during the final decade of his life was personal, eclectic, and prodigious. It was also entirely anonymous. When he gave the money to build a building, he did not permit his name to be engraved in stone above the door or even to be revealed publicly. In the mid-1960s, for example, he gave Caltech the money for a center for the study of chemical physics, his field of concentration, but stipulated that the building be named for Alfred Amos Noyes, the professor whose teaching had influenced him the most. (The few buildings that do bear Carlson's name were built after his death.) Absolute anonymity was a condition of almost all his gifts. He quietly paid off the mortgages of impoverished old ladies. He made large contributions to organizations that promoted world peace. He supported numerous civil rights organizations, and he bought apartment buildings in Washington, D.C., and New York City so that the buildings could be racially integrated. He gave millions to the United Negro College Fund, and he made direct contributions to individual black colleges. He (and his will) provided most of the funding during the sixties and seventies for the Robert Maynard Hutchins Center for the Study of Democratic Institutions. He supported the Fellowship of Reconciliation and other pacifist organizations. He gave money to schools, hospitals, libraries, and international relief agencies. The list of his beneficiaries was long, and he himself weighed every request.

In 1960, as the success of the 914 was becoming a major business news story, Carlson received a letter from Otto Kornei, his old Astoria lab assistant, who had helped him make the first xerographic print in 1938. The two men had sporadically but cordially kept up with each other over the years. In 1956, Carlson had taken Kornei and his wife out to dinner during a visit to Cleveland, and he had surprised and delighted Kornei by giving him a hundred Haloid shares (a gift that, if Kornei held on to it, would have been worth more than $22,000 by the date of his 1960 letter and more than $1 million by 1972). At that dinner, Kornei told Carlson that he was planning to leave his job at Brush Manufacturing, where he had worked since 1939. Carlson offered to help him get a job at Haloid if he wanted one, and Kornei listed Carlson as a reference when he applied for the job he ultimately took, at IBM. "It will certainly interest you that the people at IBM were much pleased to learn of my early and close association with Xerography," Kornei wrote in 1956. "You can be sure that I will try to promote this field further in its application to the special needs of my new employer."

The tone of Kornei's 1960 letter was sharply different. In it he accused Carlson of perpetrating what he described as "a phantastic injustice" and thereby cheating him out of a fortune: "Today, I cannot help but being bitter about the part I played in the development of Xerography. I feel like the man who has plowed rough ground and seeded it and has received but a minute share in the harvest. Since the harvest has turned out to be a spectacular bumpercrop I have been reproaching myself even more for having deprived my wife, my son and myself of financial means which I forfeited so readily, 'just to be nice.' "

Carlson was stunned. Nothing between the two men had changed since 1956—or, for that matter, since 1939—except that xerography, to Kornei's surprise, had become a commercial success. Kornei had voluntarily left Carlson's employment after six months because he felt the idea had no future, and when the two men dissolved their agreement later that year, each had believed that doing so was personally advantageous: Kornei had wanted to develop his electron-scanning invention by himself, and Carlson was hoping to sell electrophotography to a major manufacturer and wanted his claim on it to be unencumbered. (See chapter 4.) That Kornei had never followed up on his own idea or sought a patent for it was not Carlson's fault. (RCA and others later made a commercial success of a similar idea.) Kornei's emotional distress was understandable, of course; twenty years earlier, he had walked away from what had now turned out to be extraordinary wealth. But Carlson had never betrayed or deceived him.

Carlson responded that he was astonished by Kornei's letter and asked, "Why have you never raised the subject before in the 21 years since you left me in New York?" He then made a calm, exhaustive explanation of why he felt he had already been more than generous—an explanation that included a characteristically lucid mathematical comparison of Kornei's involvement in xerography (six months of part-time work) and Carlson's own (thirteen years, thirty-two patented inventions, and $20,000 of his own money) and assigned proportional cash values to each. Kornei's lengthy response, a few weeks later, was less emotionally fraught than his original letter had been but was equally aggrieved. "I believe it cannot be hard to understand," he wrote, "why I feel bitter and disappointed: because I acted like a friend—and you like a businessman." Carlson, after being advised by a lawyer that he needn't do anything at all, responded with two curt sentences: "I have your letter of July 25. Specifically what is it that you want?" Kornei asked for six hundred additional shares of Haloid Xerox stock; Carlson sent him five hundred (along with a detailed explanation of why six hundred shares would have exceeded the promised payout in the agreement that Kornei had forsaken in 1939).

Kornei was overjoyed. He responded, "If I were Diogenes, the Greek philosopher who carried around a lantern to search for an honest man I could now blow out the candle—because I found the man." Carlson never spoke ill of Kornei and, in fact, continued to go out of his way to give Kornei credit when he recounted the early history of his invention, but the entire exchange, including the comparison to Diogenes, must have upset him deeply: he had been an honest man all along.

At least Kornei had a plausible claim on Carlson's generosity; hundreds of other supplicants wrote to him simply because they had read in the newspaper that he was rich. ("A French lady has also written me trying to interest me in a portable shower bath," he noted in a letter to his cousin Roy in 1966. "I'm not sure whether she will demonstrate it *in person.*") Dorris urged him to hire a staff, or at any rate an assistant, to screen his correspondence, but he insisted on reading all the solicitations himself and making his own decisions; he explained that other people would have no reason to be careful with the money. "I think it was a form of suffering, really, for him and me," Dorris said. "But he considered it a trust." He seldom sought even his wife's advice. In a speech she made at a hospital dedication after his death, she said, "Only once in a very great while would he ask my opinion about a particular cause, a particular donation he wanted to make, a large one, a gift to an organization or an individual. So one day I said to him—you see, it was a very rare occasion he even let me know what he was giving, as I wasn't interested—but when he did ask me I said, 'Chet, you realize, of course, that you ask me only about those causes which you *know* I am in agreement with you about.' He laughed heartily. I should say, he chuckled."

Both Carlsons also made substantial contributions to spiritual and parapsychological groups that were of particular interest to Dorris—some of which had become important to him as well. Dorris had always had a powerful mystical side, which had never been fully engaged by any organized religion. She meditated, studied Eastern philosophers, and pursued her own, idiosyncratic inclinations, with increasing participation from him. "The spiritual life is the only thing I'm interested in, really," she said in her seventies. "I am not interested in anything else. The rest I do because I have to do it." She had believed since childhood that she possessed psychic and other paranormal powers. Carlson was skeptical, she felt, but he helped her test her abilities, and she believed that he was psychic, too. ("Many scientists are, you know," she said once.) He would make simple drawings and seal them in envelopes before going to work, and after he had left the house Dorris would attempt to visualize what he had drawn. "I would lie down with a box of these drawings beside me," she explained, "and after exercising a certain discipline of the mind, I would reach out and with eyes closed take an envelope, hold it in my hand, and demand an answer from myself as to what it was." Her rate of success, she reported, was high. She also often had premonitions and other visions, and she believed that when she was asleep she frequently left what she called her "physical body."

It is impossible to say exactly what Carlson felt about the more eccentric of his wife's beliefs—Dorris herself was never certain what he thought—but he did not dismiss them, and he treated some of them, including psychic phenomena, as subjects worthy of scientific investigation. In 1965, he visited a "dream laboratory" at a hospital in Brooklyn, where experimenters were trying to determine whether the content of subjects' dreams could be influenced by telepathic suggestion. "I was the subject one night and the results were quite interesting," he wrote in a letter to Roy. "Both I and the two experimenters picked the same painting print as most closely matching my dreams. When the [telepathic 'sender'] came in it turned out that she had been looking at that one, chosen from a dozen others."

He also increasingly shared his wife's interest in spirituality and in the ancient Hindu texts known as the Vedanta, or the Upanishads, and in Zen Buddhism. He had devoted much thought throughout his life to human suffering, both as a fact and as an ontological issue, and he took deep personal comfort in meditation and quiet contemplation—activities that complemented his solitary outlook and his preference for modesty and simplicity. Once, upon returning from a Buddhist retreat he had attended by himself, he felt so happy and so emotionally rejuvenated that he picked up Dorris and swung her around—a gesture that was at odds with his normally placid demeanor and with his spinal arthritis, which prevented him from dancing and had given him a permanent stoop. Dorris was astonished, and so was the housekeeper, who gasped, "Oh, Mr. Carlson!"

Carlson's spiritual explorations enabled him, in the last decade of his life, to come to terms with the extraordinary difficulties and disappointments he had endured as a child and as a young man. In a 1959 letter to his old roommate Larry Dumond, who was enduring a variety of vexing personal problems, he wrote, "During the past few years, my concept of myself, the world, science, and human life has been greatly altered from what it was when we used to see each other more frequently. I do not think I have many answers, and surely I have no cut-and-dried formula, but I do see that some of the sufferings that I went through, and that my parents went through, were blessings in disguise which have enriched and deepened my life and have finally provided a philosophy which is a raincoat in time of difficulty."

Later in the same letter, Carlson summarized that philosophy: "Continue to do your best to do what seems to be the right thing, but when it comes to things beyond your control leave everything to God, or providence, or whatever name you choose to call the supreme power of the universe. Have absolute faith and trust that he will take care of everything. He knows what is best. When you leave home in the morning, do not feel uneasy. Try to have absolute faith that he is taking charge, and erase from your mind the slightest feeling of anxiety in any situation which is beyond your control. If possible, while riding in a bus, close your eyes for a few minutes and strive for absolute calmness, then think 'Thy will be done' and mean it completely and absolutely. Accept the premise that he is running things and that he knows much better what is right for each of us than we do. I have known of cases where, seemingly, miracles have taken place when a person surrenders himself completely. But that is of less importance than its internal effect on you. You will have a new sense of security and independence which nothing can break. Eventually your inner calmness and power will radiate to others and they will reflect it back."

IN GIVING AWAY HIS MONEY, Carlson was minutely attentive to detail, keeping comprehensive records of every transaction and personally filing all his correspondence. This meticulousness had been a part of his character for most of his life, and it was evident in nearly everything he did. In the front of his pocket calendar for 1949, for example, he recorded not only his name, address, and telephone number, but also his hat size (7 ⅜), sleeve length (33 inches), shoe size (9 ½), watch make (Elgin), and the weight of his car (2,995 pounds), among other personal details. Whenever he bought gasoline he recorded the date, the car's mileage, the location, and the cost. For thirteen years he kept track of his and Dorris's weight ("in pajamas"), and he made a note when, in 1960, he bought a new scale. Throughout his life, he took genuine pleasure from fussy activities that most people dread. Dorris recalled, "Invariably on New Year's Day, immediately after breakfast, he would say with a certain kind of smile on his face, 'Well, now today I begin the income tax.' I don't think he failed to do this a single time in the years that we were together, unless it was the times we were down with my mother and family on New Year's Day and away from home." Carlson would go into his office and begin pulling his records together. "He didn't seem to resent having to do this at all. I notice so many people get rather disturbed at tax time, but he always said it with a smile, as if to say, 'Well, here's a challenge'— almost as if he were going to enjoy it." That had been his mother's attitude concerning the many profound difficulties in her life, and it was also his.

Carlson was equally methodical about travel. Before leaving home, he would type a list of everything he intended to take and would note the weights of the heavier items (his wool slacks weighed a pound and a half, as did his pajamas). His lists were single spaced in two columns and, including handwritten addenda, typically ran more than a page. He was dazzlingly thorough; among the enumerated items for a 1960 trip to Europe were "2 keys for each bag," "toothbrush, toothpaste," "socks 7 pr," and "map of Europe." (He originally listed "tie clasp" under "Miscellaneous" but later moved it to "Wear.") He noted on a later list that his Tally-Ho garment bag, when empty except for its four hangers, weighed ten pounds with its stiffeners installed and nine and a half pounds without.

Much of the traveling that Carlson did was Xerox related. He almost always accepted invitations to participate in corporate events or to make public speeches about xerography—not because he wanted to promote himself or glorify his accomplishments, but because he found it difficult to turn down sincere requests from anyone. Among the few requests he did turn down were offers of awards and honorary university degrees; friends of his sometimes had to pick up a medal or citation he'd been given at ceremonies he had decided not to attend. People who knew him only from the office or from private encounters were often surprised to discover, when they heard him lecture, that he was a funny, natural, and effective public speaker. (In a talk to the Society of Professional Scientists and Engineers in 1964, he said, "Right now I feel something like the English peer who dreamed that he was addressing the House of Lords and woke up and found that he was. I can hardly wait to hear what I will have to say.") In 1958, his cousin Roy accompanied him on a Xerox-sponsored European trip, which included a stop at the World's Fair, in Brussels. Rank Xerox had a booth at the fair, and when the two men stopped to see it a young salesman was describing the history of xerography and the unusual life of its inventor. Dorris, recounting what Roy told her later, said, "In Chet's usual manner he stood listening carefully, and he would nod his head every now and then in appreciation, as though he were hearing it for the first time. When the man had finished his story, Chet said thank you and they walked away." Roy later told his cousin that in similar circumstances he would have spoken up and identified himself as the inventor, and that doing so would have pleased the salesman, who presumably would have been happy to meet the great man whose life story he had just recounted. Carlson replied, "He might have been happy for a little while, but it was his story and his show, and I would have been taking the light away from him and putting it on myself." When Roy repeated this story later, in Madrid, to some representatives of another European office equipment company, they remarked that Carlson's modesty was even more impressive than his invention.

Dorris was not an enthusiastic traveler, and she almost never accompanied her husband when he went on long trips or left the country. Without her he took several trips to Europe and visited India, the Soviet Union, and Alaska. Together they traveled to the Thousand Islands region along the St. Lawrence River, went on a cruise, and took a car trip to California (in their Studebaker). During the California trip, Carlson, among other things, went camping with his old Riverside Junior College mentor, Professor Bliss, and visited two of the houses where he and his father had lived number of unexpected household improvements. He had always insisted that automatic garage door openers were frivolous, but now he had one installed. He had the furnace replaced, and the men who took away the old one told Dorris that it was in perfect condition and nearly as clean as if it had never been used. For a long time Dorris had believed that the two guest bedrooms, which were upstairs, were too hot in the summer and that reroofing the house with white singles might make them cooler; Carlson had objected to the idea of replacing a serviceable roof, but now, without saying anything about it, he had the house reshingled in white. Dorris didn't connect these modifications as they occurred, but she realized later that her husband had been preparing, with customary thoughtfulness, for the event that she preferred to refer to as "leaving his physical body." He also accelerated the pace at which he gave away possessions and discarded old papers—a regular chore of his for several years, and one that he noted on his desk calendar and asked his secretary at Xerox to remind him to perform.

Although Dorris knew that her husband had suffered a heart attack, she never knew how poor his health truly was. He kept the diagnosis to himself and asked his doctor to do the same. When he visited his cardiac specialist at Strong Memorial Hospital in Rochester, he sometimes had an assistant drive him, and when she asked him how the appointment had gone, he said, "Oh, fine. Everything is getting along very well." In fact, he was gravely ill; at the end of his life, he was taking five medications related to his condition: Atromid-S, Cardilate, nitroglycerin, Peritrate, and Questran. He smoked, though not heavily, and got little real exercise, although for a time, on his doctor's advice, he did walk a mile a day. He did the walking in his yard, by making ten round trips between a certain fir tree and a forsythia bush, whose separation, 270 feet, he had measured. (He also measured, and recorded in one of his notebooks, the average length of his stride: twenty-six inches). Despite this regimen, he looked considerably older than his age, became tired after almost any physical exertion, and suffered chest pains.

In September 1968, the Carlsons traveled to New York City—mostly on Xerox business, but also simply to spend some time in the city where they had met. After lunch one day, Dorris and a friend left Carlson in the restaurant to pay the check while they walked to a nearby jewelry store to look at something the friend was thinking of buying for his wife. Dorris got back to their hotel, the Sherry-Netherland, before her husband did. As she stood by the front door waiting for him, she saw him cross Fifth Avenue toward Central Park, buy a balloon from a vendor near one of the entrances, and take the balloon into the park. She waited for him a while, then went up to their room alone. When he returned she asked him where he had been. He said, "I thought I would go into the park a moment," then added, "I bought a balloon, and I set it free, and I watched it for as long as I could see it. It went so high it went over the skyscrapers and disappeared." As he said this, Dorris recalled, he "had a beautiful smile on his face."

Dorris felt later that he must have had a comforting premonition of his own death—which came two days later, on September 19, during the same trip to New York. He was sixty-two years old. He attended business meetings during the morning, then had several hours to fill before he was due to meet Dorris again, late in the afternoon. He went to the Festival Theatre, on West 57th Street, to see a two-year-old British comedy called *He Who Rides a Tiger*, starring Tom Bell and Judi Dench, and when the lights came up at the end of the film, the usher who found him slumped in his seat assumed that he was asleep.

Dorris arranged a small, informal service in New York City; it was attended by just half a dozen people, among them the physicist Fred Schwertz, who no longer worked at Xerox but had always been fond of Carlson and had asked to be present. A few days later, in Rochester, Carlson's ashes were buried during another very private, simple ceremony. Dorris said, "He tiptoed into life and tiptoed out again."

A much larger memorial service was held on September 26, in the auditorium at Xerox headquarters in downtown Rochester. Among the speakers were Joseph Wilson, who said that Carlson had "demonstrated to all of us that the great ideas are those of the individual, no matter how strong an organization may be," and John Dessauer, who ranked Carlson as an inventor with Thomas Edison and Alexander Graham Bell. Wilson also read condolence notes from others, among them U Thant, the secretary-general of the United Nations, who had been a friend of Carlson's and a particular admirer of his generosity in behalf of world peace. Thant later amplified his expression of grief: "To know Chester Carlson was to like him, to love him, and to respect him. He was generally known as the inventor of xerography, and although it was an extraordinary achievement in the technological and scientific field, I respected him more as a man of exceptional moral stature and as a humanist. His concern for the future of the human situation was genuine, and his dedication to the principles of the United Nations was profound. He belonged to that rare breed of leaders who generate in our hearts faith in man and hope for the future."

JOSEPH WILSON HIMSELF DIED just three years later, at the age of sixty-one, also of a heart attack. He was attending a small luncheon in the Manhattan apartment of Nelson and Happy Rockefeller, and he died at the table. Wilson had stepped down as the chief executive officer of Xerox Corporation five years before, after suffering his second heart attack, but his death nevertheless marked an ominous transition at the company—a company he had created almost through the power of his will. Peter McColough, who had taken his place as the CEO in 1966, now took his place as the chairman of the board, and a former Ford Motor Co. executive named Archie McCardell, who had joined Xerox in 1968, became the president. This change had actually been planned shortly before Wilson died—McColough and Wilson had discussed it a few days earlier—but it was portentous nevertheless. McCardell's ascendance definitively ended what might be thought of as the 914 era at Xerox; it represented the final snipping of Haloid DNA from the company's genome.

In the mid-1990s, a high-technology multimillionaire I interviewed told me that he thought the major American automobile manufacturers could be tried for actual treason. His indictment was broad: decades-long scorn for public safety, complicity in the heedless destruction of natural resources, premeditated poisoning of the population with lead, shoddy manufacturing, willful deceit, inculcation of wretched labor relations, remorselessly excessive compensation of executives, even (by way of Robert McNamara, who was the president of Ford before he became John F. Kennedy's secretary of defense) the war in Vietnam. In the past couple of decades, a good way to develop a reputation as an enlightened corporate leader has been to undo anything that looked like something a big American car company might have done.

McCardell was the archetype of the benighted American automobile executive, and his tenure at Xerox, which lasted until 1977, is almost universally viewed as a dark period in the company's history. He filled Xerox's executive offices with other hubristic Ford men, brought the company's relations with labor unions to a low point, and in almost every conceivable way did what he could to turn Xerox into a car company that made copiers. Xerox's troubles after the early boom years weren't all McCardell's doing, by any means. In fact, the infatuation with Ford men originated with Mc-

Colough, who also had a fetishistic regard for MBAs and PhDs, and who permanently bifurcated the company in 1969 by moving its corporate headquarters from Rochester to Stamford, Connecticut, while leaving the labs and factories in Webster. But McCardell personified the company's troubles. And after six years as president, he left Xerox to become the head of International Harvester, where he instigated a similar series of management disasters, including a ruinous five-month strike, and, in just five years, led a profitable corporation to the brink of bankruptcy. When International Harvester's board finally forced him out, in 1983, an old nemesis of his at Xerox threw a celebratory party that had to be broken up by the police.

Xerox's corporate history since the introduction of the 914 has been tortuous,* and the company's ups and downs have been the subject of numerous magazine articles, books, business school case studies, and doctoral dissertations. In the sixties and seventies, the company's leaders became convinced that Xerox was dangerously dependent on xerography, which they (along with most business pundits at the time) feared might become obsolete at any moment. With a pile of cash that seemed virtually inexhaustible, those leaders found many interesting ways to make huge, unproductive investments. As is now well-known, the personal computer, the laser printer, the computer mouse, the graphical user interface, and the corporate computer network were all either invented or nearly invented by Xerox researchers (mostly at the company's Palo Alto Research Center, in California) but were never developed into serious commercial products by Xerox itself. The company's efforts were not for nothing—at this very moment, I am using a personal computer, a laser printer, a mouse, a graphical user interface, and a

---

*A $10,000 investment in Xerox stock in 1960 was worth $1 million by 1972; a million investment in Xerox stock in 1972 was worth less than $500,000 by 2001.

computer network—but they didn't do Xerox much good. In addition, beginning in the early seventies, the company's dominance of the copying market was tested many times, not least in three major lawsuits. First, Xerox sued IBM for patent infringement; then, in 1972, the Federal Trade Commission sued Xerox for violating antitrust laws; finally, in 1973, SCM Corporation, which had turned down several opportunities to develop xerography itself, sued Xerox for keeping it out of the copying business. All these suits dragged on for years, in part because the invention of xerography had made it possible for lawyers to turn pretrial discovery into an open-ended orgy of photocopying. Xerox prevailed in the IBM and SCM cases, but in a 1975 settlement with the FTC it agreed to give licenses to its competitors. In the early eighties, Xerox abandoned the historically unprofitable small copier market to the Japanese, who then not only figured out how to make the market profitable but also used small copiers to learn how to build big copiers, which they subsequently threw back at Xerox. Shortly afterward, Xerox regrouped and rededicated itself under the leadership of CEO David Kearns, and made Rochester, in the mid-1980s, one of the few American cities with a positive balance of trade. The current chief executive, Anne Mulcahy, is widely viewed by old-timers at the company as Joe Wilson's true heir.

Management consultants, business school professors, and business writers love Xerox because the company's experience can be used to support almost any observation they care to make about the business world. For example, the well-known business writer Jack Trout, the author of a popular management guide called *Differentiate or Die*, has written that Xerox's big mistake in the seventies was attempting to do the thing that well-known business writers of that era were constantly telling it to do, which was to move beyond copying. "If you're known for one thing," Trout has argued, "the market will not give you another thing." This seems plausible, as

Science. The SX-70, the most popular Polaroid camera ever sold, was introduced two years after that, in 1970, the year before Joe Wilson died. In 1972, *Fortune* wrote that "the mere production of the SX-70 must already be counted as one of the most remarkable accomplishments in industrial history. The project involved a series of scientific discoveries, inventions, and technological innovations in fields as disparate as chemistry, optics, and electronics." In 1976—the year Xerox reached its settlement with the FTC— Kodak came out with instant cameras called EK4 and EK6, and Polaroid sued for patent infringement, in a landmark case that resulted (a decade later) in Kodak's being ordered to cease all manufacturing and selling of instant cameras and film, and to pay Polaroid damages of more than $900 million. In 1977, Polaroid introduced the OneStep, a streamlined and updated version of the SX-70, and promoted it in a television advertising campaign featuring James Garner and Mariette Hartley—an effective campaign that helped OneStep become the best-selling camera in the United States four years in a row and convinced most TV viewers that Garner and Hartley were married. (When Hartley was pregnant with her second child, in 1978, she sometimes wore a T-shirt that said, THIS IS NOT JAMES GARNER'S BABY.)

And then other technologies overcame it. "One-hour" processing of ordinary film—available in kiosks at shopping malls, at newsstands, in drugstores—turned the OneStep almost into a party trick. Regular prints were cheaper and higher in quality than Polaroid prints, and you could click off more than one in a row, and you could shoot a roll in the morning and have your snapshots in the afternoon. Then digital photography further crippled Edwin Land's invention. Polaroid's revenues increased into the early 1990s, then leveled off and began to decline. On October 12, 2000, Polaroid Corporation filed for Chapter 11 bankruptcy. In 2003, the reorganized company had a little over $750 million in sales, about the same as in 1974.

In 1972, *Life* put Land and his SX-70 on its cover under the headline "A Genius and His Magic Camera." Today, an SX-70 seems almost as obscurely archaic as a copying press. My son bought one on eBay a few years ago because the father of a friend of his had told him he could use it to make long-exposure prints on blueprint paper; later, disappointed, he threw it away. Polaroid sells a popular novelty camera called the i-Zone, which takes instant pictures the size of postage stamps, and it has a significant commercial imaging business. But no one today thinks of Polaroid as the future of photography.

Xerography, in contrast, is still growing. Despite the crises that Xerox Corporation has endured, the number of copies made all over the world on xerographic machines manufactured by Xerox, its predecessors, and its competitors has increased by a significant percentage every year since Carlson and Kornei peeled away that first scrap of waxed paper in Astoria back in 1938. In 1955, five years before the introduction of the 914, the world made about twenty million copies, almost all of them by nonxerographic means; in 1965, five years after the introduction of the 914, it made nine and a half billion, almost all xerographically. Five hundred and fifty billion in 1984. Seven hundred billion in 1985. More than two trillion in 2004. Add another trillion or two for the output of laser printers and you end up with something like five hundred xerographically produced pages *this year* for every human on earth. The world now produces more xerographic pages every day than it did in all of 1963, the year when the staggeringly successful 914 was joined by the hugely popular 813.

Worldwide growth in copy volume has been made possible by major advances in xerographic technology—an impressive fact when you consider that more than a few scientists who looked into the process in the fifties doubted that it could be made to work at all. The first full-color xerographic copier, the Xerox 6500, was introduced in 1973. The Xerox 9900, introduced in 1984, could turn out 360 two-sided, collated, and stapled copies in about the same length of time that an average operator had once needed to make a single copy on an Ox Box. The Xerox DocuTech 6180, a "production publisher" introduced in 1997, can, when combined with an optional Xerox SquareFold Booklet Maker, produce "saddle-stapled booklets with a unique square spine edge" at a rate of up to 180 pages a minute—whole bound books at twenty-five times the printing speed of a 914.

The most advanced Xerox machine so far is the Xerox Docu-Color iGen3, which was introduced in 2001. The iGen3 is a digital printing system rather than a copier, but it operates xerographically. It can handle "digital production press runs at 100 pages per minute, and produces 6,000 full-color, 8½-by-11-inch impressions per hour," according to a press release. It can be used to turn out finished offset-quality multipage four-color brochures, for example, and the brochures can be customized on the fly. Inside the machine, four "imaging stations" lay down cyan, magenta, yellow, and black toners on an electrostatically charged photoconductive belt, from which the powders are transferred, all at once, onto paper. The underlying imaging technology, by which a monochromatic process is employed to make full-color prints, is hard to explain, but essentially it involves separating a polychromatic image into the three complementary colors (plus black) in order to "enable one color to be recorded and then developing with colored powder to produce a copy of that color, then repeating for each other color and superimposing the dust images on the same copy sheet."

That, at any rate, is how Chester Carlson described it in his second electrophotography patent, which he filed on April 4, 1939.

Sources

I wrote an essay about xerography in the February 1986 issue of *The Atlantic Monthly*. In it I observed that the Xerox machine is an extraordinary device, yet we take it for granted. "The usual cure for this sort of neglect," I continued, "is to focus obsessive attention on the subject for a short time and then never think about it again. This is what I intend to do."

A pretty funny line—and I really did intend to forget about xerography once the article was finished. Over the years, though, I kept thinking about it, and about the man who invented it, and about the scientists and engineers who made it work, and about the obscure company that gambled everything to turn it into a product. Much has been written about the Xerox Corporation since the eighties, but almost all of it has concerned what happened to the company after it became a success. The truly interesting story, I continue to think, is how the company became a success in the first place. The Xerox machine is one of the most remarkable, most unlikely inventions ever, and it really did transform life as we know it. So after almost twenty years, I decided to focus obsessive attention on the subject once again.

The surprisingly absorbing early history of copying and duplicating has been written about fairly extensively. Among the best
books: *A Complete Course of Lithography*, by Alois Senefelder (New
York: Da Capo Press, 1977)—a facsimile edition of the author's own
1819 English translation; *Thomas Jefferson and His Copying Machines*,
by Silvio A. Bedini (Charlottesville, Va.: University Press of Virginia, 1984); *Before Photocopying: The Art & History of Mechanical
Copying, 1780–1938*, by Barbara Rhodes and William Wells Streeter
(New Castle, Del.: Oak Knoll Press, 1999), which thoroughly cov-
ers the period between James Watt and Chester Carlson and includes more than a thousand illustrations, which all by themselves
constitute a chronicle not only of copying but also of nineteenth-
century advertising, marketing, manufacturing, and general business practices; and *The Origin of Stencil Duplicating*, by W. B.
Proudfoot (London: Hutchinson & Co., 1972)—which proves that
old technologies often survive long after something better has made
them "obsolete," since Proudfoot, writing a dozen years after the
introduction of the 914, treats stencil duplicating as the state of the
art and doesn't mention xerography.

Some of the most detailed writing about early copying and duplicating methods comes from librarians and conservationists, who
have a professional interest in document preservation. See in particular various books by Luis R. Nadeau, who is the author of the two-
volume *Encyclopedia of Printing, Photographic, and Photochemical
Processes*, among a great many other works. There are also entire libraries filled with books about the history of manual copying and
mechanical printing. One (reasonably) interesting book on a related
topic is *The Book on the Book Shelf*, by Henry Petroski (New York: Alfred A. Knopf, 1999), which really is a history of the bookshelf. Petroski, whose admirable tolerance for unlikely subjects may be
greater than yours, has also written a book about the pencil. (It's
called *The Pencil*, and it was also published by Knopf, in 1990.)

Most of what I know about Chester Carlson's private life comes,
directly or indirectly, from Catherine B. Carlson, who is the
adopted daughter of Dorris Carlson. (Catherine knew both Carlsons for the last fifteen years of Chester's life. She was adopted in

adulthood, after Chester's death. Dorris died in 1998, at the age of ninety-four.) Catherine is the chairman of the Chester and Dorris Carlson Charitable Trust, which continues the Carlsons' philanthropy. She is also the able guardian of Chester Carlson's memory. She gave me free access to a large cache of wonderful material: numerous interviews (a number of which she herself conducted, many of them with people now dead); family documents; unpublished letters, memoirs, and autobiographical sketches; copies of speeches given by both Carlsons; copies of Chester Carlson's notebooks and other papers (which now belong to the New York Public Library and are available on microfilm there and at the library of the University of Rochester); interview notes for a biography of Chester Carlson by another writer, now deceased, which was contracted for by a major publishing house in the early eighties but was never published; interviews with many former Haloid and Xerox employees; her own memories of the Carlsons and their relatives and friends; photographs of Carlson; and much more. Catherine's kindness to me is all the more remarkable because my 1986 *Atlantic* article gave her (and Dorris Carlson) several solid reasons not to trust me. I hope I have corrected the factual errors in my original essay and not introduced too many new ones.

Some of the most useful items Catherine showed me were documents related to Lawrence Dumond, who was Chester Carlson's roommate in New York for a few years in the thirties and was a friend, off and on, for a number of years after that. In 1947 and 1948, Dumond made extensive notes for a magazine article about Carlson and his inventions; he was never able to interest a publisher in the idea, but his notes still exist, along with Carlson's handwritten corrections and annotations. Catherine Carlson also interviewed Dumond at length after Carlson's death, and he gave her copies of old letters and other documents. She kindly made all of this material available to me.

Carlson himself did a fair amount of autobiographical writing, some of which he included in speeches, but most of which he never made public. Long before he became a success, he made occasional written summaries of the major events of his life. These and other personal documents of his were very useful to me. Also useful was a lengthy interview with Carlson that was conducted in New York City on December 16, 1965, by Joseph J. Ermenc, who was then a professor at Dartmouth College. In 2001, that interview was reprinted in the *Law Review* (volume 44, number 2) of New York Law School, where Carlson earned his law degree in 1939. An incomplete list of biographical publications about Carlson (along with a list of his patents and other interesting items) is available at www.lib.rochester.edu.

While working on my *Atlantic* article back in the eighties, I interviewed many people at Xerox, among them Horace Becker, Hal Bogdonoff, Bob Gundlach, and John Rutkus. I also interviewed a number of retired executives who, sadly, have since died, and I spent a great deal of time rummaging through interesting odds and ends at the company's corporate headquarters, in Stamford, Connecticut. More recently, Bob Gundlach and Horace Becker, in particular, have been generous with their time.

Personal recollections are just about the least reliable source of historical information; I have been able to cross-check many of the principals' memories with contemporary documents and, in some cases, with interviews that they and others gave at other times—in fact, in five different decades. Even cross-checked interviews must be considered fallible, since human memory simply doesn't work all that well, but likely errors and misrecollections do pop out when you have multiple accounts to compare. One thing I've noticed, in this and other research projects: People tend to mentally update dollar amounts as the decades go by, so that $100 in 1930 will have become $1,000 by 1965 or 1975.

An excellent source of information concerning the creation of the 914 is an unpublished typescript called "The Autobiography of the Xerox Machine." It's a collection of personal recollections (ahem) of key figures in the development of the 914, and it was compiled in the 1970s by a Xerox employee named David Allison. Xerox originally intended to publish it as a celebratory book of some kind but apparently shelved the project after Xerox's lawyers decided the interviews might provide succor to competitors then lining up to sue the company for monopolizing the copying business. I was allowed to take extensive notes in the Xerox archives in Webster, although not to make my own copy of the typescript. In those archives, where I did a great deal of feverish laptop typing, I was aided immeasurably by Ann A. Neal, the company's archivist, who helped me make sense of a mountain of information, and I was led to Ann by Marcia DeMinco, in the company's corporate public relations department. Ann and Marcia tracked down many of the Haloid and Xerox photographs and other illustrations in the book. Xerox has produced more history than it quite knows what to do with; maybe an ambitious history of science graduate student looking for a PhD thesis topic will choose xerography. If so, Catherine Carlson, Ann Neal, and Marcia DeMinco may be able to lead him or her to several dissertations' worth of the raw material.

An extremely valuable source of information and personal recollections about the history of xerography and Xerox is a privately published book called *From Dreams to Riches: The Story of Xerography*, which was written in 1998 by Erik M. Pell, a physicist who worked at Xerox from 1961 until 1989. Pell did a truly prodigious amount of research, interviewed many people who are no longer alive or no longer capable of being interviewed, and assembled in one document an awe-inspiring amount of fascinating information about a fascinating company. I came across a mention of Pell's book while idly roaming the Internet, found his e-mail address through Google, and bought one of the last copies directly from him. I hope he decides to reissue it. Another helpful Xerox memoir, never published, is *My Daddy Worked at Haloid: My Years at Xerox*, by Jack Kinsella, also a physicist, who worked at the company from 1956 until 1986. The most reliable commercially published account of the boom years is probably John Brooks's profile of the company, "Xerox Xerox Xerox Xerox," which appeared in the April 1, 1967, issue of *The New Yorker* and was reprinted two years later in a now hard-to-find collection of Brooks's writing called *Business Adventures: Twelve Classic Tales from the Worlds of Wall Street & the Modern American Corporation* (New York: Weybright and Talley, 1969). A nice book for kids is *Chester Carlson and the Development of Xerography*, by

Susan Zannos (Bear, Del.: Mitchell Lane, 2003). For more about the Battelle Memorial Institute, you might want to try to track down *Science in the Service of Mankind: The Battelle Story* (Lexington, Mass.: D. C. Heath, 1972).

The ultimate source of many published accounts of early Xerox history is John Dessauer's memoir, *My Years with Xerox: The Billions Nobody Wanted* (New York: Doubleday, 1971). The book is entertaining but by no means canonical; more than a few members of Dessauer's staff at the time viewed large parts of it as semifictional. The book is notably untrustworthy on details of Carlson's life. For example, Dessauer (or his ghostwriter, Oscar Schisgall) says that Carlson met his first wife, Elsa, whom Dessauer calls "Linda," when she came to the door of his apartment to complain about the smell of his sulfur experiments—a charming story, but not an accurate one. Dessauer himself acknowledged to Dorris Carlson that the account was fanciful, but he said he felt his version was more dramatic, and he kept it in the book. He took a similarly creative approach to several episodes in Xerox's history, and his book sometimes treats Carlson in a way that strikes me as condescending, even dismissive.

Sol Linowitz's book, *The Making of a Public Man* (Boston: Little Brown, 1985), which he wrote with help from the best-selling business writer Martin Mayer, relies on Dessauer's book for biographical details about Carlson (although Linowitz nevertheless manages to change Elsa's name from "Linda" to "Janet"). Linowitz's account of the early xerography years is brief and somewhat confusingly organized but is often more engaging than Dessauer's. Still, it contains some obvious inaccuracies, which may be the result of misunderstandings by Mayer. For example, Linowitz says at one point that exposing a photoconductive plate (during that early demonstration he attended at Battelle) caused "some feeble off-white lines" to appear on the surface of the plate—an impossibility, unless Linowitz in those days was able to see electrons. But Linowitz's own life story is inspiring—it includes not only his years at Xerox but also his appointment by Lyndon Johnson as U.S. ambassador to the Organization of American States and his leading role in negotiating the Panama Canal Treaty, among a great many other achievements—and it's still going on.

Two frighteningly thorough, equation-filled books about the science of xerography are *Electrophotography*, by R. M. Schaffert (New York: Focal Press, 1965), and *Xerography and Related Processes*, edited by John H. Dessauer and Harold E. Clark (New York: Focal Press, 1965). The first chapter of *Xerography* is a comprehensive "History of Electrostatic Recording" by Chester Carlson—to whom the book is also dedicated. Erik Pell, Bob Gundlach, Fred Hudson, Ernest Lehmann, Clyde Mayo, George Mott, Frederick Schwertz, and Lewis Walkup are among the other contributors.

Much has been written about Xerox Corporation as a business— its remarkable success in the sixties and early seventies, its troubles in the late seventies, its renewal in the eighties, its troubles in the nineties, its worse troubles since then, its further renewal under Anne Mulcahy, and so forth. The best-known book is probably *Xerox: American Samurai*, by Gary Jacobson and John Hillkirk (New York: Macmillan, 1986), which focuses on Xerox's hard-won success at competing with the Japanese in the eighties. The book is a hodgepodge, but there are many interesting parts. Also: *Prophets in the Dark: How Xerox Reinvented Itself and Beat Back the Japanese*, by David T. Kearns and David A. Nadler (New York: HarperCollins, 1992). Kearns was the (widely beloved) chief executive officer of Xerox from 1982 to 1990. Two books have been written about the triumphs and travails of Xerox's Palo Alto Research Center: *Fumbling the Future: How Xerox Invented, Then Ignored, the First Personal Computer*, by Douglas K. Smith and Robert C. Alexander (New York: Author's Choice Press, 1999); *Dealers of Lightning: Xerox PARC and the Dawn of the Computer Age*, by Michael Hiltzick (New York: HarperCollins, 1999).

On the copyright page of my copy of Dessauer and Clark's *Xerography*, after the standard boilerplate warning about not reproducing any part of the book without written permission from the publishers, someone has written in pencil, "You're kidding." (I'm not kidding.)

Index

A. B. Dick, 44, 58, 81*n*, 102, 181
Addressograph-Multigraph
    Corporation, 151–52, 157
Agfa (German manufacturer), 124,
    181
Alcoa, 218–19
The Amateur Chemists' Press
    (magazine), 59, 61
American Photocopy, 181
anthracene, 100, 116, 137, 137*n*, 138,
    155
antitrust laws, 279
Apeco, 181
Arthur D. Little: report of, 219–20,
    222, 223, 240
Astoria, Queens: Carlson's laboratory
    in, 94–102, 115, 137, 155, 165, 282
Austin & Dix, 71–72
automobile manufacturers, American,
    277
Autostat copier, 10

backup copiers, 243, 247
ball-rolling analogy, Gundlach's,
    165–66
Baltimore Social Security Office,
    copying at, 223–24

Battelle, Gordon, 113–14, 125
Battelle Memorial Institute: activities
    of, 114–15; and Battelle-Haloid
    public announcement about
    xerography, 146–48; Carlson's
    agreements with, 117–18, 133,
    141, 143, 156; Carlson's concerns
    about, 141, 188; Carlson's early
    discussions/presentation to,
    110–11, 115–21; Carlson's
    relationship with, 193, 194, 256;
    creation of, 114;
    electrophotography research at,
    118–20, 127, 129–30, 135–39,
    145; graphic arts at, 115–16; and
    Haloid, 126, 127–30, 140, 143–45,
    183, 193–94, 259–60; and IBM,
    199; Linowitz's views about
    reasearch at, 127; lithography
    research at, 156; military contracts
    of, 135–36, 189, 200; mission of,
    114; public announcement, 188;
    and RCA Electrofax, 176, 179;
    and royalties, 117, 127, 143, 193,
    259, 260; size of, 114; skepticism
    about Carlson's ideas at, 120–21,
    136; and toner problems, 215;

Battelle Memorial Institute *(cont.)*
trustees of, 114; wealth of, 194;
and World War II, 118;
Xeroprinter of, 189–90. *See also
specific person*
Bausch & Lomb, 123, 221, 225
Becker, Horace: early days at Haloid
of, 229; and 914 Copier, 205–6,
207–8, 210–11, 217, 218–19, 228,
230, 232–34, 235, 242;
professional background of, 206
Bedini, Silvio A., 30, 31
Beidler, George, 79–81
Bell & Howell, 220–22, 253
Bell, Alexander Graham, 276
Bell Laboratories, 67–71, 91, 95,
176
Benson, Robert, 211
Bixby, William, 136–37, 138, 139
blind: xerography-based system of
printing for, 186
Bliss, Howard, 64–65, 272
blueprinting, 9, 47–48, 158, 180
Bogdonoff, Harold, 184–86, 263
"bomb-bay doors," 210
"book press." *See* copying press
Borden, Norman, 59
Boston Security Analysts Society:
Wilson speech at, 255–56, 257
Brooks, John, 9, 89, 139, 187, 206,
244
Bruning (Charles) Company, 107–8,
181
Brush Development Company, 101,
265
brushes: fur, 118, 209–12, 242;
magnetic, 175–76, 178
"business scheme": of Bell Labs
employees, 71
Business Week magazine, 247

California Institute of Technology,
63, 64, 65–67, 74, 264
Camera No. 1, 168
Camera No. 4, 168
Cameron, George, 125–26
Canon Inc., 4–5
Canon PC-10 copier, 4–6, 10

carbon paper: decline in use of, 7,
240, 252; and development of
aniline inks, 41; and development
of duplication technology, 179,
180; and hectographs, 47;
invention of, 9, 37–38; and 914
Copier, 220; and Ox Box, 151,
156; and potential applications of
photoelectricity, 116; recipe for,
38; and typewriters, 39–40
Carlson, Chester Floyd: aspirations
of, 56–58, 66, 263; birth of, 48, 50;
childhood and youth of, 50–63;
college jobs of, 63–64, 65–66;
death of, 274–76, 280; early
education of, 52, 54–55, 56, 63;
early jobs of, 55–56, 59, 62; family
history of, 49–50; as family
provider, 56; favorite plaything of,
58; as feeling unproductive, 263;
health of, 53, 62–63, 110, 273,
274–75; homes/apartments of,
91–94, 102, 183, 259, 261–62,
273–74; inventive process of,
185–86, 185*n*; as inventor of
xerography, 12; keys to success
and personal fulfillment for,
66–67; literature as career for,
262*n*; marriages of, 72–73,
131–33; mentors of, 64; moves to
Rochester, 141; "personal history"
of, 62; personality of, 54, 61,
64–65, 72, 89, 103, 108, 141, 184,
186, 262, 263, 269, 270–71, 272,
274–75; philanthropy of, 260,
263–64, 267, 270; philosophy of,
269–70; physical appearance of,
61; as public speaker, 271–72; self-
image/criticism of, 64–65, 66, 69;
separation and divorce of, 109–10,
131; spirituality/parapsychology
interests of, 267, 268–69; travels
of, 271, 272–73, 275; wealth of,
194, 259–61, 262–63; writings/
publications of, 56, 58, 59, 61, 262*n*
Carlson, Dorris Helen Hudgins
(second wife): Carlson's courtship
and marriage to, 131–33; and

Carlson's death, 275–76; and
Carlson's health, 273, 274; and
Carlson's personality, 142, 186,
262, 270; and Carlson's
philanthropy, 267; Carlson's
relationship with, 133, 267, 268,
269, 273; and Carlson's travels,
272; and Carlson's wealth, 259,
260–61, 262–63; and
Electrophotography Participation
Fund, 143*n*; as help to Carlson on
experiments, 136; and IBM-
Carlson relationship, 188; and
move to Rochester, 141; person
and professional background of,
131–32; and spirituality/
parapsychology, 267–68;
travels of, 272, 273
Carlson, Ellen Josephine Hawkins
(mother), 50–55, 62, 63, 271, 273
Carlson, Elsa von Mallon (first wife),
62, 72–73, 74, 91–92, 94, 95, 102,
109–10, 131
Carlson, Olof Adolph: and Carlson
on East Coast, 67; Carlson's
relationship with, 62; death of, 71;
early history of, 49–50; health of,
50–51, 52, 54, 55, 56, 62–63;
marriage of, 50; in Mexico, 51–53,
273; moving of family of, 50–55;
personality of, 50; physical
appearance of, 50–51; in
Riverside, 63–64; in San
Bernardino, 54, 67, 71
Carlson, Roy (cousin), 57, 71, 73,
108, 109, 263, 267, 268, 272
Carlyle, Thomas, 19
Catan, Paul, 206
CBS Reports, 252
Center for the Study of Democratic
Institutions, 264
chimpanzee commercial, 251
China, 18, 18*n*, 20
Clark, Donald, 239, 247, 248, 249,
251, 252
Clark, Harold E.: and Carlson's
inventive process, 185*n*; and
competitors of Haloid, 181–82;

and Copyflo, 190; description of
Carlson's ideas by, 89–90; early
xerography research of, 184; on
Haloid-Carlson relationship, 187;
hiring of, 184; hiring of Gundlach
by, 163; and internal studies of
xerography, 222; and 914 Copier,
199, 208, 238–39, 241; and Ox
Box, 155; and paper handling
problems, 208; and photoreceptor
research, 139–40; and "small
copier committee," 192–93;
writings of, 178
Closter, Laurens, 18*n*
Collier's: Dumond's story rejected by,
131
computer mouse, 278–79
Coolidge, Calvin, 37, 185
Copese copier, 10, 181
copiers: desktop, 256; as duplicating
machines, 36; duplicators
distinguished from, 35–36; first
photographic, 79–81; full-color,
283; language and writing as
oldest, 1, 2; marketing of, 250*n*;
personal, 4–8; and photography,
79. *See also* office copiers; *specific
manufacturer or model*
copper plates, 36
Copyflo (Haloid): as competition
with Haloid's other models, 191;
complications with, 191; cost of,
189, 189*n*; development of,
189–91; manufacturing/assembly
of, 216, 216*n*, 254; and 914
Copier, 200, 209, 213, 214–15;
optical system in, 221; paper
handling in, 202; photoreceptors
in, 190, 200; promotion of, 247;
sales/leasing of, 189*n*, 192, 236,
246; size of, 189, 190–91; toner in,
214–15; and Verifax, 189
copying: in ancient times, 15–16;
Carlson's early thoughts about, 70;
Carlson's experiments with, 70;
Carlson's thoughts about
chemical, 82–83; and copies
distinguished from originals, 8;

copying *(cont.)*
    and democracy, 30; and
    duplicating, 39–40; duplicating
    distinguished from, 35–36, 39–40;
    importance of, 30, 257; in
    medieval Europe, 16–17; in
    nineteenth century, 47–48; and
    photostats, 81*n*; as potential
    application of photoelectricity,
    116; worldwide growth in volume
    of, 282–83. *See also specific technology*
copying pencil, 41
copying press, 31–33, 34, 36–37, 40,
    41, 179, 250*n*
Copymation, 181
Copyrama exhibition, 247
Copytron, 181
Cormac, 181
corona charging, 118, 119, 173, 174,
    177, 209
corporate computer network, 278–79
Cotteneude (French inventor), 27–28
Crosby Frisian Fur Co., 210–11, 210*n*
cuff links, nickel, 241
Curtin, David, 235
Cyclostyle, 44–45

da Vinci, Leonardo, 26
Daguerre, Louis, 78–79
Darwin, Charles, 37
Darwin, Erasmus, 27, 32
Davis, John, 254
Davy, Humphry, 78
Dayton, Russell W., 110–11, 115,
    120–21, 280
Debbie commercial, 249–51
democracy: and copying, 30
Dennis, Ken, 142
desktop copiers: development of, 256
Dessauer, John: Battalle visit by, 126;
    and Battelle-Haloid public
    announcement about xerography,
    146–48; and Carlson as consultant
    at Haloid, 141; and Carlson's
    death, 276; on Carlson's financial
    affairs, 142; and Carlson's
    personality, 141; Carlson's
    pressures on, 187; commitment to

xerography of, 187; and Copyflo,
    247; electrophotography research
    of, 130; function of department
    of, 183; and Haloid-Battelle-
    Carlson agreement, 128; and
    Haloid-IBM relationship, 188;
    and Haloid's change of name, 194;
    and lack of xerography lab at
    Haloid, 183; learns about
    Carlson's ideas, 121–22, 123–24;
    and leasing of machines, 237;
    memoir of, 126; and metering
    machines, 244*n*; and military
    funding for electrophotography
    research, 135; and 914 Copier,
    199; and Ox Box, 149, 150–51,
    155; personal and professional
    background of, 124, 130; and
    RCA Electrofax, 176, 178–79; and
    Rutkus hiring, 199; and "small
    copier committee," 192–93
Dial-A-Matic Autostat, 10, 181
diazo process, 48, 125, 181
Dick, A. B., 44
dictation, 17
diffusion transfer, 181
Ditto Co., 15, 47, 81*n*, 153, 181
Docu-Color iGen3, 283
DocuTech 6180, 283
Dumond, Lawrence "Larry," 68, 70,
    72, 73, 90, 90*n*, 130–31, 135*n*, 269
duplication/duplicators: of Carlson's
    early newspaper, 58; Carlson's
    early thoughts about, 61; copying
    distinguished from, 35–36, 39–40;
    copying machines as, 36;
    development of technology about,
    179–80; with Edison's Electric
    Pen, 42, 44; and evolution of
    civilization, 1–2; gelatin, 45–47;
    and 914 Copier, 220, 241; offset,
    151–56, 153*n*, 220, 241, 253; as
    potential application of
    photoelectricity, 116; spirit, 47,
    81*n*, 116, 180, 220, 241; stencil,
    42, 58, 81*n*, 116, 180; and uses of
    xerography, 104. *See also type of
    duplication*

Dupliton copier, 10
Durez Plastics and Chemicals, 163
dye transfer process, 181
dyes: aniline, 40–42, 99; synthetic, 41, 42
Dymo label maker, 58

E. Remington & Sons, 39
Eastman, George, 123
Eastman Kodak: and attempts to obtain sponsors and licensees, 117–18; bulletin of, 121; cafeteria at, 164, 186; commitment to photography of, 187; and customer tolerance, 243; founding of, 123; Haloid as competitor of, 121, 123–24, 125, 181–82, 192, 246, 256; instant cameras of, 281–82; lack of interest in electrophotography at, 129; military contracts of, 200; photography research at, 82; and Photostat, 81, 123, 124; Rochester as home of, 123; and studies about copying, 223; in twenty-first century, 280. *See also* Verifax
Edison Mimeographs, 44
Edison, Thomas, 42, 44, 56, 114, 182*n*, 276
Edison's Electric Pen, 42, 44, 182*n*
813 Copier, 220, 255, 282
Eimer & Amend, 92
Einstein, Albert, 83, 84
Electro-Stat, 181
Electrofax (RCA), 175–79, 181, 188–89
electron photography. *See* electrophotography; xerography
electron-scanning invention, 101, 265–66
Electronics (magazine), 95
Electronics World (magazine), 121*n*
electrophotography: Battelle research about, 127; Carlson convinced of success of, 99; Carlson-Kornei work on, 95–101; Carlson's analogy about, 90*n*; Carlson's attempts to produce a working

model of, 104–8, 109; Carlson's early experiments with, 91–94; and Carlson's early thoughs about copying, 84–89; Dumond's article about Carlson and, 130–31; first copy from, 98–99; lack of scientific interest in, 129, 140; military funding for research on, 135–36; name change to xerography of, 145–46; overview about, 83–85; potential applications of, 9, 104, 116–17, 131; scientists'/corporations' reactions to idea of, 104–9. *See also* Battelle Memorial Institute; Haloid Company; photoconductors
Electrophotography Participation Fund, 143, 260
electrostatics: Carlson-Kornei experiments on, 95–101, 100*n*; Carlson's knowledge of, 88; in early xerography models, 171, 172, 175; and 914 Copier, 197, 202–4, 205, 209; and RCA Electrofax, 178; and Xerox Docu-Color iGen3, 283
engravings, 21
Ermenc, Joseph J., 61, 67, 74
Ernst & Ernst: report by, 222, 223, 240

facsimile transmission, 104
Federal Trade Commission (FTC), 250–51, 279, 281
Fellowship of Reconciliation, 264
fiber-optics: as light source in xerography, 12
"film on the drum," 213–15
fire extinguishers, 210
football commercial, 251–52
Forbes magazine, 196–97
Ford Motor Company, 155, 277–78
Fortune magazine, 12, 247, 254, 260, 281
Foto-Flo system, 191
Frankfort black, 38, 40
Franklin, Benjamin, 33–34

full-color copiers, 283
fusers, 232–34, 236
Fust, Johann, 18*n*

Galileo, 25
Garfield, Simon, 40*n*
Garner, James, 281
gelatin duplicator, 45–47
General Electric, 102, 192, 218
Georgius, 26
Gestetner Co., 44–45
Gestetner, David, 44–45
Gevaert, 181
Gillett, Horace, 114, 115
Glavin, John, 222–24, 234, 236–37, 241
Gloverville, New York, 211–12, 211*n*
government, U.S.: first copiers owned by, 34
graphical user interface, 278–79
Great Depression: Carlson's jobs during, 67–75
Greig, H. G., 176–78
Gundlach, Bob: ball-rolling analogy of, 165–66; birth of, 162; dedication to Haloid of, 163; demonstrations of early xerography models by, 167–75; early Haloid career of, 163, 164–65; and Haloid's physical plant, 195; Hollenbeck research of, 164–75; and Model D processor, 254; and 914 Copier, 203, 205, 212, 214; nonxerographic method of making prints demonstrated by, 174–75; and paper handling problems, 203; patents of, 161, 165, 166–67, 205; personal and professional background of, 162–64; physical appearance of, 161; and RCA Electrofax, 178; and toner problems, 209, 214
Gundlach, Emanuel, 162
Gutenberg Bible, 20, 179
Gutenberg, Johannes, 9–10, 18–19, 18*n*, 20, 21, 36, 89, 116*n*

Haloid Company: and Battelle, 126, 127–30, 140, 143–45, 183, 193–94, 259–60; and Battelle-Haloid public announcement about xerography, 146–48, 188, 280; board of, 187, 191, 194, 235, 246; Carlson as consultant at, 141–42, 183, 259; Carlson's agreement with, 126–29; Carlson's laboratory at, 184–86; Carlson's relationship with, 186–88, 193, 194, 256; changes name to Xerox Corporation, 10, 194, 252; commercial partners of, 125; commitment to xerography at, 187–88, 222; competitors of, 121, 123–24, 125, 175–82, 192, 223, 246, 256; diversification at, 123–24; Eastman Kodak as competitor of, 121, 123–24, 125, 181–82, 192, 246, 256; expansion of, 122, 199; founding of, 122; Hollenbeck laboratory of, 164–75, 178, 184, 195; and IBM, 188–89, 192, 193, 219–20, 222, 246; identity and purpose of, 256; in-house stock buying at, 245–46; internal office copying at, 224–25; lack of xerography laboratory at, 183; and licensing negotiations, 144–45, 176, 193, 196, 219; manufacturing/production at, 215–19, 227–29, 230–35, 255; military contracts for, 135, 136, 189, 200; and office copier development, 156; patent department at, 145, 183, 184; physical plant of, 195–96, 228, 229–30; physics at, 164–75; products of, 122–23; psychological-testing of employees at, 229; and RCA, 175–79; research and development at, 120, 127, 129–30, 135–36, 145, 183–86, 187, 188–89, 193–94, 200, 227–28; revenues of, 156, 192, 235–36, 241, 256; and royalties, 193;

sales and marketing at, 156–58, 237, 245–52; skepticism about xerography at, 140, 159, 187, 191, 246, 255–56; trademark for, 145–46; in World War II, 135. *See also* Rectigraphs; Xerox Corporation; *specific person or equipment item*
Harding, Warren G., 114
Harris-Seybold Company, 117
Hartley, Mariette, 281
Hartnett, John, 145, 146, 157–59, 235, 237
Hawkins, Ellen Josephine. *See* Carlson, Ellen Josephine Hawkins
Hawkins, John Isaac, 28–29
Hawkins, Oscar, 63
Hawkins, Ruth, 68
Hazard, Ebenezer, 30
hectographs, 45–47, 116
Helsley, Phil, 72
Herschel, John Frederick William, 48
Hertz, Heinrich, 83–84
Hesketh, William, 248, 250–51
Hollenbeck laboratory (Haloid), 164–75, 178, 184, 195
Hudgins, Dorris Helen. *See* Carlson, Dorris Helen Hudgins
Hudson, Fred, 232

IBM: and Battelle, 199; Carlson's early discussions with, 102, 103–5, 107; and customer tolerance, 243; and desktop copiers, 256; early PCs of, 7–8; and Haloid, 188–89, 192, 193, 219–20, 222, 246; interest in xerography at, 188; Kornei at, 265; lack of interest in electrophotography at, 129, 171; and manufacturing at Haloid, 215–16; size of, 253; Xerox lawsuit against, 279
icongraphy, 174–75
illustrations: reproduction of medieval, 20–21
income taxes, Carlson's, 270–71
India: printing in, 18
industrialization, 179–80

ink-jet printers, 11, 86
inks, 17, 33, 41, 42, 83. *See also type of printing*
Insalaco, Michael, 215
instant cameras, 281–82
intaglio, 20–21, 22, 116
International Harvester, 191, 278
inventive process, 185–86, 185*n*
inventor/inventions: Carlson sees, as solving personal difficulties, 74–75; Carlson's desire to be, 56–58; Carlson's early ideas for, 57–58, 69–70; and reinvention of Carlson's inventions, 141

Jacobson, Gary, 252
Japan, 254, 279
Jefferson, Thomas, 29–30, 31, 34, 37, 39
Jones, Stan, 77*n*

Kearns, David, 279
Keuffel & Esser, 181
Kinsella, Jack, 138, 195
Kleenex facial tissues, story about, 57*n*
Klizas, John F., 216*n*, 229
Klugman, Jack, 4
Korea, 18*n*
Kornei, Otto: accuses Carlson of cheating him, 265; as assistant to Carlson, 95–101, 100*n*, 118, 119, 120, 137, 146, 155, 165, 282; Carlson's agreement with, 95, 96, 101–2, 265–66; Carlson's relationship with, 101, 264–65, 266–67; demonstration kit of, 102–3, 104, 115; and electron-scanning invention, 101, 265–66; Haloid stock of, 265, 266; at IBM, 265; in 1960s, 264–67
Kuhns, Harold, 227, 228, 229, 237

LaMaster, Slater, 68
Land, Edwin, 280–82
Langer, Nicholas, 121, 121*n*, 123–24, 125
laser printers, 11, 12, 139*n*, 252, 278–79, 282

leasing of machines, 236, 236n, 237, 243
Lehmann, Ernest, 163, 164
Library of Alexandria (Egypt), 2
Lichtenberg figure, 87
Lichtenberg, George Christoph, 86–87
Life magazine, 282
linotype: invention of, 116n
Linowitz, Sol M.: and advertising of 914 Copier, 248; and Battelle-Haloid agreements, 126–27, 128, 143–44, 193–94; Carlson's pressures on, 187; and differences between Wilson and Carlson, 256; and electrophotography name changed to xerography, 136; and Haloid-IBM relationship, 188; as Haloid lawyer, 126; Haloid responsibilities of, 183; and Haloid's change of name, 194; and Haloid's commitment to xerography, 222; and IBM-Haloid negotiations, 219; and international sales, 254; and lack of interest in electrophotography, 128–29; and licensing negotiations, 144–45, 196; and military funding for electrophotography research, 135; and Ox Box, 155, 156; and potential use of xerography, 144; and Rank, 254; and RCA Electrofax, 176, 179
Lith-Master. *See* Ox Box
lithography: Battelle research about, 156; and Carlson-Kornei experiments, 100; and copying distinguished from duplicating, 35; decline in use of, 24; and development of duplication technology, 179; and early models of Haloid machines, 167n; and Haloid's revenues, 192; importance of, 23; invention and development of, 21–24; and Kornei's experiments, 155; and photography, 78; and polygraphs,

81n; and potential uses of xerography, 104, 116. *See also* Ox Box
Lois, George, 249
Lunar Society, 32
lycopodium powder, 97–99, 97n, 119–20

M. F. Kuhn Corporation, 122
Mallon, Elsa von. *See* Carlson, Elsa von Mallon
Mallory. *See* P. R. Mallory & Co.
Mayo, Clyde, 221, 228
McCardell, Archie, 277–78
McColough, C. Peter, 227, 252–53
McNamara, Robert, 277
Mergenthaler, Ottmar, 116n
Mergenthaler Linotype Company, 115–16, 206, 217
metal type, 20
metering machines, 237, 238, 244, 244N
methyl alcohol: in duplicators, 47
Mexico: Carlson family in, 51–53; Carlson's visit to, 273
Michelangelo, 26
microfilm, 200
Microtronics Laboratory, 125
Miller, Carl, 180
mimeograph, 44, 70, 81n
Model A Copier. *See* Ox Box
Model B Copier, 167n
Model C Copier, 167n
Model D processor, 167–68, 167n, 172, 174, 192, 196, 236, 254
monks. *See* scribes/monks
Motion Picture Association of America, 240
Mott, George, 204, 205, 213, 214, 231–32
movable type, 9, 19, 89, 116n
Mulcahy, Anne, 279
Multilith Offset Duplicator, 151–56
multiple-copy features, 174

NBC, 252
New York City: Carlson's last trip to, 275

New York Law School: Carlson as
student at, 73–74, 95, 102
New York magazine, 81*n*
The New York Times, 103, 116*n*, 130,
131
The New Yorker magazine, 9, 244
nickel cuff links, 241
Nickerson, Pauline, 52
Niépce, Joseph Nicéphore,
78–79
914 Office Copier: and backup
machines, 243, 247; blueprints for,
217; complaints about, 242–43;
contributions of suppliers to,
217–18; cost of, 235, 236*n*;
customer tolerance concerning,
242–44; development of, 197,
199–204, 227–29, 280, 282; as
duplicator, 241; field test for, 225;
as first office copier, 10; first order
from paying customer for, 237;
funding for development of, 156,
227; international sales of, 254;
leasing of, 236, 236*n*, 243;
maintenance/service for, 242, 243,
255; manufacturing/production
of, 215–19, 227–29, 230–35, 255;
metering of, 237, 238; number of,
254; operators of, 10, 225, 238,
244; optical system in, 221–22;
paper handling problems in,
202–4, 205–9; photoreceptors in,
11, 200, 201, 209–12, 213–15,
216, 217–19, 221, 231–32;
potential markets for, 219–25;
printing speed of, 283;
refurbished, 254; sales and
marketing of, 246–52; shipping of,
237–38; skepticism about, 12,
220–22; Smithsonian Institution
induction of, 161; as success,
152–53, 241, 242, 252–53,
254–55; toner for, 205, 208, 210,
213–15, 231–32, 242; unreliability
of, 10, 241–42, 244; usage of,
238–40
9900 Copier, 283
Noyes, Alfred Amos, 264

office copiers: Carlson sees invention
of, as solving personal difficulties,
74–75; and development of
duplication technology, 180; early,
10; early Xerox, 8–9; first U.S.
government-owned, 34; and
Haloid-Battelle-Carlson
agreement, 128; Haloid's interest
in development of, 156; monks as,
9. *See also specific model*
offset printing, 151–56, 153*n*, 220,
241, 253
Oliver, George, 218
1000 Copier, 254
Optical Society of America, 146–48,
188
optical system, 221–22
O'Reilly, Samuel F., 182*n*
originals: and copies, 8
Oughton, C. David, 126
Ox Box: appearance of, 150–51;
camera on, 168; cleaning of plate
in, 173; compared to modern
copiers, 283; development of,
148–59; and development of
duplication technology, 180; and
development of early models,
167*n*; field testing of, 151, 168;
limitations of, 165; and
lithography, 151–56, 153*n*, 180;
maintenance/service for, 243;
manufacturing/assembly of, 215,
254; operating manual for,
149–50, 170; paper for, 202;
photoreceptors in, 190, 210;
promotional materials for, 150;
and RCA Electrofax, 177;
rejection of, 151; sales of, 156–58,
246; and skepticism about 914
Copier, 256; toner for, 150, 154,
172

P. R. Mallory & Co., 72, 82, 95, 110,
111, 115, 121*n*, 129
pacifism, 264
Palo Alto Research Center (Xerox),
278
pantographs, 25–28, 32*n*, 36

paper: and Carlson's early thoughts about copying, 83; for Copyflo, 202; Haloid, 122–23, 246; invention of, 16; for 914 Copier, 205–9; for Ox Box, 202; problems with handling, 202–4, 205–9; and RCA Electrofax, 177; Xerox brand name, 208
Papert, Koenig & Lois, 249
papyrograph, 42
papyrus, 15, 208
parchment, 15–16
Pasadena, California: Carlson and father move to, 65–67
patent lawyer, Carlson as: in Bell Labs patent department, 69, 70; as self-employed, 129, 141
patents: of Bogdonoff, 185; covering selenium in xerography, 139–40; of Gundlach, 161, 165, 166–67, 205; at Haloid, 183, 184; and RCA Electrofax, 175–76, 177; of Rutkus, 205; of Senefelder, 23; of Watt, 32; of Wedgwood, 37
patents, Carlson: and Battelle, 111, 193; and Carlson's work at Haloid, 141; and Dumond's affidavit, 90; first, 90–91, 94, 103; fourth, 105; and Kornei-Carlson experiments, 96, 100; and Langer's work, 121; and lithography, 155; as model patent, 91; and 914 Copier, 12; photoconductor methods in, 139; and photoreceptors, 118; possible applications of, 116; and reenactments of Carlson's work, 89; second, 100, 283; and size of machine on applications, 105; time limits on, 12, 130, 141, 187, 193
Peale, Charles Willson, 28–29, 37
Pell, Erik M., 108, 122, 124–25, 141, 221
penknives, 28
Perkin, William Henry, 40
personal computers, 278–79
personal copiers, 4–8
Petty, William, 26–27

Philadelphia Centennial Exposition (1876), 48
philanthropy: of Carlson, 260, 263–64, 267, 270
photoconductivity/photoconductors: and Battelle research, 135, 137–39; Carlson-Kornei experiments with, 95–101, 100n; and Carlson's early thoughs about copying, 87–88; ingredients in, 137n; paper for, 188–89; and RCA Electrofax, 177, 178; and Schaffert's reactions to Carlson's presentation, 116; and Xerox Docu-Color iGen3, 283. See also selenium
photocopies: as generic term, 81n
photoelectricity. See electrophotography; xerography
photography: Carlson's early thoughts/uses of, 64, 75, 82; and development of duplication technology, 180; and first copying machines, 79–81; importance of, 79; instant, 280–82; invention of, 77–79; limitations of, 82; and lithography, 78; as nineteenth-century copying technology, 47; pictorial images as emphasis of early, 79; and xerography, 11, 104. See also Eastman Kodak; photoelectricity; Polaroid Corporation; xerography
photoreceptors: and Battelle research, 118–19, 136–37; cleaning of, 209–12; in Copyflo, 190, 200; and Gundlach's research, 165–66; and Haloid-Battelle-Carlson agreement, 128; lamps for, 217–18; and manufacturing/production problems, 216, 231–32; in 914 Copier, 11, 200, 201, 209–12, 213–15, 216, 217–19, 221, 231–32; in Ox Box, 190, 210; and RCA Electrofax, 177–78; selenium in, 11–12, 137–40, 137n, 139n, 147–48, 177–78, 190, 196,

200, 201, 213, 218; in xerography, 11–12
Photostat Corporation, 81, 81*n*, 82, 116, 122, 123–24, 156, 158
photostat (generic term), 81*n*
Picasso advertising, 248–49
Pico, 223
Pitney-Bowes, 237
Polaroid Corporation, 280–82
polygraphs, 28–29, 30–31, 81*n*, 179
portable copiers: copying presses as, 34
Precision Instrument Company, 105
printing: Carlson's early jobs in, 59; of first modern book, 18, 18*n*; invention of mechanical, 18–19; and potential uses of xerography, 104. *See also* movable type; *type of printing*
printing press: Carlson refurbishes old, 59, 61; development of, 15, 19–20, 36
Proudfoot, W. B., 44, 45
public information: and role of copying in democracy, 30
puffer, 205–6, 207, 210

quill pens, 28, 38

Radio & TV News (magazine), 121*n*
Radio News (magazine), 121, 121*n*, 123–24
Rank Xerox, 253–54, 272
Ray, Man, 77
RCA, 102, 178, 192, 253, 266. *See also* Electrofax
Rectigraph Company, 123, 124, 125
Rectigraphs: and Carlson's patent work, 82; cost of, 80; as first photographic copying, 79–81; Foto-Flo as similar to, 191; and Haloid's military contracts, 135; manufacturing of, 215; and 914 Copier, 246; old Haloid plant for, 164, 184, 195; as "photocopies," 81*n*; popularity of, 122; and sales of Ox Boxes, 157, 158; size of, 80; and Wilson's interest in Carlson's ideas, 125

Reinhardt, Jack, 232–34
relief printing, 20, 22, 116
REMCO Hectographic Copier, 45, 45*n*
Remington Rand, 181
Rhodes, Barbara, 41
Richard, George, 126
Riverside, California: Carlson and father in, 63–65; Carlson's visit to, 272–73
Riverside Junior College, 63–65, 88, 261, 272
Rochester Gas & Electric, 225
Rochester Times-Union, 252
Rockefeller, Happy, 276
Rockefeller, Nelson, 276
royalties, 117, 127, 143, 193, 259, 260
Rubel, Ira A., 153*n*
Rutkus, John, 199–201, 205–6, 207, 215
Rutledge, John, 245–46

sales and marketing, Haloid, 191, 237, 242, 245–52
San Bernardino, California: Carlson family in, 54, 55–63; Carlson's father moves to, 67; death of father in, 71
Schaffert, Roland M.: and attempts to obtain sponsors and licensees, 117–18; and Battelle-Haloid public announcement about xerography, 147; and Battelle's commitment to electrophotography, 136; and Battelle's development of Carlson's ideas, 119; and Haloid-Battelle-Carlson agreement, 128; professional background of, 115–16, 206; reactions to Carlson's ideas by, 115–17, 120; as significant contributor to serography, 126; and Xeroprinter, 189–90
Schapirographs, 46
Scheiner, Christoph, 25–26
Schwertz, Frederick A., 142, 222, 229, 275–76

Science Museum (London, England),
  32*n*
SCM Corporation, 279
scribes/monks, 9, 15, 16–18, 19–20,
  36
scriptoriums, 16–17, 19
seismic recording, 125
selenium: and cleaning of plate, 173,
  173*n*, 174; in early xerography
  models, 150, 167, 173, 173*n*, 174;
  and 914 Copier, 200, 201, 205,
  218, 242; in photoreceptors,
  11–12, 137–40, 137*n*, 139*n*,
  147–48, 177–78, 190, 196, 200,
  201, 213, 218; and RCA
  Electrofax, 177–78
Selenyi, Paul, 86, 87, 89, 97
Senefelder, Alois, 21–23, 152, 153
Senefelder, Gleissner & Co., 23
720 Copier, 254
Shakespeare, William, 19
Shepardson, Donald, 201, 217, 224
Sholes & Gliddon, 39
Signal Corps, U.S., 135–36, 135*n*,
  140
silver halide process, 83, 136, 153, 181
Simplex (index typewriter), 58–59, 68
6500 Copier, 283
"small copier committee," 192–93,
  222, 235
small copier market, 279
Smith, Adam, 34
Smith Corona, 181
Smithsonian Institution, 99*n*, 106*n*,
  161
Society of Professional Scientists and
  Engineers: Carlson speech to,
  271–72
"sorts," 19
spirit duplicators, 47, 116, 180, 220,
  241
spirituality/parapsychology, 267–69
Sponheim, Abbot of, 20
SPS Technologies, Inc., 237, 239
SquareFold Booklet Maker, 283
St. Augustine, 17
Standard Master-Making Equipment.
  See Model D processor

Standard Press Steel, 237, 239
stencil duplicators, 42, 58, 81*n*, 116,
  180
Stylographic Manifold Writer
  (Wedgwood), 37
sulfur, 96–97, 100, 116, 137, 137*n*,
  138
sword hygrometer, 208

tattoos, 182, 182*n*
Taubes, Ernest, 125–26
Taylor Instruments, 225
technology: as creating demand, 241;
  self-sustaining feedback loop of,
  179–80
television, 177, 249–52
Thermo-Fax (3M), 10, 180–82, 182*n*,
  189*n*, 219, 220, 223, 237, 238, 256
This and That (newspaper), 58, 59
3M, 129, 180–82, 223, 243. *See also*
  Thermo-Fax
Todd Equipment Company, 156
Tone Tray, 165–66
toner: and Battelle's research about
  lithography, 156; Carlson's
  research on, 183; characteristics
  of, 214; for Copyflo, 214–15; in
  early xerography models, 169,
  170, 171, 172, 173, 174, 175; and
  manufacturing/production
  problems, 231–32; for 914 Copier,
  205, 208, 210, 213–15, 231–32,
  242; for Ox Box, 150, 154, 172;
  and paper handling problems,
  205, 208, 210; and RCA
  Electrofax, 178; and Xerox Docu-
  Color iGen3, 283. *See also*
  lycopodium powder
trademark: Xerox as, 244
transparent materials: importance of,
  12–13
travels: of Carlson, 271, 272–73
Trout, Jack, 279–80
Twain, Mark, 39
"Two-Minute Minnie," 136
2400 Copier, 255
typesetting: cold, photography-based,
  116*n*; invention of, 18*n*

typewriters, 9, 37, 38–40, 41–42, 58–59, 68, 180

U Thant, 276
United Kingdom, 254
United Nations, 276
United Negro College Fund, 264
University of Rochester, 225, 240, 253
U.S. Patent and Trademark Office, 110, 133

van der Waals forces, 171
van der Waals, Johannes Diderik, 171
Van Wagner, Ed, 195
vellum, 16
Verifax (Eastman Kodak), 10, 181–82, 189, 220, 223, 236, 237, 238, 256
videocassette recorders (VCRs), 240–41
videotapes, 131

Walkup, Lewis E., 155, 156, 197
The Wall Street Journal, 185
Washington, George, 34
wasps: and inks, 17
Watson, Thomas Jr., 188
Watt, James, 31–33, 32n, 34, 36, 44, 250n
Wedgwood, Ralph, 37–38
Wedgwood, Thomas, 77–78
Wells, William, 41
White House: copying presses in, 36–37
Wildroot Cream-Oil, 162
Williams, Clyde, 115
Wilson, Joseph C.: aspirations of, 125; Battelle visit by, 126; and Battelle-Haloid contract renegotiation, 143–44; and Battelle-Haloid public announcement about xerography, 145, 147, 148; Boston Security Analysts Society speech of, 255–56, 257; Carlson hired as consultant by, 141; Carlson's agreement with, 126–29; and

Carlson's death, 276; Carlson's relationship with, 140–41, 187, 256–57; commitment to xerography of, 140–41, 187, 192, 193, 196, 235, 257; and competitors of Haloid, 181, 182, 192; and Copyflo, 191; death of, 276–77, 281; and desktop copiers, 256; early interest/enthusiasm about Carlson's ideas of, 124, 125–26, 128, 129; and electrophotography name changed to xerography, 136, 145; Forbes presentation by, 196–97; and Gundlach's hiring, 163; as Haloid president, 124; and Haloid's physical plant, 195–96, 229; health of, 158–59; and IBM, 188–89, 219, 220; and internal studies of xerography, 222; and manufacturing at Haloid, 217; McColough as successor to, 227, 277; and metering machines, 237; and military funding for electrophotography research, 135; Mulcahy as true heir of, 279; and new name for Haloid, 194; and 914 Copier, 197, 217, 220, 222, 228, 229, 230, 234, 236n, 255–56; and Ox Box, 150, 151, 155, 158;personality of, 234–35; and potential use of xerography, 144; and RCA Electrofax, 176, 179; reputation of, 124–25; as researcher, 130; and revenues, 253; and sublicensees, 145; and Xerox as trademark, 146. See also Haloid Company
Wise, Edward, 120, 126
woodblocks, 18, 20, 22, 33–34, 35
World War II, 109, 114–15, 118, 135, 162–63
World's Fair (Brussels, 1958), 272
Wren, Christopher, 26
writing, 2

x-radiography, 104
XC 1045 Copier, 6

xerography: advances in technology of, 282–83; Battelle-Haloid public announcement about, 145–48, 188, 280; Carlson's contributions to, 186–87; characteristics of, 10; as commercial triumph, 262; competing processes to, 175–82; early models of, 164–75; electrophotography name changed to, 145–46; examples of copiers using, 10–11; *Forbes* views about, 196–97; importance of, 13; light sources in, 11–12; limitations of, 165; and lithography, 24, 167*n*; optimism about, 197; "secret formula" for, 183; skepticism about, 12, 120–21, 136, 140, 159, 187, 191, 196, 246, 255–56; studies about, 219–25; as success, 282; trademark for, 145–46; uniqueness of, 11, 89–90, 280–83; uses of, 9, 104, 144, 186, 240; and xeroxes as generic term, 81*n*. *See also* electrophotography; *specific person or topic*

Xeroprinter (Batelle), 189–90
Xerox: as generic term, 81*n*; as trademark, 244
Xerox Corporation: big mistake of, 279–80; as example in history of corporations, 278–80; expansion of, 255; founding of, 10; Haloid changes name to, 10, 194, 252; headquarters of, 278; inventions of, 278–79; investment in stock of, 278*n*; lawsuits of, 279, 281; McCardell era in, 277–78; NYSE listing of, 252*n*; physical plant of, 254, 255; public image of, 252; revenues for, 253, 255; size of, 253; stock option program at, 253; use of xerography by, 10, 11; and Wilson's death, 276–77

Young, C. J., 176–78

zinc oxide, 137*n*, 177
Zuccato, Eugenio de, 42

David Owen is a staff writer for *The New Yorker* and the author of a dozen books, among them *The Walls Around Us*, *My Usual Game*, *The Chosen One*, and *The First National Bank of Dad*. He lives in northwest Connecticut with his wife, the writer Ann Hodgman, and their two children.